Blessed are the Poor
in Spirit: for their's is the
KINGDOM
of
Heaven.
St. Matt.
5.3.

DOLLS
and Dolls' Houses

DOLLS
and Dolls' Houses

Constance Eileen King

CHARTWELL BOOKS, INC.

Acknowledgments

AUTHOR'S ACKNOWLEDGMENTS

As individual museums are credited in the captions to the illustrations, I would especially like to express my gratitude to the collectors who have given much of their own time in allowing items in their collections to be photographed. In particular I would thank my American collector friend Jean Steiro, who went to great trouble to organize photographs and also provided more than adequate material for their description. In England Jan Olsen, Joy Stanford, Vera Kramer and Georgia Palmer have all earned my thanks for giving me so much of their time, while firms such as Pedigree Dolls, Chad Valley, Spear's and Dean's all kindly allowed access to their catalogues: while Christie's of South Kensington allowed the photography of various saleroom items. Dolls' house collectors will no doubt be relieved to learn that Ann Sharp's house, referred to in the text, is now in the possession of Captain Bulwer Long, a descendant of the original owner, and his co-operation is also gratefully acknowledged. The publishers have allowed me a completely free choice of illustrations, which has allowed for the broadest possible examination of dolls and dolls' houses. My very special thanks is for my husband, who drove me to so many European museums during the research for the book.

PHOTOGRAPHIC ACKNOWLEDGMENTS

Art Institute of Chicago 136 top left; Ashmolean Museum, Oxford 6, 33 top, 133 left and right, 134 left; Bayerisches Nationalmuseum, Munich 27, 28 top and bottom, 29 top and bottom, 53; British Museum, London 32 left and right; Cambridge Museum of Archaeology and Ethnology 138; Chester County Historical Society, West Chester, Pennsylvania 203, 206 top and bottom, 208 top; Christies, London 80 bottom left; Colchester and Essex Museum 238 top, 240, 243 top and bottom; Essex Institute, Salem, Massachusetts 205; Fotofast, Bologna 184 left and right, 186 left and right, 187 top; Germanisches Nationalmuseum, Nurnberg 145, 146 right, 147 top left, top right and bottom, 149, 150 top, 151; Haags Gemeentemuseum, The Hague 156 top left, lower left and right, 157 top and bottom, 158; Hamlyn Group Picture Library endpapers, 2–3, 17 bottom right, 33 bottom, 70, 107 bottom, 135 top, 139 left, 140 left and right, 141 bottom, 142 right, 163 top; Hamlyn Group–Derek Balmer 11, 13 bottom, 17 top right, 35 right, 36 left, 40 top, 41 top, 46 right, 47 bottom, 55, 56 right, 98, 229 left and right, 239 bottom, 245, 246 top; Hamlyn Group–GGS Photography 230 bottom, 231 top left, 235 top and bottom; Hamlyn Group–Kenn Skrupky 20 left and right, 21 top and bottom, 23, 24, 25, 26 top and bottom, 35 left, 58 bottom, 59 bottom, 92, 93 left and right, 114 right, 116 left and right, 117 left and right, 118 top and bottom, 119, 120 left, 122, 123, 124, 129, 130, 216, 217, 227; Historical Society of Delaware, Wilmington 210 top and bottom; Historical Society of Pennsylvania 36 right; Historisches Museum, Basel 146 left, 196 left and right; Independence National Historical Park Collection, Philadelphia, Pennsylvania 212 top right and bottom right; Institut National de Recherche et de Documentation Pédagogiques, Paris 187 bottom; International Society for Educational Information, Tokyo 7; Japan Information Centre, London 9 upper right and lower right; Japan National Tourist Organization 9 top, 10 left and right, 136 top right and bottom, 137; A. F. Kersting, London 175 bottom; Livrustkammaren, Stockholm 34 top; London Museum 141 top, 142 left, 237 top and bottom, 238 bottom left; Lyme Historical Society, Old Lyme, Connecticut 202 bottom; Margaret Woodbury Strong Museum, New York 212 top left and bottom left, 215 top and bottom; Minnesota Historical Society, St Paul 209 left and right; Missouri Historical Society, St Louis 213; Musée des Arts Decoratifs, Paris 188 top and bottom, 189 left, 197, 199 left; Musée National des Arts et Traditions Populaires, Paris 190 bottom, 191, 192 right; Museum of Science and Industry, Chicago, Illinois 219, 220; Museum of the City of New York 201, 202 top, 211, 214; National Monuments Record 170 bottom, 171 top; National Museum of Finland, Helsinki 144 left, 185, 193 centre and bottom, 194 top, 198 top and centre; National Trust 170 top, 172 top left, top right and bottom, 173; Nordiska Museet, Stockholm 190 top, 192 upper left and lower left, 193 top, 194 bottom, 195 right; Norfolk Museums Service, Norwich 164 left and right, 166 top and bottom, 167 left and right, 168 left and right, 169 top and bottom, 171 bottom; Openluchtmuseum, Genk 189 right; Anthony Panting, London 135 bottom; Plymouth Antiquarian Society, Massachusetts 208 bottom; Prestel Verlag, Munich 22 top and bottom; Puppentheatersammlung der Stadt München 79 left, 102; Rijksmuseum, Amsterdam 150 upper right and lower right, 152 left and right, 153 left and right, 154 top and bottom, 155, 159 left, upper right and bottom right, 161; Rutherford B. Hayes Library, Fremont, Ohio 222, 223, 224 left and right; Schweizerisches Museum für Volkskunde, Basel 198 bottom; Shelburne Museum, Vermont 221; Smithsonian Institution, Washington, D.C. 207; Victoria and Albert Museum, London 52, 148; Wenham Historical Association, Massachusetts 204, 218 top, centre and bottom, Margaret Whitley 144 right; Honor Wilson 12.

The photographs on pages 178, 179, 180 right and 181 are reproduced by Gracious Permission of Her Majesty the Queen. The photograph on page 230 top is Crown Copyright and is reproduced with permission of the Controller of Her Majesty's Stationery Office.

The remaining photographs were taken for the Hamlyn Group by Graham Portlock.

Published in 1989 by
Chartwell Books, Inc.
A Division of Book Sales, Inc.
110 Enterprise Avenue
Secaucus, New Jersey 07094

© 1977 The Hamlyn Publishing Group Limited

ISBN 1 55521 393 6

Produced by Mandarin Offset.
Printed and bound in Hong Kong.

Contents

The Artistry of Ceremonial Dolls

A fragment of a typical early jointed doll with additional detail to the hair. Graeco-Roman period, found at Kerch in the Crimea. Ashmolean Museum, Oxford.

Opposite:
Tableau of the Girls' Festival showing a modern Japanese child with her doll in front of the traditional setting. The Girls' Festival dolls are always arranged on a red cloth and the boys on a green. Society for Educational Information, Tokyo.

A figure that was a miniature representation of the human body quickly became endowed with the attributes of life by unsophisticated people, so that we see, in most early civilizations, doll-like statuettes used both in ancestor worship and in propitiatory ceremonies. Legends developed around such images that told how, at certain times, they moved or spoke of their own accord and were consequently regarded with fear and superstition. Many of the early statuettes and crudely carved images present problems of attribution, as they could have been either a child's toy or some kind of votive offering. As civilization developed, the divergence of standard between a play doll and a ceremonial figure became more obvious, as the most skilled artists were employed to fashion the models that were to form the climax of various ceremonies. At the Roman *lectisternium*, for instance, gods made with realistic wax heads and wearing fine clothes were entertained, while in Greece women carried fine statuettes of Adonis for ceremonies in his honour.

At peasant farms in Norway, it was customary, until the mid-19th century, to honour *fakse* and *hernos*, house gods that were made half life-size and carved of wood. On Christmas Eve the model was placed in a position of honour and a libation, in the form of beer, poured into a hollow in its head. Figures such as these and those seen in Czech and Polish peasant culture and known as *dziady* (old men), are typical of the ceremonies, part idolatry, part ancestor worship, seen in most civilizations. The early Christian church was very aware of the immediate impact of such primitive ceremonies and did not discourage the tales told by simple people of crucifixes that spoke and shed blood and figures of saints which moved.

Many ceremonies that involved the use of doll-like figures have origins that are lost in antiquity, so that although the ritual was often continued, the significance has disappeared and what remains is an enjoyable social tradition. In this context, the Boys' and Girls' Festivals in Japan, which still survive within a modern industrial economy are suggested: an ancient ceremony taking place quite frequently in a corner of a room that is also occupied by a very modern television set.

The first Japanese literary reference to young girls who played with dolls, and annual events at which dolls were displayed, dates to the 8th or 9th century. The Edo Period (1603–1867) was highly prosperous and dolls were produced in great number, often by skilled artists, while the simple clay dolls, said to bring good luck, were made in over a

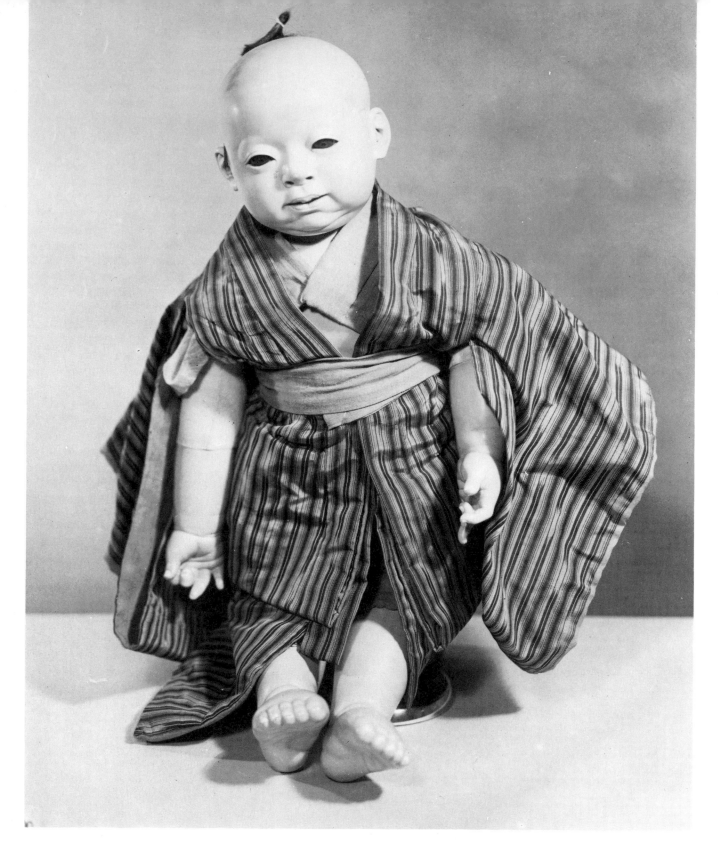

A Japanese boy doll; one of those made with realistic genital detail which his clothing conceals in this example. Bald-headed but with tufts of hair at crown and above ears. Swivel, composition head and glass eyes. Legs and arms articulated by fabric inserts that allow the doll to bow. Doll in Wonderland, Brighton.

hundred different regions. As it was a time of peace, the Edo period was characterized by a very large number of festivals at which dolls were paraded and displayed on impressive floats or in small carts. An interesting survival of these ceremonies is still celebrated in Kyoto where there is also a doll temple that exhibits a fine collection of examples, made in the Edo period, to the public.

As Japan has such a long history of dollmaking, it is hardly surprising that there are many collectors who not only assemble the products of their own country but also buy interesting dolls made in other parts of the world as souvenirs. Every region of Japan has its own traditional figures, and there are now specialist shops where a wide

8

variety can be purchased. Even department stores often have an area where such figures are displayed for local rather than for the tourist trade. Many European antique dolls are now bought by Japanese antique dealers for customers who collect good dolls from all over the world. The native ceremonial dolls are very highly considered, and a pair is frequently given as a wedding present. The general acceptance of dolls as works of art is evidenced by their display at the Nitten Art Exhibition since its establishment in 1936.

Most of the figures made purely for ceremonial or ornamental use have fixed immovable limbs and include isho, gosho and kyodo figures. The isho dolls – those costumed in elegant kimonos – are probably the most familiar to Europeans as they are often bought as tourist gifts. In better examples the body and limbs are carved of wood though they can also be made of a mixture of paulownia sawdust and paste. Gofum, a white substance made of pulverised oyster shell, is then painted over the parts of the body that can be seen. The kimono can be either painted or sewn, and the costumes range from characters seen in the Kabuki theatre to wedding kimonos. Kimekomi dolls were made in the 18th century in a very idiosyncratic manner by cutting grooves in the doll's body into which the ends of cloth, used to build up the shape of the kimono, were pasted. This method meant that very convincing folds could be suggested without the bulk involved in correctly sewn garments. This type of figure is thought to have developed from the early Saga dolls, probably first made by the skilled craftsman Sumino Ryoi, *circa* 1700. These figurines, measuring about eleven inches high, were carved of wood and given a smooth surface by a layer of gofum. The clothes were then painted and further enhanced by an application of gold leaf. A wide range of characters was made, including all sorts of tradespeople as well as gods.

Above:
A tableau of items displayed for the Boy's Festival and including, besides the symbolic carp, uniforms, shields, etc. Japan Tourist Office.

Right:
A boy with his tableau assembled for the Festival. He wears modern dress, in contrast to the ancient traditions of the ceremony. Japan Tourist Office.

Below right:
A group of small girls and their relatives sitting in front of the Girls' Festival arrangement. Japan Tourist Office.

The manufacture of dolls was a strictly governed trade, and skills were passed down from father to son, rather as in the guild system in England. The Fukuoka region has a long tradition in the making of delicately painted clay dolls which are based on traditional themes, such as old folk songs. In the Miharu district of the Fukushima Prefecture on the island of Honshu, extremely primitive figures are still made. The origin of this craft is ancient and the dolls created are known as 'Miharu Toys' and include images of Daruma, founder of the Zen sect of Buddhism, as well as the usual more doll like figures known as Hariko. The traditional Japanese paper, washi, is used for the manufacture of these brilliantly painted papier mâché dolls that were first made in the early 18th century by local farmers, who were taught the skill by experts invited from Edo (now Tokyo) by the Lord of the Miharu clan. While teaching their more advanced skills to the farmers the experts lived in Dekoyashiki, doll's houses.

Today, five families still make Miharu toys from the hundreds of wooden moulds that they have inherited. A few are made in factories in Miharu, though even in this case most of the finishing is completed by women at home. The process used in the manufacture of these figures is the exact opposite of that used for instance in Germany, as here the paper is laid *over* the wooden shape and then lifted off when dry. Brilliant primary colours are used for their decoration, though some are more subtly painted in soft blues and greys. There is great interest in Japan in these ancient methods of dollmaking even though the original function of the figures is almost impossible to assess.

The Sakura Ningyo, or cherry dolls, built over a wire frame and with painted silk faces, that can be found in gift shops all over the world, give a very false picture of the traditional Japanese figures that are often much more primitive in concept. The cherry dolls are made with great skill and often represent the warriors' handmaiden from the Kabuki drama, who carries a warrior's helmet aloft, and is costumed in brilliantly coloured silks.

Below:
The sharing of traditional wine and sweetmeats at the Girls' Festival, celebrated on the 3rd day of the 3rd month. Japan Tourist Office.

Below right:
Many pieces of well-made furniture are included in the Girls' Festival arrangement as well as dolls. Japan Tourist Office.

Group of six dolls dressed in the costumes of a wedding of 1887. The men are waxed compositions, while the women are composition. All have fixed glass eyes and wigs. Original costumes made in detail for what were basically cheap dolls. Blaise Castle House Museum, Bristol.

It might be thought that the ancient Japanese children's festivals would have died out, yet most homes still display sets of dolls on Girls' Day, Hina Matsuri, observed on the third day of the third month of the year. This festival was once purely for girls but in modern Japan is enjoyed by the whole family. The sets of dolls, some of which have been passed down as heirlooms and were sometimes stored for safety from earthquakes in small brick built rooms, are put on display in the best room. If parents have not themselves inherited a set of dolls, they buy a set for any girls born within the year, and they are sometimes given as gifts by friends and relatives; consequently a complete group often includes dolls from several different periods.

In a full set are at least fifteen figures, all dressed in ancient costume. The most important and the most highly valued are the Dairi-sama representing the Emperor and Empress, who sit at the top of a tiered display platform that is traditionally covered with a red cloth. The Empress wears a red and white kimono, that is said to represent the sacred mountain of Fujiyama at sunrise. In very early sets historic and legendary figures also appear. The doll stand measures between five and seven feet wide and is known as the hina dan; on the lower tiers sit court dignitaries, ministers, court ladies and musicians, all placed in strict order of social precedence, the lowest orders represented by three poorly dressed menials. The Emperor and Empress are usually displayed against miniature folding screens which form an effective background for their brilliantly costumed figures. A variety of delicacies in beautifully decorated miniature boxes are arranged on the lower shelves while candlesticks and vases of peach blossom, symbolising happiness in marriage add to the effect. Peach blossom is also put in vases as it signifies the feminine characteristics of softness, mildness and peacefulness.

Above:
A modern portrait doll representing
Princess Anne, modelled by Carolyn
Jane McSweeney and produced by
Honor Wilson. The legs, arms and
head are ceramic and the body is
made of leather. The wig is mohair;
the costume is silk decorated with
pearls, while the tiara, which was
especially commissioned for the doll,
is hallmarked silver. Courtesy of
Honor Wilson.

Opposite:
A 10-inch tall, poured-wax lady
dressed, according to tradition, in
imitation of a costume worn by the
Empress Eugenie. She has painted
blue eyes and a finely plaited fair
wig. The fabric body is very much
shaped to the waist. The wax feet
are painted with black ballet-type
slippers with crossed ribbons, and
the dress of pink silk is trimmed with
lace and muslin. Tunbridge Wells
Museum.

The display is on show for about a week and the daughters and their
friends, clad in new kimonos, gather before it and solemnly practice
the rules of etiquette between singing, eating green rice cakes and
drinking sweetened white rice wine, and playing games. As with
many of the ceremonies in which dolls play a central role, the actual
significance of the festival has changed and it is now an appealing
ceremonial feast to the Emperor and Empress, though originally it
probably had religious significance. It is believed to have represented
some kind of purification ceremony with its accompanying dedication
of the child to national deities.

The Boys' Festival, celebrated on the fifth day of the fifth month,
the month of the Iris, is thought to date back to 593–629 AD. Very
different values to those of peacefulness and mildness were inculcated
in this ceremony, whose traditions were linked to Bushido, the old
code of chivalry. Terrifyingly warlike figures are displayed, though
the purpose of the festival in the modern period is said to be chivalrous
rather than militaristic. Since the Second World War the festival has
become a national holiday, and is now known as Children's Day. The
ceremony developed from a traditional display outside houses on the
Festival of the Iris, displays that became so lavish that they were
eventually replaced by miniatures. Later the ceremony became
associated with the day on which the birth of sons was also celebrated.
Coloured paper carp are flown outside the house, originally one for
each son according to his age. The determination of this fish (in
Japanese legend, at any rate) in fighting its way up waterfalls sym-
bolises how in life a boy should be ambitious and willing to overcome
obstacles.

This encouragement of manliness is seen in the fierce aspect of the
dolls included in the display, such as Shoki, the slayer of demons and,
the most popular figure today, Kintoki, a sort of strong boy, able to
perform feats of strength. In some versions the Empress Jingu, a
Japanese Boadicaea, appears in full armour. The giant Benkei, loaded
down with arms, is also a very popular character. The warriors are
again displayed in the best room on a stand covered with a green cloth
and surrounded by groups of helmets, armour and swords. The un-
packing of the dolls for both festivals is an occasion of great excitement
and the traditions and ceremonial of the country are taught in an
interesting way as the figures are revealed.

In Europe, ceremonial events have occasioned the creation of edible
figures that were not only cheap to produce but also provided some
sustenance for the children enjoying the festivities. The making of
edible figures in human form has a very long tradition, but has been
frowned upon in certain periods, such as in Norway in the 13th
century when the ceremonial baking of bread in man's image was
forbidden. A very large figure made of dough known as the Tallsack
was paraded in the streets of the Riesengebirge regions of Germany
on Palm Sundays until the beginning of the 20th century. The eyes
were formed of currants and the arms were modelled so that an egg
could be clasped to the chest. Gingerbread figures have charmed
children for many centuries, as a little extra decoration in the form of
gilding or icing-sugar hair could transform the basic shape into a
particular saint or hero. Special moulds were also made so that King
George III, for instance, could be shown on horseback (he was King
of Hanover as well as King of England). In Germany, the three holy
virgins, St Einbede, St Warbede and St Willebede were still popular
in gingerbread well into the 20th century. Max von Boehn recounts how
on his twelfth birthday, Schreiber received a gingerbread man as big
as himself. In Vienna, at the fair of St Nicholas, held on 6 December,
life-sized figures representing the saint were made of gingerbread,
chocolate and even cake.

Right:
Miniature wedding procession of the
1860s. The porcelain men have pink
lustre heads, while the women are
fair-haired 'parians'. All the costumes
are original, and the figures are
4 inches tall. Blaise Castle House
Museum, Bristol.

Figures of sugar, marzipan and gum tragacanth were made not only as dolls but also as centre pieces for banquets, complete rooms sometimes being moulded from a mixture of sugar, meal and gum and peopled with miniature figures, the whole setting being painted. Some moulded dolls were made in two halves and a small trinket or a moral text concealed. In spite of the prohibition of the Koran, children in Islamic countries still buy gaily coloured sugar figures in the streets on the feast day of Mohammed, Mohammed himself being forced to recognize the importance of dolls in a girl's life by his nine-year-old wife Ayesha, who brought her dolls with her into the harem.

The collector has to study the edible dolls of the past in prints and in written references, though the moulds from which they were made can still occasionally be found. Pollock's Toy museum in London has a set of gingerbread moulds, while those used for chocolate and made of metal can usually be bought cheaply as they are not as decorative as those carved of wood. Queen Victoria, sailors, children in snow-suits and even Mickey Mouse were all cast from metal moulds, which in themselves could form an interesting and inexpensive collection.

Commemorative dolls, made to celebrate a special occasion, were necessarily produced over a relatively short period and are therefore, even if made comparatively recently, of interest, though often surprisingly difficult to locate. The coronation of the Queen in 1953 encouraged a great flurry of dollmaking, Dean's Rag Book Company of Rye, for instance, producing a doll in Peeress' robes, a Beefeater of the Tower of London, a Guardsman and a London Policeman, all 42 inches high, in honour of the occasion. Doll collectors were catered for by a firm known as the Chelsea Art Dollmakers which produced an artistic 18-inch portrait doll of the Queen. As the design of the Queen's dress was kept secret until Coronation Day, the first dolls of this edition were not correctly costumed, but another dress was later issued in imitation of the white and gold dress decorated with lilies that was worn. Each doll carried silver regalia set with semi-precious stones and the embroidery, worked by women in the Balearic Islands, included some 5,000 individually sewn pearls on each figure. The Queen's head was modelled by Mario Ricciardi while other artists were responsible for the robes and regalia. Each doll was made to order and the edition, which was the idea of Captain Xavier Puslowski, was numbered.

As a child, the Queen had inspired a firm of dollmakers to create a play-doll in her image. In 1930 Chad Valley issued a 17-inch portrait doll 'Approved by Her Royal Highness the Duchess of York. The favourite doll of all. Charmingly dressed and beautifully made.' This early version showed a chubby child with short curly blonde hair wearing a pearl necklace and a frock with tiers of frills from hem to waist. The 'Royal Dolls' made in 1938 were produced in much greater number so it is this early version that is difficult to find. In their 1938 catalogue Chad Valley declared 'We have pleasure in announcing that the Princess Elizabeth and Princess Margaret Rose Dolls have been approved by their Majesties the King and Queen and the Prince Edward doll by HRH the Duke of Kent. The dolls are made in velveteen, fully jointed. Chad Valley heads, especially modelled from likenesses of the originals, fitted with curly hand-woven wigs and dressed in clothes as worn at the present time by the Royal children themselves. The princesses are supplied either in blue or in pink colour schemes.'

Princess Elizabeth could be obtained either 18 or 21 inches high wearing a hat and a double-breasted coat over a flowered dress or dressed in a party frock. Princess Margaret was made only in the 16-inch size but again costumed either in a hat and coat or in a party frock. Prince Edward of Kent appears by the number of surviving dolls to have been made in a much smaller quantity and measured only 15 inches. He wore a summer or winter-weight suit composed of

When General C. L. Herbert was British Resident in Baghdad in 1868 his wife heard that the ladies of the Sultan's harem had nothing to do. She therefore sent to London for this group of dolls, and the ladies employed their hours in costuming them. Tunbridge Wells Museum.

short trousers and belted top. The pressed felt heads of these dolls were extremely effective and the characters are still recognisable today, despite some fading, especially in contrast with those made, for example, in America by Madame Alexander whose composition versions are only recognisable by the labels they carried.

Other Royal ladies have inspired dollmakers: in 1935 a rag doll nine inches high representing Queen Mary was issued by Liberty and Co. and though a not very flattering caricature, was effective as a doll. In the States a completely improbable version of Prince Philip was made in plastic. Princess Anne and Princess Margaret in their wedding dresses have inspired several costumiers of dolls to create their own miniature versions. At the London Museum is a wax portrait of Queen Anne, whose costume is worked in great detail in paper filigree, while

15

A pair of commercially made figures with composition heads modelled as portraits of Salisbury and Gladstone, leaders of the Conservative and Liberal parties respectively. The detail of the arms is printed. The figures, which are 8½ inches tall, are costumed as boxers or wrestlers of the period. Tunbridge Wells Museum.

Queen Victoria in the form of a wax doll can be seen at the Bethnal Green Museum. Such accurate portrait dolls are now very difficult to find and much treasured, though many old dolls claimed in families to be portraits of Victoria are found to have little resemblance and have usually only been dressed to represent her.

Paper dolls such as that portraying the French Empress Eugenie, and published in 1860 by G. W. Faber, are interesting in that the printer was able to recreate several of the costumes she wore in precise detail in coloured lithography. The Faber editions are liked by collectors because of their rich colours and the gilt decorated gift-boxes in which the dolls were sold. Much later in the century the German Crown Prince and Princess were sold with their portraits and costumes printed on a sheet of card for cutting out.

The only dolls that most boys were allowed to treasure in the 19th and early 20th centuries were those representing national heroes, or costumed as soldiers and sailors. The Pierotti family, of Italian origin, who made poured-wax dolls, created several very effective portrait figures representing for instance Lord Roberts, British Commander-in-Chief during the Boer War, in the full dress of a Field-Marshal with red felt jacket and white kid trousers. At the beginning of the First World War they also made a doll portraying Lord Kitchener dressed in equally detailed costume. The amount of work lavished on the portrait heads, such as cleverly detailed wrinkles and hair, beards, moustaches and eyebrows created by delicately inserted hair, might lead to the supposition that these were display figures, but their intention appears to have been purely as rather expensive playthings.

Right:
Waxed composition boy wearing the uniform of Colston's Boys School, Bristol, founded by Edward Colston in 1708. The doll is 19th century and wears the original school uniform of the 18th. Blaise Castle House Museum, Bristol.

Below:
A shoulder bisque with well-painted eyes and distinct modelling of the fair hair. The fabric body is filled with sawdust. She is dressed in the costume of the 1890s, and said to represent 'The New Woman', later manifested in the Suffragette movement. Tunbridge Wells Museum.

Below right:
Printed rag soldiers made in England in 1916 by Samuel Finberg & Co, representing soldiers of the First World War. Bethnal Green Museum, London.

'Dolly Joins the Forces' opened to show the variety of uniforms—also the very poor quality of the wartime printing. Author's collection.

Above:
A paper dressing-doll sold in the form of an economically produced booklet during the last war. Author's collection.

Opposite:
Advertising dolls with composition shoulder-heads, created to promote the sale of Bisto gravy powder and known as the 'Bisto Kids'. The heads are modelled to suggest that the Kids are sniffing Bisto with relish. Doll in Wonderland, Brighton.

Several less spectacular versions of Lord Kitchener were made, usually in composition, by other firms, as he made a quickly recognizable figure with his large moustache and military uniform. Belgian refugees in England during the First World War made representations of the famous French Marshal Joffre complete with his full range of medals. In the USA at this time, Sophia Delavan made War Nurses and Orphan dolls, while in England Dean's made cut-out rag dolls representing the British Tommy and, especially for Boots the chemist, a wounded soldier wearing a red bedroom slipper on his injured foot. In Germany the officer dolls made by Steiff bore the firm's characteristic seam down the front of the face. Many German bisque dolls are found dressed by their original owners in the nurses' costumes of the war years, while the English makers of bisque dolls during the same period sold many dressed in uniform.

During the Second World War there was a proliferation of dolls in service uniforms and in siren suits worn by some members of the public. An engaging propaganda booklet, published to encourage young girls to join the women's services, provided a cut-out doll with the smart uniforms of the three services—all printed with the greatest economy and on the cheapest of paper. Norah Wellings produced Harry the Hawk, an air force mascot in aid of the Royal Air Force Comforts. A very large number of these rag dolls must have been sold as they are quite easy to find. In the United States the Freundlick Novelty Corporation created General MacArthur in composition complete with a moulded hat, making a very convincing portrait.

Stage and screen personalities have provided doll-makers with a wealth of subject matter since the time of the ballerina Fanny Elssler, in the 1840s. She was portrayed in porcelain in a ballet position, sometimes with moulded flowers in her hair. This is a rare and desirable doll as the face is modelled with rather more character than is usually found on dolls of this material. This dancer was also made as a paper doll and sold in a box, with the details written both in French and English. Fanny, in this version, was dressed only in a chemise and a variety of costumes and headdresses was supplied. Though there are many porcelain dolls said to resemble the 19th-century singer Jenny Lind,

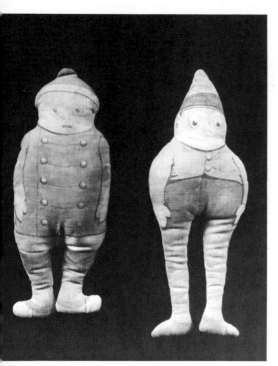

there are none that can be positively claimed as true portraits. This entertainer, who ravished the heart even of the critical Queen Victoria, was, however, made in paper. An example in the Nordiska Museet, Stockholm, includes some twenty different costumes showing Jenny as various opera characters. Another paper version of her is probably of American manufacture and shows her for example as Donna Anna in *Don Giovanni* and Alice in *Robert le Diable*.

In the same period the popularity of Tom Thumb was reflected in the paper dolls issued by McLoughlin Brothers of New York, a set that included not only the dwarf himself, who, incidentally, also charmed Queen Victoria, but also Mrs Lavinia Thumb and Minnie Warren, her sister and bridesmaid. A poured-wax doll in an American collection is also believed to have been made in his image.

The American gentleman's admiration for the daring ladies of the stage in the 1880s is perpetuated in a series of mildly alluring articulated paper dolls whose very sweet and innocent faces are contradicted by plunging necklines and rather suggestive poses. Ada Rehan wears saucy black stockings and long gloves, while Fanny Davenport and Rose Coughlin wear rather less adventurous knee-length drawers. These dolls measure 14 inches high and were intended to be costumed in scraps of lace and silk. They are stamped 'Patented 1880'.

Gramophone records, films and radio meant that, by the early 20th century, the names of entertainers were familiar to a very large number of children, and the dollmakers were quick to realize the sales potential of toys made in the image of people who were known to the masses. Dean's Rag Book Company made a series of dolls, with their Evripose joints, that included George Robey and Jackie Coogan, the celebrated boy actor of Chaplin's *The Kid*. In 1937 Lupino Lane was added to the Evripose Tru-to-Life range and Will Hay, in academic gown and wielding a cane and book, was included in 1938. A particular character was sometimes brought quite suddenly to public attention, such as Buster Brown, who appeared in a cartoon in the New York Herald and was made in rag by the Art Fabric Mills in America and, in 1927, by Dean's in England, but here 'Brought recently into the foreground by Film Comedies in which his antics are brought up to date for a generation too young to remember the Outcault cartoons. Dressed in high grade felt and silk,' boasted the catalogue for that year.

Many of the bisque-headed dolls found in original Scottish costumes depended for their inspiration on the impact of the singer Harry Lauder, who captivated audiences in the first half of the 20th century. Lupino Lane, as he appeared in *Me and My Girl* wearing a check suit and a bowler, made an amusing souvenir rag doll.

Shirley Temple was the star who made the greatest impression on the dollmakers as she was herself represented almost as a doll in her films. Her image inspired mothers all over the world to dress their own children in Shirley Temple frocks and torture their hair into Shirley Temple curls. The only really fine doll known to have been created as a portrait was a figure made of wax over a composition base and given blue glass eyes. This portrait doll was used for the promotion of her films and was given the refinement of inserted lashes and brows. The commercially produced versions are almost all made of composition substances and have suffered colour changes and sometimes the flaking and cracking associated with this medium. An early version shows her as a plump child with two upper and three lower teeth. This doll has a shoulder head that is impressed with her name and mounted on a cloth torso with composition arms and legs. She also was made in a flirty-eyed version that was costumed in a crinoline dress and pink hat, as she was seen in her *Little Colonel* role. When the film *Hurricane* was released in 1937 there was a fashion in Polynesian-style beauty as represented by Dorothy Lamour, and a chocolate brown version was marketed in America by Ideal. When Shirley Temples are found with their hair net and badge, and in good condition, they are collectable. Their popularity among collectors encouraged the Ideal Toy Company to reissue the doll in vinyl in 1967. Another recently made vinyl model was not liked by Mrs Shirley Temple Black and an alternative was designed that was marked 'Hong Kong, Ideal Doll'. This re-issue of a doll that is basically so dated is an interesting phenomenon which, one feels, rests more on the nostalgia of doll collectors and parents rather than on any appeal to the modern child, apart from that exerted by any pretty toy.

Charlie Chaplin inspired the creation of much more vigorous dolls, though there is a wide variety of standard among the versions produced. To my personal taste, that made in 1915 by Louis Amberg & Son of Ohio showing the actor in a rather quizzical mood, is the most effective.

An extremely beautiful Bavarian
Christ-child dating from the end of
the 18th century. Its very small size
is unusual—the poured-wax figure
measures only some 3¾ inches.
Private Collection, Munich.

Left:
A wax Christ-child with inset glass
eyes and carved hair. Known as The
Augustinian Child or The Gracious
Child, it was venerated in the
Augustinian church in Munich from
1624 until 1870. Length with halo,
25 inches. The Burgersaal, Munich.

Opposite:
A group of printed fabric dolls that
were earned by submitting four
package tops or labels from 'Aunt
Jemima' products such as Self Rising
Flour and Buckwheat Flour plus 25
cents. All four dolls were sent if a
complete set of labels was sent in.
The dolls represented Aunt Jemima,
Uncle Mose, Diana and Wade, and
the Cream of Wheat Chef. Blandings
House Museum, Wisconsin.

A composition Campbell Kid and a larger Scootles that was one of the creations of Rose O'Neill. Scootles is unmarked as it was sold with a tie-on label. Campbell Kids were originally drawn to advertise Campbell's Soups. This 12½-inch example wears its original yellow fur-fabric dress. Painted black eyes, moulded shoes and socks. Unmarked but attributed to Horsman. Scootles measured 12½ inches. Blanding House Museum, Wisconsin.

'Charlot' dolls were made also in France after a successful tour, while in England Dean's made an 11½-inch version complete with hat and stick and with a 'Tru-to-Life' face for a mere 1/-, or 5p in current coinage.

Joe E. Brown, Gene Autry, Deanna Durbin, Margaret O'Brien, Jane Withers, Sonja Henie, and Juanita Quigley, a child star of the 30s, were all imitated in doll form by American manufacturers. The collecting of mid-twentieth-century dolls is not yet popular in Europe, though all these portrait editions are sought avidly in America. The characterization in these composition heads is usually very good, and it would appear to be the medium itself that lacks appeal, as the all-bisque dolls made to represent characters such as Lord Plushbottom, with moulded waistcoat, tails and spectacles, and Mr Bailey the Boss, are collected on both sides of the Atlantic with interest. Among the more recently made American dolls Joe Louis with a well modelled latex head, a heavily padded cloth body and huge boxing gloves, is a particular favourite.

Many celebrities have been commemorated in doll form, such as that made with a bisque head in 1912 and dressed to portray the Norwegian explorer Nansen. In the 1920s some charming all-bisque figures with moulded aviators hats and goggles were inspired by the achievements of Amelia Earhart. In the mid-nineteenth century, Mrs Bloomer caused great controversy by her choice of what were considered masculine garments. An interesting doll in the collection of Mary Hillier is believed to be dressed in imitation of Amelia Bloomer, and bears a note stating that it was bought at the 'International Exhibition held at Hyde Park in 1851'. It was in this year that the fashion made its appearance in England and under a headline 'Bloomerism at the Crystal Palace', *The Times* drew readers' attention to three ladies dressed in the new style who had appeared in the open space near

the Exhibition. They were 'Persons of some station in society and bore with considerable good humour the taunts which were freely directed towards them.' An enterprising doll costumier must have realized the sales potential of such an event and dressed his waxed composition in long cream silk trousers under a conventional shell pink skirt.

Although individuals often claim that dolls in family possession were made as portraits of celebrities, these claims can only rarely be supported and, on examination, what is often discovered is a standard doll that has gathered tales about its origin over the years. One doll that is a definite portrait is that in the Goodwill Industries doll museum, Colorado, representing George Washington on horseback. As this figure has a German bisque head it must have originally been produced in some numbers, apparently as a *bonbonnière*, as the head of the papier-mâché horse lifts off. Generally, as the communication of fashions and ideas was much slower in the 19th century, it was not economical for a manufacturer to produce a doll that would only be popular in one country, and this accounts for their extreme rarity.

Several modern American dollmakers have attempted to fill this gap by producing retrospective portraits in porcelain and bisque. An attractive porcelain ballet dancer wearing flowers in the moulded hair and representing Madame Taglioni, is made by Suzanne Gibson, while Carol Nordell makes composition and wax figures representing, among others, Teddy Roosevelt and well-known characters from American paintings. The most collectable of the American reproduction china dolls are those designed by Martha Oathaut Ayres, particularly of George and Martha Washington and produced by Emma St Clear at the Humpty Dumpty Doll's Hospital.

Today, with so many television programmes shown to both American and British audiences, toymakers are able to create dolls in the likeness of popular characters that are instantly recognized by thou-

'Lettie Lane' was designed by Sheila Young and appeared in the *Ladies' Home Journal* in America from 1908 to 1915. Lettie was 6 inches tall and is seen in this photograph surrounded by a group of her play dolls. Daisy, the doll to Lettie's right, was issued as a bisque-headed doll between 1911 and 1912. The bisque version was 18 inches tall and could be earned by any girl who secured three magazine subscriptions and sent in $4.50. Blanding House Museum, Wisconsin.

'Maggie' and 'Jiggs' made by Schoenhut. Jiggs, some 7 inches tall, carries his original pail marked 'Corned Beef and Cabbage'. The cartoon strip called 'Bringing up Father' was created in 1912 by George McManus and copyrighted in 1924 by International Feature Services Inc. Blanding House Museum, Wisconsin.

Goldilocks and the Three Bears, printed in bright colours on fabric and sold as an advertisement for Kellogg's Corn Flakes. Marked 1925. Goldilocks is 14 inches tall. Blanding House Museum, Wisconsin.

sands of children; Chad Valley, for instance, in their 1976 catalogue offering Barapapa and Baramama from the BBC cartoon series. The collecting of modern dolls such as these could provide a child with an interesting hobby, and, in later years, an absorbing commentary on the changes in popular entertainment.

A saint's image, sometimes in the form of a play doll, was considered, both in the 18th and 19th centuries, an appropriate gift, especially at Christmas for a Christian child. In a painting by Greuze of 1760 is seen a small girl holding a doll representing a monk, while in 1741 a picture by Chardin showed a girl with a doll dressed as a Carmelite nun. Young visitors to convents and monasteries were sometimes given such figures, often costumed in intricate detail by women of the order. When clay dolls dating to the 14th century were discovered in Nuremberg, small figures of monks, obviously intended as toys, were included in the group. A doll dressed as a nun was also a good preparation for a child taken to see a relative who had joined a religious order as the dark costumes were often frightening.

A particularly interesting pair, of 1710–1720 and made of wood and papier mâché, were sold at Sotheby's in April 1974. One wore the habit of a Canoness of St Augustine in full choir robes and a winter cloak, while the undergarments were sewn in precise detail, even to a handkerchief in a pocket. It is difficult to decide whether such a figure was made as some kind of a gift for important visitors or, as is often thought, as models that could be used by nuns when making a particular habit. Late 19th-century dolls are sometimes found dressed in detail almost as precise as in the early 18th century examples and these are definitely intended as playthings, as their acquisition is often remembered: it would therefore appear likely that many of those dating from the 18th century were also, despite the high standard of their clothes, made originally as religious toys, possibly to encourage a girl to take the veil.

The majority of religious dolls, especially those made of wood and costumed in paper, are not unattractive and must have provided some comfort for a lonely child. Many of those made of wax, which cracks and discolours, can have only remained attractive for a comparatively short time and children must have often inherited dolls of quite frightening appearance. A wax doll, representing an old shrivelled crone wearing the Sacred Heart on her breast, was given to the natural daughter of Lord Byron and Mary Shelley's half-sister Claire Clairmont in the 1820s by the nuns at her convent at Bagnacavallo. When Allegra died, the doll was passed on to yet another child, who cannot have slept peacefully with such a terrifying figure watching over her, and it seems very possible that such dolls were intended as a means of frightening a wayward young soul into complete obedience.

The infant Jesus is almost invariably a chubby smiling baby whose presence in the nursery must have delighted many children. Finer quality figures show the child naked and sometimes with genital detail, lying on a silk or velvet cushion and protected by a glass shade. In such examples the wax modelling is of the most precise quality and hair, lashes and brows are often inserted. Frequently one hand is raised in blessing and occasionally the mouth is modelled slightly open to reveal small bone teeth. Wax figures, made as portraits of loved children or even to commemorate those lost during childhood, are also found set out in a similar manner under a glass shade. These can usually be differentiated from an Infant Jesus by the less spiritual expression and the fact that some sex-concealing drapery or garment is often worn, these figures often being made with no sexual detail at all, a detail that was traditionally accepted on the Holy Child. Some remains of a halo are also frequently visible, though it was sometimes attached only by a delicate wire.

An earthenware crib representing the Adoration of the Shepherds, made in 1772 by the Viennese Johann Georg Dorfmeister. It comes from Cilli—formerly Untersteiermark, and now Celje—in Slovenia. Bayerisches Nationalmuseum, Munich.

These two figures from a crèche setting show the skill characteristic of the 18th-century makers. The woman is signed 'F 3 H', and the man was made by Francesco Viva and dated 1778. Bayerisches Nationalmuseum, Munich.

Cheaper versions of the Infant were made in a variety of materials including wood, earthenware, papier mâché and waxed composition. A charming example, in its original matchwood box covered with patterned paper, was sold at Christie's in 1976. As the figure was still wrapped in its original tissue, both the costume and the poured-wax head had escaped the usual discolouring, even the metal spangles forming the halo and part of the swaddling bands still retaining their brilliance of colour. The head was modelled with simplicity and the black irisless eyes were shown with the lids slightly lowered. A rudimentary cone shape formed the body that was wrapped in pink ribbon and lace. The box carried an inscription relating that the doll was given as a gift to a child in 1825.

Swaddling figures were often given as baptismal or birth gifts and the materials from which they were made varies from the most exquisitely carved ivory to gaudily decorated and roughly made figures whittled from a block of wood. The majority of the wooden swaddling figures were made in Germany, especially in Berchtesgaden where at the Heimatsmuseum several examples can be seen attached to a 19th-century pedlars pack. In this case the figures are lathe turned to a simple skittle shape, but have a wide base so that the doll can stand. Similar carved dolls were also made at Oberammergau, the Erzebirge and in Czechoslovakia.

Clay figures discovered in Nuremberg and dating from the 15th century are thought to be some kind of baptismal gifts, as several are moulded with a cavity at chest level just large enough to hold a coin as a present for a child. Though some wooden swaddling babies were imported in the late 19th and early 20th centuries from Germany, they were never popular in England as christening gifts and their place appears to have been taken by the earthenware cradles, sometimes left empty so that a token could be enclosed and often with the child's date of birth written in slip on the side.

Writing in 1908, Mrs Nevill Jackson mentions how, in the toy markets of Spain, Italy and France there were at Christmas time hundreds of playthings representing the Infant Christ in his cradle. 'Miniature images of the Magi, with almost grotesquely black faces and oriental turbans are sold in thousands . . . votive hearts, arms and legs and so forth in tinsel, composition, lead and wood are to be purchased in Spain and Italy in all seasons of the year.' St Theodora in glittering armour, St Florians with buckets, St John with a lamb and St Laurence with a gridiron could all be obtained cheaply. She comments that these dolls were carved in some instances by cottage workers while the painting and decorating was carried out at the great warehouses and that 'Frequently the makers of the large figures for church use are also the purveyors of religious toys for children.'

The setting up of doll-like images in churches as votive offerings was a practice continued into the 20th century according to Max von Boehn who recorded particularly realistic life-size figures at the Church of the Fourteen Saints at Lichtenfels, as well as more usual hollow wax offerings. At this time 17th-century moulds were still in use at the studio of the court wax modeller in Munich and were decorated according to the wealth of the worshipper: some figures of this type being cast in silver and gold though the majority were always wax. In 1736 the Emperor Charles VII set up a statue of his first-born prince that corresponded with the actual weight of the child. Many of these votive figures are of children, either because they were desired, or in order to protect them, perhaps in illness. Very early examples wear a type of swaddling dress and have little shape except in the moulding of the head.

Despite the English 19th-century dislike of religious statuary, the image of St Nicholas never lost popularity as a Christmas gift. Many

Above:
A crib made in Aix-en-Provence, contained in a decorative case. The landscape and grotto are made of canvas and paper. They are decorated with the dust of glass and rock crystal, and ornamented with artificial flowers, snail shells and glass animals. Bayerisches Nationalmuseum, Munich.

Right:
A scene from a typical 18th-century Neapolitan crib showing tradespeople at work while musicians play in front of the shrine. The setting is complete, even to the pug dog and the carcasses of animals. Bayerisches Nationalmuseum, Munich.

versions are of papier mâché cast from a simple two-piece mould, while small bisque versions were intended as cake decorations. An old gentleman who had once owned a toy shop showed me an enchanting figure he had used as the centrepiece of his window display until 1925 when the business closed. It was a figure of Santa Claus, made around 1900 and standing behind a sack of toys. The papier mâché figure was articulated and as a simple musical movement played he bent forward and lifted out a toy. Similar versions of this figure can be seen, including one which shows the saint mounted on a horse whose head nods.

The most desirable to collectors of the Father Christmas dolls are those made of bisque in Germany by an unknown maker. Heavy modelling of the old man's character façe is accentuated by red painted lines and the portrait is completed by bright glass eyes that twinkle convincingly. This unknown firm also produced another interesting doll representing Uncle Sam.

The setting up of extravagant groups of figures to form a nativity scene is mainly associated with Continental countries, in particular Germany and Italy. Great nobles in Italy competed with each other in an effort to produce the largest and most costly *presepio*, the native term for a crèche, one noblewoman even sacrificing part of her own wardrobe in order to costume the figures in sufficient splendour.

It is thought that the crib scene was originated by St Francis of Assisi who wished to make the story of Christmas clear, even to those who could not read. The early arrangements were probably quite simple, but steadily gained in complexity until not only the Holy Family, the Magi and Shepherds were included but also villagers, street traders, animals and birds as well as, quite frequently, a figure of the person, sometimes a prince, who commissioned the scene. Many of the Italian figures have terracotta heads that were sometimes signed by the artist on the inside of the shoulder plate, while others, especially those of German origin, were carved and painted wood or even plaster. When the costumes became shabby they were often re-made by nuns in preparation for the next Christmas display, and it is therefore not always possible to date them purely by the style of dress. The crèche figures can be differentiated from early dolls by the realism of their body proportions and the delicacy of the hands, often modelled with the fingers spread well apart. While 18th-century play dolls are quite primitive, the crèche figures were made as realistically as possible to please discerning adults. Sadly, despite their artistry, the current monetary value of such images is low, as many are too small to be used as statuary by decorators and the majority of collectors require only one or two examples from the large number that have survived.

A letter from John Locke to John Strachy in 1664 would suggest that early figures were rather different from the 18th-century examples with which collectors are more familiar. 'Near to the high altar in the principal church at Cleeves, was a little altar for the service of Christmas Day. The scene was a stable wherein was an ox, an ass, a cradle, the Virgin, Joseph, the Babe, shepherds and angels dramatis personae. Had they but given it motion it had been a perfect puppet play and might have deserved pence a piece; for they were the same size and make that our English puppets are; and I am convinced that these shepherds and this Joseph are kin to that Judith and Holophernes which I had seen at Bartholomew Fair.'

Even allowing for Locke's disapproval of the images, the inference that jointed dolls of the period made both in France and England were virtually indistinguishable from one another is interesting, and also suggests a wider divergence of standard between crèche figures than is realised, as obviously the churches would have preserved their best examples.

Dolls
in an Adult Image

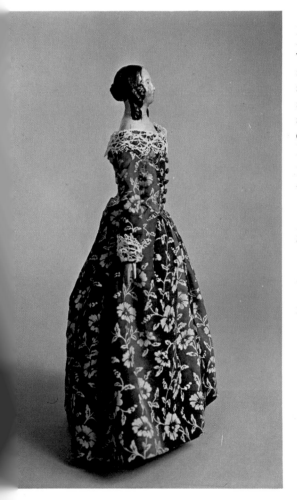

A papier-mâché lady with a moulded bun and ringlets. The eyes are painted, the body is leather, and the lower arms and legs are carved from wood. Leather and wood are separated by orange bands. The flowered blue dress is made of cotton. Collection Mrs Jan Olsen.

Simple models of the human form, sometimes with articulated joints, have been found in the remains of early civilization but their intention, whether as toys or as fertility symbols, is often almost impossible to assess. The play dolls of the Egyptians were made of wood and linen and given embroidered faces with hair of fabric threads. These dolls are of great interest, as they illustrate how, from the earliest times, adults have fashioned simple rag dolls to amuse a child. They have occasionally survived in Egypt because of the hot dry climate but it is likely that they were made in many countries. An Egypto-Roman example made of coarse hessian, now in the Victoria and Albert Museum, dating from the 3rd or 4th century, was discovered in the grave of a child together with a ball. The majority of surviving early Greek dolls are made of clay; the head and torso being modelled together while the simple limbs swing from pivot joints by string or wire. There was an established commercial manufacture of dolls, and vendors travelled the whole of the Greek world with a variety of wares. A few examples, obviously made for richer children, are modelled in some detail, with ornate headdresses, though the majority are of the most rudimentary kind.

At the Ashmolean in Oxford, there are several alabaster lady dolls dated *circa* 343 BC whose construction differs from that of the terracotta figures. The alabasters have well-shaped legs that are fixed in position, while the lower arms are jointed to the rigid torso just above elbow level, thus providing the doll with a much more elegant shoulder shape for costuming than is usually seen. A particularly fine example has pierced ears and one arm carved, for realism, in a very slightly raised position.

At puberty Roman girls dedicated their dolls to Mercury, Jupiter and Diana and surviving examples are of similar construction to the Greek terracottas, though there is an oak doll, wearing a gold bangle, of such superb artistry that it must represent a prestige product of the period. A very beautifully ornamented small ivory doll was discovered in the sarcophagus of the Empress Maria, the consort of Honorius, while a carved wooden example over 2 feet high was found in the grave of another Roman girl. Male as well as female dolls are found in Roman remains, though whether they were intended as boys' playthings is not known. However, it is obvious from the variety of surviving examples of dolls made in different materials that the Romans as well as the Greeks supported a lively doll-making trade.

After the fall of the Roman Empire we pass into a period from
which examples are almost non-existent, not, I would think, because
children ceased to own them but mainly because the early Christian
church frowned on such pagan practices as burying a child with its
toys. Despite the apparent lack of civilized order, many of the old
trading routes were kept open and the luxuries of life were still available to the wealthy. In England, simple dolls of wood were probably
sold at the great fairs which were a feature of life in the Anglo-Saxon
period. In the 12th-century *Hortus Deliciarum* of the Abbess Herrad
there is an illustration of two boys, playing at a table with jointed
knights controlled by crossed strings, indicating that some quite
sophisticated toys were available at the time.

Puppet shows were a great centre of attraction at the medieval fairs
and children must have longed for dolls similar to the figures they saw
on stage. Some of the 14th–15th century clay dolls discovered under
the pavements of Nuremberg in the 19th century represent elegant
women wearing fashionable dress. The *Hortus Sanitatis* of 1491 shows
a Nuremberg dollmaker at work carving wooden jointed figures that
would probably have been costumed before sale. German writers
extolled the beauty of certain dolls in the medieval period and it is
obvious that surviving examples can give little idea of those made to
the highest standard. A written account refers to a mannequin figure
ordered by Isabella of Bavaria on the occasion of her marriage to
Charles VI of France. The doll was to be dressed in Paris in the height
of fashion and sent to England to show Isabella's friend, another
Isabella, the young queen of Richard II, the costume of the court.
In 1396 the court valet to Charles VI, who was responsible for the
dressing of the figure, received 500 francs for a similar commission.
As there is rarely any reference to size in such accounts it is difficult
to establish whether the figures were in miniature or full-sized so the
clothes could be worn.

Wax, wood and composition were all used as dollmaking materials
in the 14th century and both Sonneberg and Nuremberg were well
established as manufacturing centres. A number of the toys distributed
by the Nuremberg merchants all over Europe were made at Oberammergau and in the Groden Valley and it is sometimes suggested that
craftsmen were forced to diversify into dolls because of a decline in the
demand for religious statuary in the area. At the great annual fairs,
such as those held in Venice and Florence, dolls in a variety of materials
were sold; those of composition, made of waste organic materials,
being rapidly destroyed by vermin.

Ott and Mess, the first recorded dollmakers, make their appearance in the 15th century and are described as Dockenmacher, a term usually used for toys in general. Dr Mannfred Bachmann comments that dollmaking, at this time, was a free craft in Germany and not limited by tight guild rules so they could be made as a side line by a variety of craftsmen. But of course, only joiners would have been allowed to make wooden dolls and potters figures of clay. Luxury dolls for the children of nobles were obtained from Paris, where a traveller commented on the 'Charming and effectively dressed dolls' seen at the Palais du Justice, where they were sold alongside other expensive items. Among noblewomen, life-sized fashion display figures, now referred to as Pandora, were popular gifts, Ann of Brittany commissioning one for Isabella of Spain.

Throughout the Renaissance the child's doll usually continued to be made in the form of an adult, though interesting exceptions begin to appear. In a woodcut from the cycle *Die Lebensalter des Menschen* of the 16th century, a girl is shown holding a doll whose costume and proportions indicate a child rather than an adult. This doll was provided with a cradle and some spare blankets. Baby dolls are also seen in the cradles of Dutch cabinet houses, though they were not very popular at this time as children preferred the finely dressed adults that can be seen in paintings such as that by the Younger Cranach. Those shown in Renaissance paintings are obviously quality dolls and they appear to be jointed at the shoulder and elbow; the faces are painted with considerable realism and the costumes are correct in detail. Several seem to have a torso that is mounted on a wire or wooden frame that is shaped to support the skirt, the complete doll being constructed in a very similar manner to women found in some crèche settings.

A rag doll, now in the Royal Armoury Collection in Stockholm, is a very rare survivor from this period and once belonged to a daughter of Charles IX. The construction is again reminiscent of crèche figures, as pink and yellow silk is wound around a wire armature. Wearing a wig of real hair, and with its features embroidered on the padded face, the doll is costumed in the style of a fashionable woman of the 1590s. The hair is braided and a pearl tiara is worn. The costume consists of a skirt and bodice together with two petticoats, one of cut and uncut velvet and another of silk taffeta. Pearls are also used for the embroidery of the loose sleeves and an embroidered ruff is carried. The underwear consists only of a linen chemise. The Royal Armoury doll thus has a very strong dual appeal, both as an interesting early doll and as an accurate costume document: throughout the development of dolls in an adult image this dual appeal is much to the fore.

The French continued to create the most lavish dolls during the 16th century and among important commissions was one from the Duchess Claudia of Lorraine who ordered some of the most beautifully costumed dolls that were available for the baby daughter of the Duchess of Bavaria. It was now more common to order expensive play dolls as prestige gifts, and an idea of the standard that was possible is indicated by the mounted knight now in the Bavarian National Museum, Munich, that wears a black leather jacket with long sleeves over the most exquisitely made miniature armour. These jointed knights appear to have been popular toys for wealthy children as several woodcuts exist showing similar figures.

Dolls carved from a single piece of wood, with no jointing, known to collectors as stump dolls, occasionally survive from this period, though completely authenticated examples are rare, and pieces of architectural carving sometimes masquerade under the title. Similar stiffly formed figures were also made of pipeclay; one, in the form of an elegant lady in a low-cut dress, dating from 1525. A woodcut of the

A particularly fine alabaster doll of unknown provenance with effective jointing of the arms. Graeco-Egyptian, of the Ptolemaic dynasty. Ashmolean Museum, Oxford.

Woodcut from the *Hortus Sanitatis* of the 15th century, showing the makers of wooden figures, presumably dolls, at work. Wellcome Museum Library, London.

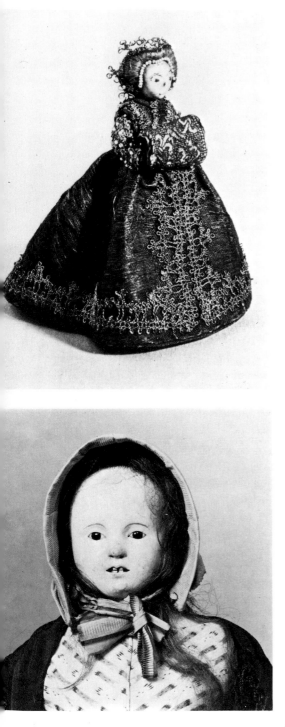

Above:
Papier-mâché shoulder-head with fixed glass eyes typical of dolls made in the Sonneberg area. Four bamboo teeth and pierced nostrils, gusseted pink leather body. The tops of the legs have an unusual metal structure, unfortunately rusted now. Doll in Wonderland, Brighton.

Top:
A doll made for the display of costume and dating from the 1590s. She wears the fashionable costume of the Swedish court, and has embroidered features and a fabric body. Royal Armoury Collection, Stockholm.

period shows a stall in a Dutch market where a mouthwatering range of jointed dolls, some almost half life-sized, and all in the form of well-costumed ladies with ruffs and farthingales, are on display. Male dolls in military costume were also offered for sale, indicating the extremely high standard available to people of moderate means.

In his *Traite d'Architecture* of 1567, Philibert Delorme mentions a technique of manufacturing dolls by pressing papier mâché into moulds. A variety of waste substances such as bran and even vegetable matter was combined as a material for moulding dolls heads, particularly in the Nuremberg area, but as the dolls were very fragile none are known to have survived.

The playthings of Louis XIII of France, born in 1601, were recorded by his doctor, Heroard, and included a fine knight on horseback and a Turkish trumpeter. When he was just over two years old, Sully presented him with a little carriage full of dolls. At the age of six he was given a small nobleman, splendidly dressed in a scented collar. Louis combed the doll's hair and commented 'I am going to marry him to Madame's doll' (Madame being his sister). After the age of seven he was considered too old to play with dolls though it appears that on occasion he continued to do so. Many of his toys came from Germany where the industry was already well established and included plaster dolls and an earthenware figure of a monk. Other royal children, such as the Duchess de Longueville, were given dolls that were accompanied by huge wardrobes.

Wax dolls of some artistry were made for the cabinet doll's houses that were popular both in Germany and Holland from the 17th century. The bodies are often of wire wrapped with silk or fabric and only the parts that are visible when costumed are made of wax. A great deal of individual characterization was given to the heads which range from rather evil old workmen to chubby babies. Those in Margaretha de Ruyter's house, at the end of the 17th century, are costumed in the most precise detail and illustrate the dress of rich burghers. One gentleman, in a full-bottomed wig, wears a close-fitting jacket with tiny buttons and sports a splendid jabot; the ladies wear silk dresses with trains over petticoats decorated with gold lace. 'Faveurs,' small bows sewn to the costumes, are worn both by adults and children. One child wears a velvet cap with a padded brim, used to protect the head when learning to walk. The costumes of workmen, nursemaids and cook are all perfectly reproduced in miniature and indicate a standard of continental wax doll making far superior to that seen in the early English baby houses.

As a modelling substance, wax was very popular, as it so convincingly represented the texture of the human skin. Various methods of colouring were evolved, the makers of portrait waxes soon discovering that pure beeswax was not suitable as it became hopelessly discoloured with age. Vasari comments on the preparation of modelling wax which could be made hard by the addition of animal fat, turps and black pitch – the animal fat making the mixture more supple while the composition was bound together by the turpentine. Though effigy waxes, created to be placed in a catafalque near the grave, had been made in England since the 13th century, there was little interest generally in portrait waxes before the 18th century, when the fashion for images of wax became popular. Among the many nobles modelled by the well-known Mrs Goldsmith was the Duchess of Richmond. Several of the 19th-century dollmakers such as the Montanari family were also artist modellers in wax and the making of dolls was possibly a useful sideline for the less-skilled members. The making of portrait waxes became popular with amateurs and a certain Mrs Salmon taught the art and sold moulds and glass eyes. A particularly beautiful poured-wax doll dating to the late 17th century was owned by a Miss

Bivar who came to England in the train of Mary of Modena in 1673.
The construction of the doll, having a stuffed fabric body and wax
hands and feet, is similar to that associated with 19th-century examples,
though the modelling of the face was reminiscent of that seen in Italian
church figures of the period, but this figure with its fine costume
decorated with silver tissue and lace is certainly a plaything. This doll
was sold at Sotheby's and was accompanied by another wax doll of the
same period wearing a white night-shift and a scarlet 'Turkish'
dressing gown trimmed with silver braid. As wax is really a rather

fragile substance for the manufacture of toys, few dolls that can be firmly dated have survived from this early period and individual examples are great treasures.

At the same sale appeared the pair of dolls that became famous because of the public appeal to match the amount for which they were originally sold and thereby enable them to be kept in Britain. 'Lord and Lady Clapham' are, at present, the most important dolls to have survived from the late 17th century, as previously the standard of wooden dolls of the period had to be studied from the so-called 'Old Pretender' doll now in the Bethnal Green Museum, with its eye catching patches and fontage. In basic construction, Lord and Lady Clapham are similar to the lady with patches, as the heads are carved disproportionately large and the features are also alike, as in fact is the painting of the eyes in all three examples, suggesting that these quality figures might have originated from one maker or at least one particular area. The great importance of Lord and Lady Clapham lies in their full documentation and in the fact that they perfectly exhibit the manner of wearing items of fashionable dress.

In a detailed costume description, the Victoria and Albert Museum comment on the almost total absence of other good visual source material for this period, whether pictorial or in the form of surviving garments. They wear what is described as 'fashionable undress' and when acquired by the museum, the 17th-century pins were still in place. Coats such as that worn by the man were introduced in the 1680s but continued to be worn until the end of the 18th century. No full-sized matching sets of breeches, waistcoat and sword belts have survived as they were usually separated and passed on to servants, so this miniature set is of extra interest. The waistcoat and breeches are made of silver tissue, probably of French origin, and lined with light blue spotted silk. The shoes are correctly made miniatures with the buckles fixed, as in some full-sized versions, with buttons. The male

Below right:
An English wooden doll with the typical flat back and irisless glass eyes, wearing the remains of a costume that appears to date from the early 18th century. Believed to have been taken to America in 1699 by Letitia Penn, daughter of William. Historical Society of Pennsylvania.

Below:
Poured-wax lady with considerable characterization in the modelling of the face. She wears a costume of around 1760 and is constructed with leather arms. The doll belonged to Elizabeth Everett of Bishopston, who married in 1782. Blaise Castle House Museum, Bristol.

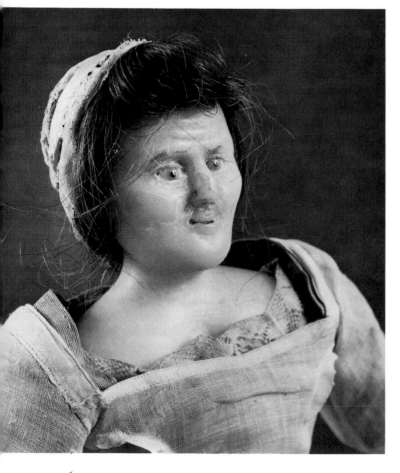

doll's shirt is given long side vents that allowed a man to wrap his shirt around his legs instead of wearing drawers. The banyan or dressing gown is made of pink satin of French or Italian origin, lined with pale blue Chinese silk. His hat is of plain felt with a silver cord bearing the makers name 'T. Bourdillon, Hosier and Hatter to His Majesty, 14 Russel Street. Covent Garden.' This hat with its street-numbered address caused me some misgiving, as the streets of London were not numbered at the time when the dolls appear to have been costumed and it seems almost certain that the hat at least was a considerably later addition. Thomas Bourdillon first appears in the records of the Guild-hall Library at this address in 1781, simply describing himself as Hatter and Hosier. In the 1793 Universal Trade Directory, however, he has adopted the style 'Hatter to his Majesty'. This would appear somewhat irregular, as the warrant holders at that time were a family called Wagner. There can be little doubt that this is the Thomas Bourdillon who made the hat, and that its date can be little earlier than 1793, as the streets in the Covent Garden area did not begin to be numbered until the 1760s.

Lady Clapham wears a double cap with lappets, a cap that is of great importance as neither a cap nor wire support in full size survive. Here in miniature can be seen the arrangement of the wire support in all its complexity and, at the back of the head, a knot of coiled hair, intertwined with pink ribbon and known as a chou. Her mantua is a style of dress introduced about 1676 and was a new fashion, as, combined with corset and petticoat, it formed a complete outfit. The V and A textile department comments 'In the absence of surviving examples, its origin is debatable but, from a consideration of the cut of this miniature, it is clear that it derives from the loose undress gown, more or less based on the Eastern Mode, which was worn informally from the middle of the 17th century. It is all the more important typologi-

Above right:
An early 19th-century Grödnertal with detailed painting of the ringlets that fall over the forehead. With the original hat and lace-trimmed costume in faded green. Collection Mrs Jan Olsen.

Above middle:
Poured-wax lady doll in effective original costume. The head has fixed glass eyes and is slightly turned to the left. The hair is inserted into the scalp and the costume is that of a bride of the 1870s. Inside the hat is a Dickins & Jones label. The body of the doll is hair-filled. Doll in Wonderland, Brighton.

Above left:
A waxed composition lady, *circa* 1845, with irisless dark eyes and the original glass earrings. The mohair wig is partly covered by a hair-net. The body is fabric and the lower parts of the arms and legs are of wood. Dressed in salmon-pink taffeta. Collection Mrs Jan Olsen.

An unusual waxed papier-mâché lady doll of the type made in the Sonneberg area, accompanied by several well-sewn items of costume all dating from about 1845. The original hair is painted in black in a very simplified manner and a fair wig is worn over this. The body is leather and the arms have a wire armature. The doll is 20 inches tall. Bethnal Green Museum, London.

Opposite:
Porcelain and wood jointed doll undressed to show construction. The front pegs that should run through the porcelain head and into the wooden torso are missing and the head is tied in place. Painted pink shoes and blue garters: the hair is upswept into a bun. 7 inches tall. Collection Mrs Jan Olsen.

cally as it stands at the beginning of the series of 18th-century gowns and from it develops the pleated English back, the sack and later, semi-formal mantua.'

The undress gown accompanying the doll was T shaped and until the costume department saw this miniature they had been unaware that any difference of cut might exist between men's and women's undress gowns of the period. The quilted petticoat has little fullness and the boned corset shows how the long narrow-waisted silhouette was achieved. The clothes of both dolls are made of the finest of fabrics available at the time and trimmed with expensive braids and ribbons. As good material was so expensive in the 17th century and even odd pieces were utilized in the costumes of women, one wonders why these attractive figures were so correctly attired, as dolls were often dressed in scraps of joined fabrics. Were they used perhaps as some kind of display model that later became a child's toy, or were they originally intended as gorgeously-equipped dolls for a very rich child? Might they have been fashion dolls? It is doubtful whether we will ever know, but Lord and Lady Clapham survive as probably the most important pair of dolls in Europe and we have to be grateful to the hundreds of people who contributed to their purchase by the museum.

It became highly fashionable in the 18th century for ladies to have their likenesses made in wax and costumed in the current mode, in imitation of those traditionally made in Paris, and exported to show the civilized world the current fashions, such figures being referred to as pandoras. French court ladies sometimes displayed two figures, one dressed in grande toilette and known as the Grande Pandore and another, La Petite Pandore, wearing negligée. In Paris there were exhibitions of costume where figures of this type, such as those made by Rose Bertin, milliner to Marie Antoinette, were displayed.

The coming of the pandora was an event eagerly anticipated by ladies of less elegant countries, who waited until they had examined the precise design on the doll before ordering their costumes. In New England, a mantua maker displayed 'A baby dressed after the newest fashion of mantuas and nightgowns and everything belonging to a dress. Lately arrived in the Captain while from London.' Whether this figure came originally from Paris or whether the New England ladies were satisfied with the English versions of current fashion is not known! One French duke is reputed to have owned 25 life-sized mannequins on which his complete wardrobe was displayed. There is a general supposition that the Grande Pandore were life-sized and the Petite Pandore smaller, but as there are so few fully authenticated examples we are very much in the realm of conjecture.

In 1712, Betty Crosstitch, a milliner, stated that she had received the French baby for the year and she claimed to have taken the utmost care to have her dressed by the most famous mantua makers and tire-women in Paris. Another milliner offered to send the doll to customers for seven shillings. This sending out of the pandora is possibly the reason why, despite the probability of a large number having been made, few survive. I was offered a very primitive example about nine years ago in Bermondsey market, but in this case the body, from the waist down, was cut in outline rather like a dummy board. The head and torso were carved in the round and the arms, with big, rather crudely carved hands, were jointed. The figure was accompanied by roughly cut, but quite authentic, patterns for 17th-century dresses, while it was costumed in a shift of coarse linen. Though of great interest to the costume historian, the figure did not appeal to me as a doll collector as the head had been repainted many times and had lost much of its charm.

An example in my own collection originally stood on a pole that fitted into the carved torso, and made up, the pandora would measure about one third of life-size. In this case the head is still completely original and the hair is carved with great skill. Good quality glass eyes are set into the wood before a layer of gesso was added. An Essex collector owns a smaller but interesting example where a similarly carved torso is mounted on a wooden slatted cone-shaped skirt which revolves on its base so that the complete costume can be shown. Many finely dressed play dolls are seen in museums wrongly described as pandoras, simply because of the high standard of their costume and this mis-description has in turn led to a wide variety of well-dressed playthings being similarly called. There is, for instance, a tendency to describe almost any well-costumed 18th-century doll as a costume or fashion figure, but it should be remembered that doll dressmaking was cultivated as a craft by some gentlewomen such as that energetic craftswoman, Mrs Delany, and we should not therefore be too eager to describe a doll as a pandora. The dolls dressed by the Powell family and now on display at the Bethnal Green Museum and the Victoria and Albert are a case in point as, despite the fact that they were dressed to reflect the fashions of their period by several generations of the same family, they were not intended as dressmaker's patterns.

Small-scale garments were sometimes used by painters in the costuming of carved wooden lay figures, figures that can usually be differentiated both from dolls and pandoras by the simplicity of feature and the very complete body articulation. The Harris Museum and Art Gallery, Preston, owns the small garments once used by the painter Arthur Devis, and in his portrait of Mr and Mrs Ricketts in the grounds of Ranelagh, the man wears a suit almost identical to the miniature clothes.

The range of people able to buy dolls for their children increased steadily during the 18th century and the dollmakers began to experiment with new methods, one of which was to coat a pressed papier mâché head with wax to give a more realistic effect. These waxed dolls began to be made around the middle of the century and have usually to be dated by their costumes, as they continued to be produced in almost identical manner to the end of the Regency period. The waxed

A pair of fine-quality English wooden dolls wearing mid-18th century costume. Note the realistic modelling of the faces and the well-carved hands, indicating a superior product of the time. Blaise Castle House Museum, Bristol.

heads have glass eyes with black pupils and usually no attempt is made to suggest the iris. One of the Powell dolls, dressed in a Brunswick dress for travelling in 1769 is of waxed composition, and I have in my own collection a doll wearing a simple muslin gown and a tall brimmed hat of a shape fashionable in the late 18th century. Were these dolls not dressed in their original costumes, they would have been attributed to the early 19th century, the period when the great mass production of such dolls began.

The majority of collectors associate the 18th century particularly with the jointed wooden dolls popularly described as Queen Annes. In fact the Queen lived for only a short period of the total time in which the dolls were made but they, like so many other antiques, have become associated with her name. The import of dolls was discouraged in the early 18th century by taxes and by 1747 the importation of painted dolls was prohibited. It is problematical whether German carved heads received their final coat of paint in England or whether the German wooden dolls of this period were different from our Queen Annes. Various suggestions have been made as to methods of distinguishing between German, English and even French craftsmanship but, on examination, none of these theories are well supported and until some concrete evidence to the contrary appears, I tend to consider that the majority were made in England where, in the main, they are now most often found.

One of the English woodturners who made such dolls is known, as he was involved in a court case over the theft of '14 naked babies and two dozen dressed babies and one jointed baby'. The use of the word baby to describe what were actually adult dolls continued in use well into the 19th century, the Philadelphia Public Ledger for 1837 still using the term 'Baby house' to describe a doll's house. Conversely, in 1782, a public auction of the goods that were part of the cargo of the brig *Proventia* included 'Two cases of dolls' suggesting that in both England and America, the terms were used alongside one another for some considerable time. William Higgs, who had lost his dolls, claimed to be able to identify his own work and usually sold to shops in Whitechapel and St Catherine's Lane. Though such wooden dolls are often grouped together, there is actually a very wide variety of standard, from some of a simple bedpost shape to others that are carved with real character and have beautifully shaped bodies with breasts and rounded stomachs.

An unusual doll with the stuffed body and wooden lower arms and legs usually associated with papier-mâché heads—in this case the head is poured wax with the moulded hairstyle of the 1840s. The figure is 10 inches high. Tunbridge Wells Museum.

A 12-inch high pedlar doll, *circa* 1835–40, with a papier-mâché head, lavishly equipped with drapery-type wares. The label reads 'Please to buy of Bristol. Ella.' Blaise Castle House Museum, Bristol.

Below right:
A fish and sea-food seller with baskets filled with seaweed and shells. The doll is a Grödnertal type, 13 inches tall, with a papier-mâché head and painted red shoes. Tunbridge Wells Museum.

Below:
A typical turned and carved wooden doll with blue glass eyes of the type popularly referred to as a Queen Anne. Brown leather arms and jointed legs. 28 inches tall. Collection Mrs Jan Olsen.

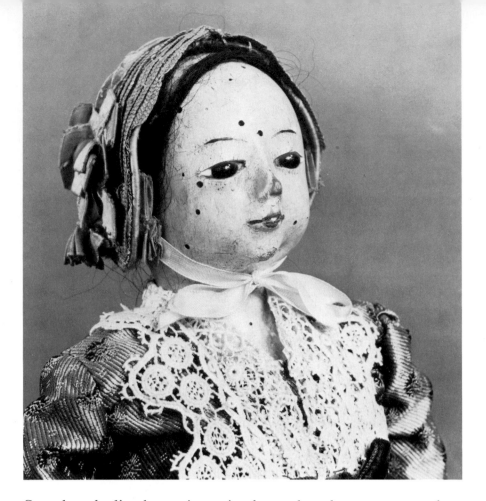

Few wooden dolls of the 18th century are carved with as much realism as this example, with its bulbous black eyes. The body is also well shaped, but the legs have been replaced, giving the doll a truncated effect. The clothes, too, are replacements, but the bonnet is old. The face disfigured by woodworm. Now 14 inches tall. Tunbridge Wells Museum.

Some have bodies that are just a simple peg shape but exert tremendous primitive charm. Part of the attractiveness of the Queen Annes lies in the fact that they can still be purchased without too much difficulty, and most serious collectors are eventually able to own an example. Late versions often have a sharply-pointed torso and the legs are suspended from the central point by means of string or wire. The arms are not always carved and can be made of leather or linen while the fingers were made of substances such as straw, bamboo or small rolls of leather. The majority were carved in wood, however, in a simple fork shape.

The swelling chest area of the turned dolls looks surprisingly effective when costumed and the sharply jutting hips help support the skirts. Some of the heads were overlaid with substantial amounts of plaster in order to give a modelled appearance. The cheapest dolls were made with eyebrows that were treated in an almost stitched manner that is completely stylised, while other examples are rendered with more subtlety, by perhaps painting in a brow lightly and then suggesting the individual hairs on the surface in a darker colour. It is by these variations in the standard of workmanship that the collector has to evaluate such dolls.

The majority of Queen Annes have black irisless glass eyes, though a few, especially those intended for baby houses, were painted. These eyes are of the simplest kind, being made by dropping a blob of molten black glass into white or from slices of a two-coloured glass rod, the eye then being fixed in position before the layer of gesso was applied. The dolls of this type made in the Regency period are often found with more realistic blue eyes, though this cannot be taken as a firm indication of date, as the occasional early doll is discovered with realistic eyes and some in late costumes were still made with brown eyes! Some early dolls are very poorly made, others that are quite late are of a high standard . . . all the collector can do is visit as many museums and study as many examples as possible until he has developed a 'feel' for quality and period that cannot be taught.

A number of Queen Annes are found dressed in costumes that include two strips of fabric or ribbon hanging from the shoulders; these are usually described as leading strings and are said to indicate a child doll. I became unhappy about this explanation after seeing sets of original dolls in baby houses with dolls made to adult height wearing these additions that were most definitely not intended to guide a faltering walker! In fact these ribbons were worn as an indication of a dependent child, who could be any age from two to thirty and have no connection with the strong leading strings that would support a child's first steps. Philippe Aries, in *Centuries of Childhood*, mentions an engraving by Guerard showing a child wearing hanging ribbons between which can be clearly seen the cords used to aid walking–the leading strings. The hanging ribbons were purely a traditional style and had more or less gone out of use by the 1780s.

As they were virtually indestructable, wooden dolls made ideal toys and continued to be played with long after the painted face had disintegrated or been washed away. A number of such playthings appear regularly on the market, quite often minus not only face but arms and legs as well–one recent example retained only its well-made corset but was obviously a treasured possession and kept in a family for hundreds of years.

In an account written by Mrs Stevenson entitled *When I was a little Girl*, published by Macmillan in 1871, she wrote, 'I never had any of those grand dolls such as children have now, with eyes that open and shut and real hair done up in curls or chignons, and wax faces and arms, and fine clothes that are stitched on their bodies in a most cruel and unfeeling way . . . I should not have known what to do with them. I could not have washed them every night in my little tin bath with the real soap tray and towels. I could not have cut scratches on their arms to make believe they had fallen down and hurt themselves. I could not have coloured their faces with red paint and then pretended they had taken scarlatina, I could not have tumbled them, clothes and all, into the water tub in the back yard and punished them and sent them to bed in disgrace. Indeed, they would not have been of the slightest domestic value to me as I could not have put them through any of the experiences I went through myself.' After reading accounts such as this regarding a child's treatment of her doll, it is little wonder so many torsos sans everything appear in the salerooms!

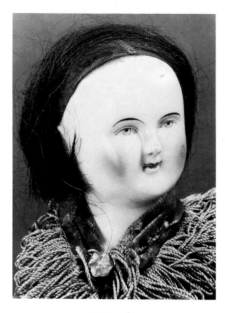

A porcelain-headed lady with the remains of the original wig concealing the black-painted spot on the crown. The body is fabric filled with sawdust, with porcelain arms. The legs are replacements and the dress is of a later date. 15 inches tall. Tunbridge Wells Museum.

Detail of 'parian' lady showing the precise modelling of the hair. Pierced ears and painted eyes. Joy Stanford Collection.

A few German dollmakers are recorded as making wooden dolls, such as Christian Freidrich Hammer, who worked in Nuremberg, and Johann Demitz. Hammer broke the rules of the guilds by painting his dolls in his own workshop and by this action freed the doll industry from the hampering restraint of the bismuth painters who had insisted that the dolls should go to their workshops for finishing. This new freedom meant that the German doll industry could begin to expand rapidly.

The most frequently found German wooden dolls of the early 19th century are those with delicate limbs and painted black hair known as Grödnertals. They were exported from Germany all over Europe and to Britain and America. These dolls are typical of the period when children from all walks of life began to be given toys of similar construction, that were mass produced on a folk basis; even Queen Victoria when a child played with dolls of this simple type, which she and her nurse costumed as noblewomen and opera singers known to them, a group that can be seen at the London Museum. The basic Grödnertal is characterized by a carved yellow comb at the top of the black hair and simple painted features. The slim bodies are jointed in small versions with simple pivots, while larger dolls have ball and socket articulation. The finest large examples have extra joints at the waist and even the neck, almost in the manner of an artist's lay figure, but in a much simplified manner. All the known Grödnertals date from the Regency period, though it is possible that their production began rather earlier, in the late 18th century. With their high-busted slim shapes and long legs they were obviously conforming to the Regency ideals of feminine beauty.

They range widely in size, from tiny examples of under an inch to others as large as forty inches, such as the superb example in the Strangers Hall, Norwich, dressed in the height of Regency fashion in a pink silk overdress and a muslin frock. From a belt hangs a miniature silver chatelaine. Some quality dolls such as this were given hairstyles carved in much more detail than was usual and ornate combs and pierced ears. Some have delicate, tendril-like ringlets that hang before the ears, while a few rare male examples have carved moustaches. Those the collector is most likely to find are of doll's-house size, but even in this small scale a surprising number of completely different expressions could be achieved by a few deft brush strokes. This variety of expression in the cheaply made dolls was exploited by the young Victoria, who used a sweet-faced example for Lady Pultney and another with a cross face for the Duchess of Orleans.

Some particularly fine Grödnertals have heads carved in considerable detail, but care should be taken in deciding whether the complicated effect is actually achieved with the chisel or by overlaying the core of the head with a layer of papier mâché that is actually moulded into shape. Either type of doll is desirable, though an intricately carved example obviously called for more skill in manufacture. I recently examined a most interesting type in a private collection which was given rather crudely carved but well-formed breasts, almost as though the maker was experimenting with an improved shape. Brotteig or plaster overlaid heads can often be distinguished by the fact that changes in atmospheric conditions sometimes cause them to crack or the plaster to flake away; some of these were decorated only with a black spot at the crown, though this type, in combination with a jointed wooden body, is very rare. Male dolls of the plaster overlaid type are also difficult to find, especially in larger sizes.

The Grödnertals were gessoed after carving, and painted in flesh colours; red, yellow or blue slippers were painted on the simply carved feet. Only the parts of the doll that could be seen when costumed were given this surface treatment, the remainder being left as plain wood.

The basic Grödnertal body continued to be used until the late 1840s, though by this time the heads, usually now of brotteig or plaster, were given updated hairstyles.

Various mixtures of rye meal, paper and waste materials were used in the manufacture of composition substances from the 18th century on. Examples from this early period, usually with leather or wooden bodies and applied wigs, are very rare, as the mass production of dolls of this type did not begin until the early 19th century. The extravagant hairstyles of the Regency Period were a challenge to the modellers, who meticulously copied the contemporary fashions – plaited buns, bunches and waves.

When a style defeated the modeller, actual hair, stiffened with some kind of size or lacquer, was applied. Once made, many of these moulds continued in use over a twenty or thirty year time-span and the figures often have to be accurately dated by their costume rather than the style of hairdressing. A few extremely rare versions were given inset glass eyes, while others were modelled bald and given wigs. Catalogues of the period also illustrate baby dolls and gentlemen with side whiskers and bald heads – unfortunately examples appear to be quite unobtainable.

Although their hairstyles varied so greatly, the basic construction of the papier mâchés remained constant and consisted of a white or pink kid body, with the lower arms and legs made of wood; the joints being neatened with strips of coloured paper. A wire armature was resorted to in very large examples in order to keep the figure rigid. As dolls of this type warp and crack very easily, collectors have usually to accept some slight damage, as absolutely perfect examples are not easy to find. Cheaper, late versions were given the simple hairstyles of the 1840s and bodies were, by that time, often made of fabric, though the gauze dresses that are often found on the very early 19th-century dolls still continued to be used.

German makers were able to produce papier-mâché dolls so economically that competition was almost pointless, though the figures were often costumed in France before sale. From about 1840, however, the French began to regain their interest in manufacture and initially

Above left:
Bisque swivel-headed Parisienne doll. The shoulder plate has moulded breasts and the feet are interestingly modelled with high heels. Metal-rimmed holes in the feet give support for standing. Late 19th century but wearing the original 18th-century-style fancy dress with a red woollen cape. Marked '3' on head. Probably by Jumeau. Christie's, London.

Above:
A black-haired porcelain lady with a jointed wooden body. The lower arms are porcelain, like the lower legs, and one hand is modelled clenched and with a hole running through so a costume accessory can be carried. She wears the original costume of beige and cream silk, with red-painted shoes. 7¾ inches tall. Bethnal Green Museum, London.

Right:
A wax doll wearing a man's costume
of the 1820s consisting of a top hat
and a luxurious fur-trimmed cape.
With fixed blue eyes and inset hair.
Blaise Castle House Museum, Bristol.

A Grödnertal-type wooden doll
wearing the remains of a German or
Swiss regional costume that was
completely made of blue, brown and
black paper. The hair is especially
interesting as it is crowned with a
neat bun-like coil of thin cord which
was then painted and varnished.
Collection Mrs Jan Olsen.

are considered to have produced very well-made gusseted bodies of
leather that allowed for greater movement. At this stage it is generally
considered that heads continued to be obtained from Germany but
that the assembly and costuming was carried out in France. This
theory is supported by the fact that similar heads are seen in German
trade catalogues of the time. Ladies' heads with bamboo teeth and glass
eyes, however, are often described as completely French; at present
there is no firm evidence to support this claim, and I am inclined
personally to feel that these heads are also of German origin. These
Franco-German dolls of the 1840s and 50s are characterized by their
plump bodies and round faces with a much more frequent use of glass
eyes.

The mass production of waxed composition dolls also began in the
early 19th century and collectors are fortunate in the large number that
have survived. The hair was often pushed into the head through a slit
cut in the crown, which has led to the term 'slit heads' being applied to
dolls of this type. The lower arms were usually made of coloured
leather to represent gloves, with individually stitched fingers, while the
bodies were very simply made from fabric. Slit heads are usually
attributed to Germany, though several English firms are recorded as
having made waxed compositions, but it would appear in so similar a
manner that the products are, at present, indistinguishable from one
another. Sleeping eyes had occasionally been used in dolls since the
18th century, but they do not appear in any number until the Regency
period, when their movement was effected either by a wire lever that
protruded at waist level, or by a system of wire and string.

Right:
English wooden doll of the Regency period in unusually fine condition, showing how strongly such faces were decorated. Blue eyes are particularly associated with the early 19th century. 21 inches tall. Joy Stanford Collection.

Bisque-headed Parisienne in striped silk day dress with a brown overskirt and bustle. Gusseted leather body. The clothes were commercially made, about 1870. Blaise Castle House Museum, Bristol.

Many dolls of this basic type do not have hair inserted in a slit but wear wigs of mohair or hair sewn to a cap of cotton or flannel. An almost white shade, with tight curls, seems by the number of surviving examples to have been very popular.

A number of waxed compositions made in the early 19th century were dressed retrospectively in a modified version of 18th-century costume, with some of the detail fixed to the body with pins. Commercially made costumes such as these were created with the intention of an eye-catching effect, and have often deteriorated badly in comparison with home-sewn dress which was made in detail. The standard of the workmanship in these clothes, made by mothers and nurses, is almost invariably high and despite the basic simplicity of the costume of the period, the clothes are interesting for their meticulous attention to detail.

A charming man doll of this type in the Strangers Hall, Norwich, has the remains of a beard implanted into the wax by a heated needle or small knife. The body is typical of that usually encountered in slit heads, though this implantation of hair is more frequently seen in the plumper dolls dating from the 1840s and later. Rather more realism began to be demanded in the late 1830s, and some of the waxed compositions were made with lower arms and legs modelled of the same substance as the head. Though this made for a more life-like figure, it also meant that much of the primitive charm of the very stylized doll was lost. More attention was also given to the bodies which were waisted and sometimes filled with hair rather than the traditional sawdust.

A fine matching pair of Parisiennes, the one undressed to show the construction of the leather-over-wood body, with the additional joints both at the waist and the ankle. The costumed doll wears a silk dress in pale pink and green. 18 inches tall. Bethnal Green Museum, London.

Slit heads were sometimes utilized in the construction of pedlar figures; these fanciful items were both made at home and commercially as ornaments, to be preserved under a glass shade. The small wares of the pedlars must have provided a continual source of wonder for young children, but would have been far too fragile for their often clumsy hands. Home-made pedlars usually wear a red flannel cape over some form of country costume and have a much softer and more haphazard appearance than those made by professionals, whose construction is much crisper. Generally, the commercially made versions are superior as the variety of wares offered is much greater and the scale of the various objects more precise. Their stock consists of items often as diverse as saws and spring bonnets, while gentlemen's braces, books and small knitted bags seem common almost to all.

The *Dolls House News*, a few years ago, illustrated a most interesting series of commercially produced cards of small items for 19th-century pedlar's trays, one holding very small Grödnertals, scissors, tape measure, penknife and knitted or crocheted baskets, while another consisted of socks and gloves of various sizes, all correctly made. If such cards of related objects could be purchased from drapers or novelty shops an explanation of the similarity of the wares between examples from different parts of the country is provided.

Although pedlars are usually described as of 18th century origin, I have, to date, seen no example that can be positively attributed to that period nor picked up any contemporary written reference except with regard to those carved of wood shown in the Bestelmeier catalogues. They therefore appear to be a fancy very much of the early 19th century, though cheaper play versions are sometimes found dating to the 1890s. One of the few known makers is C & H White of Milton, Portsmouth, who made a series of dolls, often with fine leather faces representing a range of produce sellers rather than the more usual pedlars. Subjects ranged from the poulterers to sellers of garden produce with appropriate costume. Grödnertals, as well as slit heads, were often utilized in the making of pedlars, a particularly fine pair coming up for sale at Sothebys in 1976 representing 'Amy Scrap. Licensed hawker No. 5367' and 'Mark Thrift. Licensed hawker. No. 7298'. These licences were issued to pedlars after 1810, which helps to give some indication of a possible date. Mark Thrift was given finely painted black sideburns and both carried well-stocked wicker baskets of goods.

Though the pedlars are often considered a purely English fashion, 'Women Pedlars with moveable heads' were offered in Hieronymus Bestelmeier's catalogue for 1800, though these were probably similar to the carved wooden figurines which he sold. In the same catalogue, a dealer in fashion goods with a boutique is also offered.

The construction of vendors, not necessarily in the form of pedlars, was of great interest to the Victorians and bazaar stalls, costermongers' carts and hat shops were all created with considerable ingenuity.

Porcelain was necessarily an expensive substance in the 18th century and, though used occasionally for the manufacture of shoulder heads, examples are so rare as to be virtually unobtainable. Toy tea sets were made of porcelain in some number, but the material does not seem to have been utilized on any scale as a dollmaking material until the 1830s. Companies such as K.P.M. (Königliche Porzellan Manufaktur, Berlin) produced some exquisite dolls in the 1830s and 40s, which are usually dated by their hairstyles. The Berlin dolls are often tinted with a soft pink glaze which makes them more realistic than the rather stark white of most porcelain heads. As in the manufacture of papier mâchés, moulds continued in use some time after a particular style had gone out of fashion, so that dolls are found in completely original clothes of a later date than the hairstyle might suggest. Porcelain dolls with black spots on the crown, often referred to as Biedermeiers, are thought to have been produced around 1840; their features are usually much finer and the painting more delicate than that found on the later dolls.

The majority of porcelain dolls are completely unmarked except with a number and are unattributable except as to country of origin, which is almost invariably Germany. A few dolls dating from the mid 19th century, with makers' marks stamped on the fabric torsos, have recently appeared. One, with an ornately moulded hairstyle incorporating entwined flowers, was stamped 'H. & Co. Patent'. A boy doll recently added to my own collection and wearing the original clothes, *circa* 1850, is marked in turquoise in an oval 'Fʳ. H. & Cie Patent' indicating a French origin. The porcelain is of very fine quality and the decoration delicate. The shoulder head is attached to the body by a single sew hole back and front, rather than the two or three that are more usually found. As European collectors become more aware of the importance of recording marks, it might eventually prove possible to attribute more porcelains.

Most of the porcelain dolls made before 1870 represent ladies, and the traditional type of construction, with a fabric body and porcelain arms, legs and head, was maintained. Very few men dolls were produced, and though hundreds of ladies were made for dolls houses, those with short hairstyles representing boys or men are seldom seen. The method of constructing the porcelain dolls was not very satisfactory, as the heavy limbs tend to crash together alarmingly when the doll is moved, and accounts for the large number found damaged. The basic doll has fairly short black hair modelled in the form of ringlets; legs are finished with flat-healed boots sometimes decorated with painted ribbons. Just below the knee a delicately painted garter might also appear. The bodies are very small waisted but have large hips to act as some extra support for the crinoline dresses that were worn when dolls of this type were in their hey day. An idea of a doll's actual date can often be estimated by reference to the fashionable shape of a woman in contemporary fashion plates.

The cream and green silk costume of this Parisienne is both effective and very well made. The leather shoes are marked 'C.C' in an oval. The 18-inch doll, which is marked '4' on the head, has a swivel neck, pierced ears and bisque lower arms. The body is gusseted kid and the eyes are blue. Tunbridge Wells Museum.

A carved and painted wooden doll of superb quality. The family of the donor had links with the court of the Old Pretender. Painted eyes, kid covered wooden arms, and lower part of the legs covered with silk to simulate stockings. The doll is even dressed with linen underwear. Late 17th century. Bethnal Green Museum, London.

Large numbers of china heads were sold loose for home assembly not only as dolls but also as pincushions. As pins were an expensive item in the 18th century many women continued to hoard them in a decorative manner by pushing them into a doll's skirt that was filled with emery powder that sharpened them and helped prevent rusting. A range of two-faced dolls, one side representing age and the other youth, would appear to have been especially made for pincushion assembly, as each example known is mounted on an emery-filled conical skirt and has wired arms. The quality of some of these heads, especially the old woman's face, is very high, with heavy modelling of wrinkles, though another version is quite mediocre. These two-faced porcelains are much more rarely found than play dolls and tend to command substantial prices.

Pedlars and swagmen carried the porcelain dolls the Germans were able to produce so cheaply into every small village in the country and, as the smallest sizes were within the price range of even the poorest children, a very large number are still found. Dolls of this type were assembled at Alfred Davis and at Josephs in Leadenhall Street and it seems probable that a number were exported in parts, to be made up in the country of destination. As there are only fleeting references to the doll trade in writings of the 19th century, it is impossible to estimate the extent of this trade and I believe that the majority were imported complete.

Very occasionally, porcelain heads are found on Grödnertal type bodies, and usually have one hand modelled closed, with a neat hole running through, possibly so that an article could be carried. This method of modelling a single hand is also seen in wax dolls made for Dutch cabinet houses and appears to be traditional rather than, as is sometimes fancifully suggested, as a special method for dolls representing Queen Victoria carrying the sceptre. Heads intended for mounting on wooden bodies can be distinguished by the single sew holes at the back, accompanied by a pair in the front of the shoulder head. Several different hairstyles are found on dolls of this type and some were made with a most attractive pink tint to the faces and arms. Among the rarer porcelains are those with very ornately moulded hairstyles, brown or even blonde hair, and, almost impossible to find, those with inset glass eyes.

The cold white porcelain could not have continued to please children indefinitely and manufacturers began to create dolls of unglazed porcelain known as bisque. Early bisque heads, dating to the 1850s, were untinted and are generally described by collectors as parians, though in fact not made of that particular substance. It was once considered that some of these parians were of French origin, but as there is little evidence to support this, it would seem that the main production was German. The construction of the bodies was almost identical to that used in porcelain dolls, but the heads were given additional detail which could be achieved very effectively in this medium. Jewelled tiaras, plumed turbans, flowers and pearls were all described in detail and tinted with great artistry. The finest examples were given pierced ears and inset glass eyes. Some of these highly-decorated heads are in fact fine pieces of porcelain, exhibiting a range of decorating techniques, such as the use of lustre in several strengths, seen even on a single head.

In order to give more realism to the parians, the manufacturers began to tint the bisque in a soft pink and this type of doll is still referred to by the term applied to them by Eleanor St George – 'blonde bisques'.

These tinted ladies were modelled with much softer features than the earlier parians and, in fact, by the 1880s, some intended to represent ladies were quite child-like in appearance. A few rare men dolls of this type are found, one even being decorated by the manufacturer with a finely painted black beard. This particular example, in the Bethnal Green Museum, has a swivel neck. Swivel necks meant that even more realism could be achieved but, as it added to the cost of the doll, it is a device only occasionally found on the type. These top quality tinted bisques are often found with grey boots rather than the more usual black. This extra attention given to the footwear indicates the slight shortening of fashionable skirts for walking, and some boots were lustre decorated for extra appeal. I have not found any adult heads of this type to be marked, and despite the obvious skill of the makers, they remain unknown.

Unglazed bisques continued to be used in doll's houses long after they had gone out of fashion in larger sizes. Even in the 1920s, untinted bisque ladies and gentlemen are seen in catalogues wearing the fashionable bobbed hairstyles of the time. This use of an outdated material continued as there was nothing else that, on this minute scale, could so perfectly reproduce individual characters. Doll's house families, complete with white-haired grandparents and perhaps

A particularly fine pair of carved wooden dolls dating from the late 17th century and wearing their very detailed original costumes. They were known by the family of the original owners as Lord and Lady Clapham. Both are 21 inches tall. Victoria and Albert Museum, London.

a visiting young soldier with a drooping yellow moustache, continued in production from the 1870s to the 1920s, but are now only occasionally found as complete families. Though not particularly valuable individually, a complete family, accurate even to the babe in arms and elder sisters and aunts, would command a high figure from a doll's house enthusiast.

While the Germans were making parians and blonde bisques, the French interest in the manufacture of dolls reawakened spectacularly in their production of perfectly equipped lady dolls known as Parisiennes. It is often suggested that the earliest French lady dolls were given German porcelain heads, but as these are so very different from those usually associated with that country, it would appear possible that the French had begun to manufacture their own. Bodies of gussetted kid were the most usual, though others are found with jointed wooden, fabric over metal, or even leather over wooden bodies. The pink-tinted porcelain heads, sometimes with swivel necks, are thought to be the earliest Parisiennes ever made: their faces are hardly beautiful, with rather pug-like noses and red nostril spots, but are appreciated by collectors as the first examples of their type. They are frequently referred to as Rohmer types, after a firm working in Paris between 1857 and 1880. Eyes of such dolls can be either painted or glass, those with painted eyes being the more popular with collectors. Authentic Rohmers are stamped on the chest 'Mme. Rohmer. Breveté S.G.D.G. Paris', the initials in translation meaning 'Without Government guarantee'. As several of the pink chinas are found with this mark, it has become the custom to refer in this way to all dolls of the type, though it is possible that they were also made by other firms. Occasionally a doll of this type with porcelain legs is found, and these are among the most desirable.

The French manufacturers all experimented with different body types as a particular advance became fashionable. Gutta percha was the most unsuccessful of the experiments as, although it was used in some quantity, the dolls have not survived in any number. Certain makers such as Fernand Gaultier, who marked his dolls 'F.G.', produced heads for assembly by other makers, so that even when a doll is stamped with a maker's name on the body this does not necessarily mean that he manufactured the complete figure. Exclusive shops, for instance, sometimes marked wares with their own stamps, so that examples are found with the name of Mlle Lavalée Peronne, who sold the finest of dolls with elaborate trousseaux at her shop 'A La Poupée de Nuremberg' on the Rue de Choiseul and who edited the publication *La Poupée Modèle*.

Bodies marked 'Simonne. No 1 à 13 Passage Délorme, Rue de Rivoli 188, Paris' have been found with heads marked both by 'F.G.' and Jumeau, and it is problematical as to whether Simonne only assembled or actually produced any complete dolls herself. When judging the quality of a Parisienne, it is therefore more sensible to rely on the

A tilting knight bearing the Holzschurer arms. The figure under the armour is made of jointed wood. It is 8 inches high, and dates from the mid-16th century. Bayerisches Nationalmuseum, Munich.

appearance of the doll rather than any mark or stamp. Some Parisiennes marked by Bru or Jumeau are of very indifferent quality while others are superb. Though a marked doll is liked, because it can be definitely attributed, the new collector should not be blinded into thinking that a doll is necessarily good simply because it carries the mark of a well-respected maker.

The Parisiennes epitomize their age of splendid bourgeois luxury, when even the child's doll was part of the heavily ornamented household. Their very complete equipages included not only a vast range of outfits for every possible social occasion but also jewellery, writing cases, sewing accessories and, in one case, even a tea set. It was the fascination of the well-made miniature costumes as well as the quality of the beautifully decorated bisque heads that caused Parisiennes to be collected from the 1920s, when this field first became popular. Early collectors often wove romantic stories around these perfectly made dolls, suggesting that they were created as fashion figures to be sent all over the world to display French costume. As prints of the period show such dolls offered for sale from street stalls and they were promoted by booklets especially aimed at children, their intention was obviously that of play.

An astonishing amount of detail was lavished on the costume of Parisiennes made in the 1860s. The sewing machine was still not in use by doll dressmakers, and the standard of needlework found in their wardrobes is of the highest quality. Braids and beaded decoration were meticulously sewn in position in garments that were perfectly made miniatures rather than effective eye-catching dresses made with the minimum amount of effort that are seen on later dolls made by, for instance, Jumeau. In the 70s and 80s, though the dolls were still lavishly equipped, less detail was put into the dress and many were machine sewn, their design being limited by the machine. Edges were much more frequently pinked with shears in order to save tedious handwork and rather less care was given to obtaining trimmings in perfect scale. The dolls themselves, however, are rather more beautiful, with longer faces and larger eyes and resemble rather haughty ladies rather than the sweet plump-cheeked woman of the 1860s.

A complete area of Paris, around the Passage Choiseul, was devoted to the manufacture of dolls' clothes and accessories; there were doll bootmakers, milliners, glovers and corset makers, all contributing to the filling of the often large trunks which accompanied the dolls. Books were published by the doll companies advising small girls of the types of clothes they should obtain to keep their plaything in the height of fashion. Among the shops selling such accessories were Au Nain Bleu and Madame Barrois. Commercially produced patterns, such as those in *La Poupée Modèle*, taught girls, under the supervision of a mother or nurse, how to create similar costumes at home. Some idea of the number of dollmakers is indicated by the fact that at the 1878 Paris Exposition fifty-seven makers showed their products.

The name Jumeau seems to be known to every antique dealer in Europe, many thinking that the only dolls of any quality originate in this particular factory. In fact Jumeaux vary in quality to a greater degree than almost any other French doll and have to be priced upon appearance rather than on a mark. The firm was established in 1842, when a partnership existed with a certain Belton. At first the company produced beautifully costumed dolls with heads obtained from other companies, but manufactured their own heads at Montreuil-sous-Bois, *circa* 1873. The Jumeau Medaille d'Or stamp found on bodies related to an award of a gold medal at the 1878 Paris Exhibition. Marked Jumeau heads have been found on stockinette-covered metal bodies and on others of leather-covered wood. One very rare type has moulded breasts and bisque lower legs with moulded high-heeled

Pink-tinted porcelain doll, 1850—60, with moulded ringlets, and painted blue eyes. She wears side-lacing boots, and is seated on a sofa of a later date. Blaise Castle House Museum, Bristol.

shoes, an unmarked example of this type of doll being illustrated. Very large eyes are a feature of their better quality Parisiennes, though other marked examples are of indifferent quality. The firm was very publicity minded, and exhibitions of their dolls in furnished rooms and miniature settings were staged all over Europe and America. This wide publicity meant that the company's name became known to a very large number, and even in 20th century catalogues the products of this firm were mentioned by name whereas those of other makers were just described with their country of origin.

Even in their own time, the luxury of many of the French lady dolls was frowned upon, E. Stevenson commenting in 1871 'I think it is very foolish to have such fine lady dolls. I went to see a little girl the other day and she brought me hers to look at. Her mama had sent for it all the way from Paris and it cost five and twenty shillings . . . This Paris doll that I was telling you about was dressed as if she was going to a party. She had a pink silk dress on with black lace over it and pink roses and a white feather in her hair, and a necklace and bracelet and a fan and bouquet and a lace pocket handkerchief and everything else that grown up ladies wear when they want to be very grand indeed . . . I did not feel respectful to this doll when I found that all its things were put together and stuck on with paste and glue and that it had no petticoats worth mentioning and very clumsy stockings which fitted as badly as possible. But worse than that, it had to be hung up by its arms in a cupboard when it was done with and the little girl was only allowed to play with it when she had her best frock on. As for kissing it, she never dare do that for fear of rubbing the paint off its cheeks.'

'Psyche', a cut-out paper doll given
away in a French fashion magazine,
circa 1835. The two-sided clothes
slipped over the head. Blaise Castle
House Museum, Bristol.

A papier-mâché shoulder head on a
leather body with wooden lower arms
and legs. The eyes are blue painted
and the hair is modelled with
exaggerated wings that are drawn
into a plaited bun at the back. The
shoulder plate is unusually low and
the breasts are indicated. The doll
wears a faded blue taffeta dress
trimmed with flowers and lace.
Tunbridge Wells Museum.

The cost of this composition or plaster doll, constructed mainly for
show, seems very high and the disgusted sigh of the old lady at French
frivolity can still be clearly felt after a hundred years. A similar attitude
to the more conventional Parisiennes is frequently encountered in
autobiographies and it seems as though the child was often both
fascinated and irritated by the grandeur of her toy. The juries at
international exhibitions also made wry comments on the fact that
such dolls were over-expensive and that children would benefit more
from a simple doll, together with fabrics from which they could
themselves construct the clothes.

A few Parisiennes were dressed as girls, in mid-calf-length coats and
dresses. Sometimes, as in the case of a lovely girl doll of fine quality
seen recently at Sothebys, the figure can be tentatively attributed by
the marking of part of the costume, in this case the original shoes being
marked with the Jumeau 'J'. These smaller girl dolls are particular
favourites, as they can be used to set up a most effective group with
lady dolls. The costumiers of a few dolls seem to have been undecided
as to whether a figure was meant to represent a lady or a girl: an example with its original trousseau in my collection having splendid
formal ladies' dresses alongside several of mid calf-length that a young
girl, but no respectable woman, of the period would have worn.

Huret devoted much attention to ploys for the promotion of sales,
such as balls and garden parties aimed at encouraging a child to make
sure that her doll was the best equipped and most fashionable at the
event. Their products were marked 'Maison Huret, No 22 Boulevard
Montmartre Paris' or '68 Rue de la Boetie'. It made several innovations,
including the registering of a patent to enable a head to turn or tilt
so that a more realistic effect could be obtained. Huret ladies are often
characterized by their plump and child-like features.

Although lady dolls were made by the firm of Bru, established in
1866 and working from the Rue Saint Denis, only rarely are adequately
marked examples found. Heads marked with an incised 'BS' are
thought possibly to have originated at their factory and a few other
dolls are authenticated by their original Bru boxes. A Parisienne with
a plump face and wearing a blue and white striped muslin frock over a
gusseted leather was found to be marked 'B Jne et Cie' on the back of
the shoulder and 'E. Depose' on the front; such marked examples are
very rare and usually fetch a higher price at auction than their quality
might suggest, purely because of the interest in a marked doll from a
firm that so rarely incised their name.

Despite the fact that the term Parisienne is usually associated with the fine bisque dolls produced by a few quality companies, other lady dolls, in a cheaper but similar vein were made by, for instance, the Lanternier company of Limoges who adapted the wooden bodies used by the finest makers into similar composition structures that are rather ugly when unclothed but surprisingly effective when costumed. The heads used on such bodies are of the simple socket type that fit into the composition torsos, and are usually made of bisque of poor quality though the actual modelling is good, and of interest as examples of an economical adaptation of a quality doll for sale to a less affluent market. Lanternier also produced lady-type heads for slim, adult-shaped jointed bodies; an example of such a doll can be seen in the collection of the Ipswich Museum.

A number of rather beautiful waxed lady dolls were made in Germany at the end of the 19th and beginning of the 20th centuries. Some were given good quality hair-filled bodies but other, later, versions were often very cheaply constructed and the bodies roughly filled with straw. The costumes of the later dolls, though effective when new, are usually of poor quality, frequently being sewn in position. A few large examples are found with the most exquisite dress precisely reflecting that of a particular period, and figures of this type are purchased very much as effective costume documents rather than fine dolls. Rather more immature lady dolls were made by the German firm of Dressel, whose work is often characterized by the presence of moulded waxed red boots of some decorative quality.

Alongside such waxed compositions, the Germans also produced bisque-headed lady dolls, though in nothing like as large a quantity. Those most frequently found are of a small size, usually under 12 inches, and are only occasionally marked. Their costume is very similar in construction to that found on the waxed dolls. An example in my collection is marked '7926' with some indistinct printed green figures. The Colemans refer to one in their collection that is marked '72' in green. The use of stamped green figures is typical of the Brothers Heubach and the shape of the incised numbers in my own example is also typical. The modelling of these heads is very effective, and the colouring and the quality of the bisque is also of a high standard. A particularly effective example was sold at Christie's, South Kensington in 1976, which measured $20\frac{1}{2}$ inches, this being unusually large for the type. The costume was accurate and highly extravagant, though it could not be removed, being sewn in place; curiously, in this case, as the figure was accompanied by a nightdress, suggesting that the whole was probably used for some kind of display. The poor quality bodies in all the mentioned dolls, in combination with a good quality head, are also typical of Gebruder Heubach's work.

Rather similar marked dolls were produced by the Kestner Company and sometimes stamped 'Gibson Girl' on the chest, a superb example from the collection of Jean Stiero being illustrated. This range was of generally better quality, as the bodies were of gussetted leather. Simon & Halbig, who had produced tinted bisque shoulder heads in the 1870s began to make more realistic wigged lady dolls in the 1880s. Early heads of this type were mounted on fabric or gussetted kid bodies and have inset glass eyes. A few unmarked dolls of excellent quality with swivel heads are thought to have been produced by Simon & Halbig, possibly for the French market. The best of their dolls are created from bisque of the most superb standard, and have a very soft quality of modelling that is not seen in the majority of French lady dolls. When ball-jointed dolls became popular, a lady-type version was produced with an accentuated waist and rather delicately suggested bosom. The heads really imitate girls rather than women, though they are classed as woman dolls by collectors.

A key-wound mechanical walking figure of an elderly gentleman with a papier-mâché head and sheepskin wig. The figure moves on wooden rollers concealed under the feet and the head turns from side to side. $11\frac{1}{2}$ inches tall. Tunbridge Wells Museum.

Above:
Bisque-headed doll with a well-equipped dressing table. Marked in red on the head 'Tête Jumeau Déposé 9'. An unusual adult-style body that is small-waisted and has a definite bust line. The body is marked 'Bébé Jumeau.S.G.D.G.' Costumed for the Philadelphia Exhibition of 1876. Doll in Wonderland, Brighton.

Right:
Bisque lady doll of the type known as a Gibson Girl, with glass eyes, leather body and bisque lower arms. She wears the original wig, and is 22 inches tall. Blanding House Museum, Wisconsin.

Bisque heads were necessarily fragile, and various efforts were made to produce a more durable material. Rubber and rubber-type substances at first seemed ideal but despite the fact that they were able to withstand the damage of childhood, they are unsatisfactory as collectors' items, as the material soon perishes. The Goodyear discovery of a method of vulcanising rubber meant that the substance could be moulded into doll shapes. Despite the fact that a number were made both in France and England, those that are most collectable are found in America, manufactured, in particular, by the India Rubber Comb Company, whose heads imitated the designs of currently popular moulded bisque heads of the 1870s.

A few effectively modelled metal doll's heads were made in the 19th century, one of which wore moulded flowers in the hair; the majority of the metal dolls however, are of the child type. Various composition mixtures were also used in the manufacture of adult dolls, though the surface treatment has often deteriorated badly. One of the most satisfactory materials, despite new discoveries, continued to be fabric, but because dolls of this type soon became dirty, even well-made figures are often ignored. The Warwick Toy Museum has a group of delightful doll's house rag dolls of the Regency period that have, by great good fortune, survived as a complete family. It was not until colour printing on fabric became really cheap, in the last quarter of the 19th century, that any mass production of rag dolls was able to begin.

The first commercially made American dolls are considered to have been made by Izannah Walker, who was making dolls as early as 1855 by soaking cheap cloth in glue or paste and pressing the mixture into a two-part mould. Layers of stockinette and wadding were then added and the shape strengthened by wood on the inside; they were decorated with oil colours. The slightly springy surface caused by the layered method of construction is an identifying feature, as are the separately applied ears. Their prim, homely faces, with curls falling on their plump cheeks, make them very popular with American collectors.

Painted fabric mask-faced dolls were also made in the States by Martha Chase. Portraits of such famous characters as George Washington were made. A two-piece Santa Claus, made in rag by Edward Peck in 1884, is thought to have inspired other makers, including Laurence & Co of Boston, who were cloth distributors and printers. The Arnold Print works of Massachusetts was one of the country's largest manufacturers of prints and dress goods and among other dolls they produced 'Palmer Cox Brownies', some twelve in number. A variety of fabric advertising dolls were made, including Rastus the Cream of Wheat Chef, and Aunt Jemima who advertised flour.

Italy is associated with rag dolls because of the pressed felt toys made by Enrico Scavini of Turin and marketed as Lenci. These dolls were created in an 'artistic manner' and included a Mozart and a Madonna and child. Over a hundred different characters including a Chinaman and Indians, were on sale by 1921. In Germany, Margaret Steiff manufactured felt-headed dolls from 1894, characterized by the seam that runs down the centre of the faces and gives her soldier dolls in particular a rather sinister appearance.

Her dolls are also recognizable by their large flat feet which enabled them to stand. A very fine example representing a fire chief with the name Steiff impressed in the leather belt can be seen at the Toy Museum in Nuremberg. This company still operates in the Federal Republic.

A pair of home-made paper dolls created from printed figures cut from a ladies magazine and representing fancy dress. The skirts are made of silk and lace; the cotton articulated legs are cut from card, and the ballet shoes are crudely painted. Tunbridge Wells Museum.

The three versions of Sindy. In the foreground is 'Active Sindy', the most expensive, with completely realistic jointing. 'Lovely Lively Sindy' wears a check skirt and is jointed, but not at the ankles. This doll is sold with a Sindy Hair Care Set. 'Funtime Sindy' is the cheapest, and wears a simple flowered frock. This version is jointed only at neck, shoulder and thigh. Pedigree Dolls, Canterbury.

In 1903, Samuel Dean launched Dean's Rag Book Company, which is still in production though no longer making dolls. Their printed rag dolls were made between 1903 and 1936 and included Old King Cole and Mr Puck of *A Midsummer Night's Dream*. In 1912, a series of dolls in Victorian style dressed as ladies were sold, each doll carrying a facsimile autograph of their designer, Pauline Guilbert. The Tru-to-Life series was introduced in 1920 and represented the firm's entry into the field of shaped dolls; both Charlie Chaplin and George Robey were included in this series.

Between the two wars, adult dolls passed almost completely out of fashion and were only seen occasionally as character dolls, representing film stars or comedians. The manufacturers appear to have decided that children really wanted sweet-faced child dolls, and the only adult dolls made in any quantity in Europe were directed very much towards ladies. Just as, in the 18th century, women had imitated their wardrobes on cut-out paper figures and Regency women toyed with isinglass dressing dolls, so in the early 20th century dolls again became of interest to fashionable ladies. Paul Poiret, the couturier, suggested

in 1910 that fashion-conscious women should carry dolls in that season. Such figures were especially costumed by Paquin and Mme Lanvin, and of course copied by other designers. A whole range of dolls continued to be made by a variety of makers, usually in the form of very long-limbed women with silk or fabric covered faces. The most alluring, with the long eyelashes set into a slit above the eye and with silk stockinette faces were made in France. In America such dolls were called Vamps or Flappers, the New York Sales Company selling a composition flapper with fashionable bobbed hair and a cigarette in its mouth. Wearing high-heeled shoes and a trouser suit of daringly masculine cut, the doll must have upset many an elderly relative!

Boudoir dolls were made in England by several firms. Dean's 1928 catalogue included 'Smart Set' dolls, among which was a duchess in leopard-skin coat and carrying a lorgnette. Another of their dolls wore leather boots and knickerbockers. Figures of this type continued in production until 1938 when Pierrot costume dolls, popular since the early 20s, were still sold. In the 20s a range with 'Marcel wave mohair wigs' was advertised. The Chad Valley Company did not become interested in boudoir dolls until the early 30s, when they appear in their catalogues as 'Carnival dolls'. Several different versions of a basic doll were sold, all gaily dressed in an updated version of a Pierrot's costume. The girl wears a short skirt with a pointed, witch-like hat and the men, who usually outnumbered her five to one, in rather stage-like outfits including flat caps and flared trousers, all parti-coloured. The dolls all have the small black painted curls on their cheeks associated with Pierrots. In 1935, Chad Valley were describing their lady dolls as 'Sofa dolls – Coldly disdainful or bewitchingly inviting, these play-things of the sophisticated Miss 1935 simply command attention. Gaily dressed with classically beautiful features, they will grace the homes of the most modern of moderns. Can dolls have personality? We say they can.'

This particular range was 21 inches high and made with pressed felt faces; the costumes were made of floral crepes, art silk and velveteen. An illustrated doll wore a huge floppy hat with a large bow of ribbon at the neck, a be-frilled jacket and very wide boudoir pyjama trousers printed with flowers. Their faces are typical of the period, with tiny rosebud mouths and sideways-glancing eyes.

Very few boudoir dolls are attributable, and the majority have to be assessed by the effectiveness of the figure and the maker's skill in exactly suggesting the period in which they were made, those dressed retrospectively in Victorian or foreign costumes being generally of less interest.

It was not until the early 60s that lady dolls, now referred to by doll-makers as fashion dolls, again became popular. Barbie was introduced by Mattel in 1959 but did not become world famous for a few years. In England, the original Sindy was designed by Dennis E. Arkinstall but the doll was updated in 1971 by Eric Griffiths, Pedigree's doll designer, whose involvement with dolls began after a career as a cartoonist and illustrator. The original Sindy was more adolescent in appearance but now has a more sophisticated, slimmer, teenage body to conform with current taste. Originally, the doll was intended to represent a fifteen to seventeen-year-old, with the image of a 'nice girl'. The staff at Pedigree dolls in Canterbury are very aware of this image that must be projected, and the sexual side is played down, even a French girl friend that was introduced, being discontinued as 'too sexy'. At one stage, Sindy was given a boyfriend called Paul, but he was not a great success, mainly, it is felt by the firm, because mothers in Europe were not as amenable to teenagers with boyfriends as their American counterparts. The designers also felt that the child resented the boy friend, as she could not then have Sindy completely to herself.

63

Opposite:
Swivel-headed dolls with moulded
hairstyles are only occasionally found;
this example is made even more
interesting by its fixed glass eyes.
The original fringed dress is worn,
with a badly fitting hat that obscures
the detail of the loosely plaited hair.
Bisque lower arms and legs with
moulded boots. Height, 14 inches.
Bethnal Green Museum, London.

Above:
Bisque-headed lady whose walking
mechanism is concealed under a
cardboard 'skirt'. The wooden base
contains two straight and one pivoted
wheel. The mechanism is marked
'Steiner Paris'. The doll has an open
mouth with two rows of teeth, and
wears the original wool dress.
Christie's, London.

A new wardrobe is designed for this doll every six months and made
in Hong Kong. Each year sales of Sindy are in excess of 5,000,000
indicating the popularity today of adult-type figures. An interesting
change, however, has taken place in the buying pattern for Sindy
accessories. In the 60s girls bought a very wide variety of outfits,
but the trend has now changed and the emphasis is upon accessories
such as hair dryers, a swimming pool and beach buggy and even a
horse. The explanation is possibly the current teenagers' lack of interest
in clothes, for what is almost a uniform of denim is regularly worn.

In 1976, the firm introduced 'The Champions', a boy and girl in
young adult form with their bodies especially constructed to sit astride
their well-jointed horses with manes that can be combed! The psychology behind this set is similar to that motivating Sindy's accessories,
and works on the theory that even if a girl lives in a very poor environ-
ment, she can enjoy, by substitution, the extravagant items that the
dolls own.

The Idealized Child

Opposite:
A well-modelled poured-wax child of the very hectic colour particularly associated with the work of the Pierrotti family. The eyes are fixed, the hair is implanted and set in groups. The lower legs and arms are of wax, and the body is hair-filled. 28 inches tall. Collection Mrs Jan Olsen.

Below:
A good-quality waxed composition child with implanted hair and fixed dark eyes. The doll has the very heavy type of limbs associated with the period after 1840. Collection Mrs Jan Olsen.

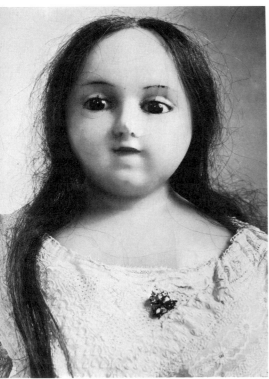

The few dolls made in the image of young children before the middle of the 19th century are of interest because of their attempted realism. Baby dolls, seen in the Dutch cabinet houses or in the 18th-century English doll's houses, are very much representations of actual children, with creased faces and, often, quite irate expressions. Portrait figures in wax were made in some number in the 18th and early 19th centuries to represent either an adored child in infancy or a young baby that had died. Several stories associating dolls of this type with particular houses are recorded; one is believed to cry when evil is near while another, thought to have supernatural associations, was practically the only object that survived when the house was burned down.

From the mid-19th century dolls ceased to be only play items and the manufacturers seem to have given much more attention to the creation of idealized figures that would attract the mother, perhaps out on a shopping expedition. The rapid increase in the number of toy shops meant that a doll could be displayed to advantage and the costume and accessories carefully arranged whereas, in the Regency period, dolls intended for general sale were necessarily of a type that could be carried in large numbers in pedlar's baskets or carts. A rather disturbing, cloying, sweetness is frequently encountered in the products of the second half of the century, a sweetness surely aimed at the adult rather than the more robust taste of a child.

Wax-dollmakers were the first to exploit the sales potential of dolls resembling beautiful children and the products of the English firms were the finest in the world. Poured wax was used as a medium for dolls from the 17th century and possibly earlier, and was often a technique practised in single families and passed down from father to son. The moulten wax was poured into a plaster or, occasionally, metal mould and allowed to cool slightly before the surplus was poured away. Moulds were usually two part, but more complicated heads necessitated extra: cheaper dolls were created with only one pouring but two, or even three, are not uncommon. Each layer had to become completely cool before the next was added, making their manufacture a relatively slow process and one that was difficult to automate in any way.

The traditional dollmaking method was followed whereby only the parts visible when the figure was costumed were made of the more costly material, and the bodies were made of stuffed fabric. It seems very unlikely that all the 19th-century English wax-dollmaking was

One of the rarest bisque-headed bébés is that marked 'A. Marque' for an unknown maker. This example has glass fixed eyes, pierced ears, and a broken line of lashes on the eyelids, which is unusual. The body is of composition, and the arms are made of bisque from the elbow down with a bisque ball joint. The doll has a very long thin body. Doll in Wonderland, Brighton.

centred in London, but no marked examples are known to me from other parts. Even in the London area, the number of known makers is relatively small and only one marked, and therefore positively attributable doll is found to a dozen or so that are unclaimed. Collectors sometimes attempt an attribution by the resemblance of a doll to another marked example but, except in the case of almost identical toys, this is unsatisfactory as even single makers often made a range of completely dissimilar figures. Makers' names are found on original boxes, stamped on the fabric chest or, occasionally, incised in the wax. Discerning collectors judge a doll on its quality rather than on the presence of a name, though it is obviously interesting to know the maker.

French and Spanish craftsmen continued to create dolls in wax during the 19th century but, until recently, interest in dolls in these countries has been minimal, and research almost non-existent, so that any really fine examples that occur tend to be given an English provenance. Their manufacture, even in England, was concentrated particularly on a few families of Mexican and Italian origin, who probably brought skills learned in the making of church and portrait figures into the making of dolls. The work of these makers is of great interest today as the dolls they produced are among the last made with a craftsman's individual care. Some firms offered to implant the hair of a particular child into the head of her doll thereby giving the figure a completely unique appeal. Some element of group production was obviously employed, such as the pouring of a row of moulds at the same time, and the sewing of piles of body parts, but, eventually, the craftsman handled each piece individually, in order to neaten mould lines and decorate the face, after its cosmetic dusting with violet powder or potato meal.

To the layman, poured-wax dolls are mainly remarkable because of the idiosyncratic method used in the creation of their wigs, human hair being implanted into the wax scalp by means of a heated needle or knife. Several hairs at a time were pressed in place and the resulting scar sealed with a warm roller or similar tool. Even an experienced worker must have taken at least a day to complete a head of medium size, which meant that the dolls were, even when new, comparatively expensive. Later, mohair, inserted usually in small bunches, was used, particularly by the Pierotti family. In some examples this insertion is quite crude and groups far bigger than any self-respecting modern maker would insert are pushed together into the scalp. In the best examples, eyelashes were implanted in the lids, a process calling for some skill. The effect of brows was given by laying hair on the wax forehead and very lightly varnishing the surface. A few poured dolls were left completely bald and provided with a more usual wig. Although such dolls were originally cheaper, they are now of interest as only rarely found. An even rarer technique involved laying hair on the slightly warmed scalp to create the effect of a boy or a young baby.

It was not only in the making but also in the costuming of poured waxes that a quality product was evidenced, as many are found in their original, commercially made dresses that were sewn in surprising detail. Expensive silks, decorated with braids, fringe and lace were frequently used, and the boots in particular made as correct miniature items. Even after the introduction of the sewing machine the makers of these expensive dolls often continued to create their costumes by hand.

The only well documented firm is that of the Pierotti family who continued to make dolls in the traditional manner until 1935. Giovanni Stefano Pierotti was born in 1730, and, according to a descendant, Irene Pierotti, worked in the wine export trade. His son, Domenico, came to England in 1770 and lived with his aunt, Mrs Castelli, who made objects of papier mâché. He was naturalised in 1810 after learning

the trade of his relatives, and set himself up in London. Anericho Cephas, his ninth child, became a portrait modeller in wax and is thought to have also made some poured-wax dolls which were shown at exhibitions. The eighth child of Anericho, Henry Pierotti, showed dolls at the Great Exhibition of 1851 and later opened a shop in Oxford Street, known as The Gallery, Crystal Palace Bazaar. Like the other dollmakers, the Pierottis also produced small decorative figures and tailors' and dressmakers' display figures. Irene Pierotti, in an interesting article in *Country Life*, commented that her grandmother continued to make dolls as a small home industry after the death of her husband from the lead poisoning that was a danger to makers in this medium, because of the white lead used to colour the wax. She was helped by two sons and three daughters, and their work was sold from various London shops. After the death of the last dollmaker in the family, his tools were given to the Museum of Childhood at Rottingdean.

Pierotti dolls are often characterized by rather delicate features and heads turned slightly to one side. The modelling is often rather tentative and little of the force seen in the better Montanaris is evident, the family obviously concentrating on the production of a beautiful child's face. The high colouring of the wax is a rather strange characteristic, as the tone is, in some cases, almost puce, and one wonders why this peculiar colour was liked. It is not unpopular with collectors, as it is so characteristic of the firm. Other marked dolls are made of quite pale wax, so it should not be thought that the heavy colouring is typical of all their dolls. When marked, the name of the firm is scratched across the shoulder plate, though the majority are identified by stamps on the chest giving the names of the shops which sold the dolls, including Morrells, Mortlocks or even Hamleys, who sold Pierottis until the 1930s.

The quality of dolls made by the Montanari family is much more exciting, as the modelling of the heads is vigorous and assured. With their massively modelled shoulders and rather heavy, sulky faces, they form a complete contrast to the sweetly pretty Pierottis. Some of their dolls were sold from the Soho Bazaar, and the firm also worked for a time from 251 Regent Street. They also exhibited work at the Great Exhibition, though a boxed example from this display which appeared

Above left:
A poured-wax doll of English manufacture, with rooted hair and fixed blue glass eyes. The body is hair stuffed, with poured lower arms and legs. The modelling of the feet is unusually good. The silk dress is original. 26 inches tall. Collection Mrs Jan Olsen.

Above:
German bisque-headed child with a jointed body, blue sleeping eyes and pierced ears, the head marked 'K & R Simon & Halbig 34'. 13½ inches tall. Author's collection.

The drooping bisque fingers and the open-closed mouths of this pair of dolls are typical of the work of the Bru company. The boy has a pink kid body and the original sheepskin wig. Bethnal Green Museum, London.

Opposite:
A poured-wax girl with fixed blue eyes and implanted fair hair. Although unmarked, it is probably of English manufacture. 21 inches tall. Author's collection.

in the saleroom was of the meanest construction and completely unlike those usually attributed to this firm. Undressed dolls shown at the Great Exhibition by Madame Montanari cost from 10 shillings to 105 shillings, while costumed dolls cost considerably more. Little wonder then that the jury considered them too expensive. At the Paris Exhibition of 1855, the claim was made by Madame Montanari that her dolls would stand all varieties of climate and could be washed in alkaline water.

Richard Montanari was referred to in the 1870s as 'A manufacturer of exhibition prize wax and rag dolls' and several other members of his family lived near his Fitzroy Square address. Like other dollmakers, the Montanaris claimed to make the Royal Wax Baby Dolls, in imitation of Queen Victoria's children and are believed to have included Princess Louise in this range. None of these Royal Baby dolls are known, and presumably they were of the basic type, but packed or labelled in some specific way.

Dark hair is found much more frequently on figures made by Montanari than on those created by the Pierottis, who preferred blond or titian hair. The arms are also heavier and the rolls of fat much more accentuated. All these comparisons, however, have to be of a general indicative kind, as the number of genuinely marked Montanaris is very small. One more definite difference is the fact that Montanari bodies are hand sewn, whereas the marked Pierottis are usually machined.

Right:
Tinted bisque shoulder-headed girl
with moulded hair, glass eyes, and
bisque lower arms and legs. The
moulded boots are decorated with
purple lustre. The doll is 11 inches
tall, and was made in Germany about
1865. Author's collection.

Below:
A German bisque-headed double-
jointed doll, 23 inches tall, with the
head marked 'S & H 1079 D.E.P.' for
Simon & Halbig. It has blue sleeping
eyes, pierced ears, and an open
mouth with four moulded teeth. The
wig is original, as is the costume,
which is topped with a feather-
stitched blue woollen cape. Author's
collection.

At the 1851 Exhibition, a prize was obtained for their 'English wax
dolls', with a layer of muslin stretched over the surface of the wax to
give a soft finish and disguise any cracks that might occur later during
play. Unfortunately, time is the usual enemy of such mixtures of
media, and when found the wax has, over the years, often stained the
surface, giving a rather unpleasant effect. Several makers are believed
to have made these wax babies, and *Playmates*, an American publication, in 1879, describes them as strong enough to be played with by a
baby. A magazine article from the same period described how a dollmaker in Shoreditch, London, worked. 'Occasionally, but not often,
she also did the covering of the faces . . . Taking up a ready made wax
face, she pressed it into a heated mould, previously lined with white
muslin, which adhered to the warm wax and came away with it. Upon
this surface her employer would paint the features and complexion.
For effecting this operation, which called for some deftness, the dollmaker was paid 6d per gross.'

By the end of the 19th century, sixteen makers of wax dolls were
recorded in London alone, employing dozens of outworkers such as
the woman mentioned above, for costuming and simple manufacturing
processes. Herbert Meech was the dollmaker to the Royal Family
though again only a few marked examples are known of his work. One
sold at Sothebys in 1976 had a most delicate face of a pale coloured wax
that gave the doll a rather consumptive air that was interesting, because so different to the usual plump-cheeked child dolls. Charles
Marsh sold dolls to C. Gooch of the Soho Bazaar, but his known pro-

'The History of Little Fanny. Exempli-
fied in a series of Figures in dress
and undress.' Printed for S & J Fuller.
Tunbridge Wells Museum.

ducts are even more confusing than those of the two main makers, as
they are all completely unalike and exactly illustrate the impossibility
of attribution by appearance, as one I examined was an almost typical
Pierotti, while another was of a distinctly Italianate appearance.

Lucy Peck was making poured wax dolls at The Doll's Home, 131
Regent Street, in 1901. She not only made her own dolls but also sold
those of other firms, Simon and Halbig dolls sometimes being found
with her labels on their bodies. Although the wire-eyed mechanism
was long since out of fashion as a method of moving eyes, Mrs Peck
was using a variation in her dolls in the early 20th century. I have not,
to date, found a Lucy Peck without the eyelets, used to protect the wax
from the pressure of the thick cotton used in sewing together the parts,
though examples of almost all other makers' work, in original condition are sometimes found without this refinement.

The essential fragility of the medium means that wax dolls are often
found in a damaged state, and this has a little less influence on value
than in the case of bisque dolls, for instance. A few years ago, collectors were eager to restore such acquisitions, to the extent of making
them appear almost new. Fortunately, dolls are now accepted as
respectable antiques and there is much less indiscriminate restoration.
It is their very fragility of substance that helps create the vision of a
Victorian child, and because of the delicate patination of the wax they
are much more evocative of their period than the still pristine bisques.

Waxed composition dolls, often representing smiling children, were
produced both in England and in Germany but it seems impossible to
differentiate between the countries of origin, as a very similar product
was made. The majority were very cheaply made, with composition
lower limbs that were sometimes also waxed. The round-faced
pumpkin-headed dolls, intended to represent women, but often more
closely resembling children, were superseded by wigged dolls, with
soft, child-like modelling of the features, sold cheaply enough to be
within the price range of all but the poorest of parents. Black or orange
boots were painted on the moulded legs, and the wax was sometimes
applied over the paint to give a softer effect, a technique that was often
also applied to the faces. The cheap, muslin bodies were often roughly
filled with straw. Not all waxed dolls were of this very cheap kind, as
some were given a much thicker coating of wax and the wigs were
implanted in the scalp as in the expensive poured dolls. Others have

well made, hair-filled bodies, and were extravagantly costumed to rival the poured dolls. Some completely unsuitable devices were sometimes employed, such as sleeping eyes weighted by lead, which often fractured the head. Dolls with interchangeable and with two and three faced heads are found in waxed composition, though their condition is rarely good, and they tend to be collected as curiosities rather than fine objects.

Late dolls, both of bisque and porcelain, were made in a more child-like image, though the bodies often continued to represent small-waisted women. Some porcelains were moulded with a name such as Bertha on the shoulder front, where it was visible when the doll was costumed, and enabled the child to invest the figure immediately with a particular character. Some were made with moulded bonnets, and yet others given wigs of mohair. Though the intention was a child-like doll, the manufacturers seem to have found difficulty in adapting their traditional techniques, and women dolls, dressed to represent children, were sold as late as the 1920s, particularly for use in doll's houses. Occasionally, a particularly child-like porcelain head is seen, but there is little idealism evident, merely an adaptation of a very basic design. A few dolls with plumed hats, in imitation of the Scottish costume worn by the royal children at Balmoral, and a popular costume of the period, were made in the 1860s and 70s, but mainly in white bisque, the majority of bonnet dolls made after 1880 also being of this substance, and made not only in a variety of sizes but also with a great range of designs, so that some collectors specialize in this category. Examples over a foot high are not often found, the majority being just a little larger than doll's house size. They are almost invariably unmarked, except with a number.

Tinted bisque dolls with glass eyes were made by several companies in the 1870s and 80s and mounted either on fabric or on leather bodies by such firms as Simon & Halbig or Dressel, Koch & Fischer. Early examples retained the traditional moulded hair, though this was soon discarded as a method in favour of wigs. Some of the most beautiful German dolls, with closed mouths and rather soulful expressions date to the closing years of the 19th century and portray children with a beauty of countenance rarely seen in real life.

Illustrations of children produced in the last quarter of the 19th century almost invariably represent them in an idealized, and rather cloyingly sentimental, manner: the child shown weeping at her mother's graveside is always beautiful and, though perhaps dressed in rags, is invariably clean. The French dollmakers created bisque dolls with huge eyes, heavy brows and immaculately curled hair, all completely idealized and with only the slightest resemblance to a real child. The more unreal the doll, the huger the eyes and the more lowering the brows, the more coveted it is by the collector.

The term bébé was used to indicate a doll representing a child somewhere between the age of eight and twelve. Probably the most appealing are those made by Bru, a company founded in 1866. Their early bébés have exquisitely modelled shoulder heads, the chest in particular being unusual, as they are modelled to represent the delicate breasts of the young adolescent, even the nipples being lightly painted, and a swivel head giving added realism. The earliest Bru's are those with leather gussetted bodies, sometimes incised Bru or at others marked with an incised circle and dot, or even a crescent, a circle and a dot. With a slightly open mouth, known to collectors as an 'Open closed' as there is no actual entry into the head, large paperweight eyes and sheepskin wigs, the products of this factory are unmistakable. Early doll collectors often removed these sheepskin wigs because of some slight damage and replaced them with ringletted real hair, an unfortunate change, as the essential character of the doll is then lost.

Above:
Closed-mouth bébé of poor quality bisque but with large eyes and heavy brows, marked 'R 806. X' on the head. The doll has the French-type jointed body with fixed wrists. The ears are pierced, and the wig is original. Tunbridge Wells Museum.

Opposite:
French bisque-headed doll with jointed body, fixed eyes and open mouth. The original costume is very decorative. Marked '* 95' for Phoenix Baby. Joy Standford Collection.

Above:
Bisque-headed bébé with open mouth, upper and lower teeth, and pierced ears. The head is incised 'J Steiner Bte. S.G.D.G. Paris'. The body, which is purple-coloured carton under the flesh colour, is marked 'Le Petit Parisien Bébé Steiner'. Doll in Wonderland, Brighton.

Opposite:
Unmarked French bisque-headed bébé with closed mouth and pierced ears. The head is particularly effective, and has similarities to dolls marked 'A.T.' The body is of composition. Doll in Wonderland, Brighton.

The early Bru body proved unsatisfactory, as the cork filled body soon assumed a crouching position and little movement of the limbs was possible. The arms usually contain a wire armature that does enable them to be bent slightly but, generally, movement is minimal. It was necessary to improve the design and a body with carved wooden lower legs and improved articulation was developed. This new type of body was more successful, as the lower arms were pivoted and the wooden lower legs, also with pivots, enabled the doll to sit and assume various positions. An advertisement for the company in 1873 mentions a new type of doll, made of leather but with carved arms and legs, which possibly refers to this type, though the majority now discovered have bisque lower arms.

In the late 1870s, several patents were recorded for body improvements including some of rubber, and coloured as well as white dolls were produced. As the basic types of doll continued to be produced alongside one another, any attempt to date the doll by its body type is difficult, and a much more accurate indication is given by the style of the costume. Without the original dress, dating to within twenty years is almost impossible. The company took great pride in its dolls' up-to-date costumes, and they are therefore a reliable guide.

The later Bru has a jointed wood and composition body with bisque lower arms and a socket head that fits into the body. The characteristic wooden feet, with well carved toes and beautifully painted toe nails, were used on this newer body type, and the makers' chest band, often found on the leather dolls, was also added. Pull-string voice boxes were sometimes given, and the earlier sheepskin wigs were replaced by curled hair or mohair. As this company was the most exclusive of the French makers, it endeavoured to maintain its position by the introduction of a large number of what must have proved very costly innovations, such as one doll that appeared to breathe and another that could 'eat and digest food', known as Bébé Gourmand, advertised in 1881, and with pull strings at the back of the head controlling the movement of the tongue. Bébé 'Le Dormeur' had eyelids that closed realistically over the eyes. Attempts were also made to create an indestructable substance that could give a beautiful surface finish, and heads were produced in rubber, composition and gutta percha. Marked Brus are very occasionally found made of these substances, and their sorry appearance proves how heavily the dolls relied on the fine quality of the bisque for their impact.

Despite the very obvious quality of the dolls, the firm obtained silver rather than gold medals at exhibitions, until, after 1883, the company passed to H. Chevrot, who, of course, continued to trade under the respected name of Bru Jne & Cie, but who obtained gold medals in profusion in centres as far apart as Paris, Liverpool and Melbourne.

The original costume, even of the early circle-dot Bru's, is nearly always disappointing with regard to the underwear, which usually consists of a cheap lace-trimmed petticoat and drawers, all the attention being lavished on the actual dress, which was usually hand sewn, because its complexity made sewing by machine too difficult. One Bru recently examined in its original costume was decorated with rows of free-hanging, tiny, white glass beads that must have proved a considerable hazard for any very young children. Silk brocades, satin, lace and fine wools trimmed with fur were all used for the extravagant outer costumes. In the mid 1880s the Bru company was advertising dolls dressed in knee-length skirts, an unflattering length as it exposed the gussetted knee joint on the leather bodied dolls, but is liked by collectors as it is so characteristic of the maker, and makes the figure very dateable. Dolls' costumes were usually adaptations of current children's styles, and the best method of dating their dress is by refer-

Closed-mouth bisque-headed Jumeau marked 'Déposé Tête Jumeau. B^te; S.G.D.G. 7 H 9'. The doll has large fixed eyes, pierced ears and fixed wrists. Joy Stanford Collection.

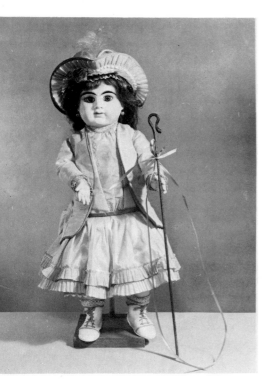

French bisque-headed bébé, with the original mohair wig, cork pate, large fixed brown eyes and composition body. The head is incised 'E 10 D', probably for Ernest Decamps, Paris. Doll in Wonderland, Brighton.

ence to reprinted fashion plates of the period rather than by the study of other dolls, as sometimes an individual maker would create his own particular version of a current style. Here one thinks particularly of those strange costumes devised by the paper-dollmaker, Raphael Tuck, in the 1880s and 90s, that bear little resemblance to the costumes of other dolls of the time. Muffs, fur coats, dressing cases and outfits for a whole variety of social and sporting occasions could be purchased at specialist shops for these expensive French bébés, that were sold basically complete, with a dress, earrings and necklace. Occasionally a rich parent would buy a doll together with a large wardrobe of clothes, but these are now almost impossible to find.

The firm of Jumeau was the greatest competitor of Bru, and their porcelain factory was also in the Montreuil area. This company put so much energy into marketing and claimed so often that their products were far superior to all others, that eventually the claims were generally accepted. As German-made dolls were far cheaper, the French saw that their main chance of survival lay in the manufacture of top quality, beautifully dressed dolls for the ever-increasing middle class, not only of France but also of England and, particularly, America. Trade exhibitions aided the manufacturers in their promotion campaigns, as their dolls were proved, by the number of medals awarded, and the general acclaim, to be the finest.

Jumeau was marketing dolls described as bébés in the 1860s, though these were probably more in the nature of lady dolls and the so called 'Bébé Jumeau' was only sold after 1879. The main showroom was at the Rue Pastourelle in Paris, where the dolls were artistically arranged in beautiful settings, and with appropriate accessories. At the 1878 Paris Exposition, a gold medal was won and it is this medal that is referred to by the *Medaille d'or* stamp found on the bodies of subsequent dolls. One of the most characteristic features of the best Jumeau are the large, peculiarly luminous eyes that were especially made at their factory by skilled women. In 1885, Jumeau as well as Bru introduced a bébé with an eyelid that closed down over the eye and was activated by a lever at the back of the head. In 1897, the more frequently found eye mechanism, that worked by means of a lead weight, was introduced. The most popular doll to collectors made by Jumeau is the so-called 'Long Face', that is found on a ball-jointed body. The early method of ball jointing was by cord, rather than the elastic that was later substituted. The Long Faced Jumeau has a peculiarly haunting expression, which is of lasting attraction, rather than the somewhat foolish appearance of some of their later dolls.

Open-mouthed dolls with teeth were considered an important advance, and were originally more expensive than the closed-mouth versions, as they involved extra manufacturing processes. Now, the collector prefers the earlier closed-mouth dolls as they are more scarce and their expressions are preferred. Some of the early closed-mouthed dolls have huge almond-shaped eyes and are described as 'almond-eyed Jumeau' in England, though in America they are called 'Portrait Jumeau'. Many Jumeau heads are unmarked and only the bodies were stamped. Some were sold in Jumeau boxes or with Jumeau ribbons, and the basic dolls are now completely without identification, except by their expressions which are very easily recognizable, though this is more difficult in later dolls when other firms in some cases actually appear to have attempted to copy the Jumeau expressions.

Although the bisque of early Jumeaux is usually of a high quality, examples from the 1890s often vary considerably, and the dolls have to be valued completely on the standard of the individual example. Coloured dolls were also made, the almond-eyed mulatto bébé being a collector's favourite. As so many French dolls were made for export to America, the rarer examples are now more readily available in that

country than in Europe. German competition was becoming very
strong by the 1890s and in 1892 the company attempted to compete on
a cheaper level by the introduction of two new models 'with a twenty
to fifty per cent difference in price' from the standard dolls, but without the firm's name. Papa and Mama voice boxes worked by pull-
strings, walking and hand-kissing dolls were all produced in an effort
to keep ahead of the market, while Edison's invention of a talking
machine in 1887 and the demonstration of the American Phonograph
at the 1889 Paris Exhibition caused the firm to incorporate the new
invention in a doll, a type that was on sale by 1894. A phonograph doll
is illustrated to show how the body was made to contain the mechanism;
by changing the wax cylinders the doll could recite different speeches.
Dolls of this type have a double appeal, both to collectors of dolls
and gramophones, so that the price obtained is always high, despite
the very basic quality of the dolls themselves. The new invention was
rather expensive and probably not sufficiently child-proof to be used
for a really wide mass production and quickly went out of favour; once
again there appear to be far more examples in American collections
than in Europe.

Designs for dresses were supervised by Madame Jumeau herself,
and the more expensive dolls costumed lavishly. Not all were sold
dressed in fine clothes and boxed examples are found wearing only

A particularly beautiful head with pierced ears and the original cork pate, marked Téte Déposé. Paris Bébé' for Danel et Cie, Seine, Paris. Doll in Wonderland, Brighton.

Below:
Jumeau bébé with the dress lifted to show the construction of a phonograph doll. Christie's, London.

Right:
An unmarked white and black tinted pair of all-bisque dolls, which measure 3 inches in height. The heads are moulded with stringing loops. These are two from a group of twenty, which came on their original shop display card. Author's collection.

the simplest and cheapest chemise, shoes and socks. Marks on Jumeaux are either incised or stamped and include the most frequently found 'Tête Jumeau', 'Breveté S.G.D.G Jumeau' or simply 'E.J', the last referring to Émile Jumeau. Later dolls are found marked only D.E.P. or with an incised 1907, but are in every way typical of the factory. A Heubach doll, made in Germany, was recently seen in the stock of a London doll dealer with the 1907 incised number and a head modelled to resemble the Jumeau of that type. Was this a straightforward copy of the more expensive product, or did such German factories occasionally make heads for French assembly? Certainly Simon & Halbig heads are occasionally found on marked Jumeau bodies, but the marked Heubach raised the question of whether they too assisted in this way.

The Steiner company, which was established in 1885, was again energetic in the registration of patents, their key-wound walking doll that moves on wheels concealed under the carton skirt, and with a double row of teeth, being very much a transitional doll, somewhere between a lady and a child. Their crying bébé, with a leather-covered body that raised its arms while crying mama, finds a place in many collections, and was obviously made in some numbers. An example sold in July 1976 at Christie's carried not only the Steiner mark but also a label relating to its seller 'Jouets Simonne, Rue de Rivoli'. There is a wide variety of standard, even in a doll such as this, some being decorated with great softness, while others are quite macabre.

A label showing a girl carrying a banner is often found on the bodies of dolls made after 1889, and a characteristic of their bébés is their use of a pate of purple cardboard, instead of the cork used by the other quality makers. Steiner also introduced a lever mechanism which controlled the eyes from the side of the head just above the ears. Before the flesh colour was applied to the bodies, a purple undercoat was used and this now shows through in areas of maximum wear. Among other Steiner characteristics are fingers of the same length and a big toe that is separated from the others. Heads were sometimes marked 'Le Parisien' and some also marked with the name Bourgoin. The company

was run by Jules Steiner and by 1872 claimed to produce five different types of bébés. The successors of Jules Steiner used Bébé Phénix as their trademark.

Some variety of faces was made by Steiner; a few resemble Schmitts, while others have eyebrow painting very reminiscent of Jumeau. The best bébés are of really superb quality and have expressions that are much more gentle than, for instance, Jumeaux. A particularly rare Steiner Arab, modelled as a man in brown bisque and with heavy brows and drooping moustache is seen in *Images of Love* written by J. and M. Selfridge.

The majority of firms manufacturing lady dolls were forced in the 1880s to add bébés to their range, as they were becoming increasingly popular with children as well as the more sentimental parents. Well known makers, such as Fernand Gaultier and Huret, both made rather plump-faced dolls, the Gaultiers in particular often being given very heavy quality bodies with quite large areas made of wood. A particularly rare series with often quite high colouring and sharply pointed faces was marked 'Marque A', and are at present completely unattributable. An example from 'Doll in Wonderland', Brighton, is illustrated. Rabery and Delphieu, already known for lady dolls, also turned to the manufacture of bébés, and made girl dolls with particularly heavy features and bodies that are often more squat than those used by the majority of French makers. The faces are frequently attractive because of their air of exasperation, which makes them recognizable in a group of bébés.

It is difficult to understand why the bisque used by the Lanternier company of Limoges is generally of such poor quality, as the firm was manufacturing in an area with a tradition of fine porcelain. The actual modelling of the heads was often attractive, yet their finished dolls were generally of a low standard. One example that was once in my own collection had the most beautiful green paperweight eyes, set in a face that closely resembled a late Jumeau. The body containing a mama-papa voice box worked by strings.

Fleischmann and Blodel, known particularly as the makers of F.den Bébé, originated in Bavaria, but opened a Paris branch of the firm also. In 1892 they registered a patent for a doll that walked and turned its head, while another threw kisses when a button was pressed.

All these makers found great difficulty in keeping prices at a level that was competitive with the German makers, and they were eventually forced to amalgamate into a company known as Société Française de Fabrication de Bébés et Jouets (S.F.B.J.), founded in 1899. Fleischmann was head of the syndicate, which included Bru, Rabery et Delphieu, Jumeau, and Pintel et Godchaux. Emphasis was placed on the streamlining of production, though the established dolls continued to be produced and marketed under their known trade names; but there was a general lowering of standard. Even more reliance also seems to have been placed on imported German heads, and some of those marked D.E.P., made at that time, more closely resemble Simon & Halbig dolls than those of the French makers, though the bodies are very much of French origin. In 1911 the company claimed to produce 5,000,000 dolls a year at the Vincennes factory and 7,000,000 a year by 1922, making the number of S.F.B.J. '60s' found in relation to other French dolls hardly surprising.

The products of the amalgamation range from dolls made from Jumeau moulds, but marked S.F.B.J., to mean and crudely made dolls of such abysmal quality that few German factories would have tried to market them. Collectors often rave about the artistry of individual French dolls, but it should be remembered, despite their obvious beauty, that these figures were objects of fine craftsmanship, produced in large numbers, rather than works of art.

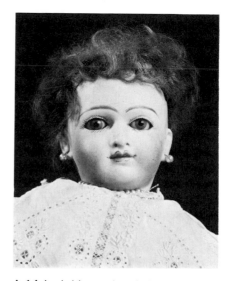

A 14-inch bisque-headed bébé marked 'Jumeau Medaille d'Or' on the body. The fixed-wrist body is ball jointed. It has pierced ears, and a closed two-tone mouth. The eyes are probably later replacements, but the white embroidered costume is original. Tunbridge Wells Museum.

Bisque-headed bébé incised 'C. N.3 J. Steiner'. The blue eyes close by means of a wire lever behind the left ear, a mechanism patented in 1880. The composition body is marked 'Le Petit Parisien' Doll in Wonderland, Brighton.

The creation of a perfect child, that would remain for all time just as originally envisaged, was very much within the ability of the makers of paper dolls. With the exception of a Regency series published by S. & J. Fuller of London and representing such characters as Little Henry and Fanny, the majority of dolls made before the last quarter of the century of this material all represented adults. The earliest cut-out dolls were produced in Germany in the mid-seventeenth century, when each individual item of costume was laid in place on the figure, a type of construction that could not long have remained popular. Standing figures with tabs for the attaching of costumes were made by the 18th century and, as dolls became more sophisticated, back as well as front views of the dress were supplied, an example named Psyche, that was included in a French fashion magazine of the early 19th century, being illustrated to show how costumes of this type were fitted.

G. W. Faber sold the most exquisitely dressed girl dolls packed in boxes colourfully decorated with prints showing the dolls in a particular costume. 'The Little Girl, dressed in the most pleasing costume' was a title that was written in four languages as well as the native German. These costumes were slipped over the head and held in place by a tissue backing, though the traditional method of tabbed fixing was also sometimes used. The Faber dolls are among the most collected in paper, as their hand-coloured costumes are so effective.

Bisque-headed French bébé with open-closed mouth, pierced ears and painted nostrils. The original cork pate is still retained. Incised 'A. 12.6' for A. Thullier, who made dolls between 1875 and 1890. Doll in Wonderland, Brighton.

Above:
French bisque-headed doll in a brown embroidered dress, with brown fixed eyes, pierced ears, and an open mouth with five teeth. Marked 4 Jullien 3'. Joy Stanford Collection.

Right:
A French bébé with effective heavy brows and the high-quality eyes particularly associated with the Jumeau factory. Many dolls produced by this firm were sold unmarked, as in this case, where the head is only marked 'S'. Collection Mrs Jan Olsen.

The majority of paper dolls were produced by firms that also published games or books, and after 1840, when lithography replaced engraving, there was a rapid increase in the number of different dolls issued, though the individual makers are often unknown, as the original boxes or wrappers are lost. An interesting variation on the usual paper doll is seen in a boxed set at Christchurch Mansion, Ipswich, described by the manufacturer as 'Floral Dressing'. The label on the box goes on 'The occupation in question which may be also justly termed attractive dressing game greatly serves to awaken and develop the children's sense of beauty . . . the dressing of the figures is entirely left to the children's own taste.' The dolls were packed into a colourful box with compartments in which flower heads of various colours, types and sizes were stored. Slots were cut in the actual costumes of the dolls into which the flower heads were pushed, eventually creating an outfit that was a mass of flower heads and which must have provided some hours of employment; very much parent-orientated, as it was both quiet and clean. Fans, hats and bags were all embellished with flowers in this dressing game that, judging by the tortuous phrasing of the label, was probably of German origin.

American printers had made such progress by the end of the 19th century that they were sometimes used instead of the traditional German by English publishers. 'Fanny Grey–A History of her life', is believed to have been the first paper doll commercially produced in America, followed by such characters as Jenny Lind, both being

German doll undressed to show the typical double-jointed body and the bisque head left open at the top for the insertion of the eye mechanism. The top of the head is covered with a cardboard pate before the wig is glued on. This 30-inch doll is marked 'C. M. Bergman Walterhausen, Germany 1916 11'. Author's collection.

actually printed in Germany but to American design. Godey's Ladies Book in 1859 included six boys and girls with their appropriate costumes, and these were the first American dolls to be given away in a magazine. The inclusion of dolls in magazines remained more popular in America than in England, the *Ladies Home Journal* for instance producing several, from Letty Lane in 1908 to the illustrated 'Fold-A-Ways' of 1922.

The 1890s saw in America the production of thousands of advertising dolls. Small girl dolls with abundant gold curls were used as advertisements for Clarks O.N.T. Spool Cotton and carried the exhortation that the child receiving the gift should ask for this product when next sent to buy cotton by her mother. Diamond Dyes and Lions Coffee were among the commodities so promoted and provide the American collector with a wide range of collectable figures.

In England, Barbour's Irish Flax Thread was advertised by a series of figures in imaginary costumes based on the flowers and fruits of various countries, the heads and arms slipping between the folded dresses. Sunlight soap also gave away a range of dolls while Germea breakfast food was advertised by a series of cut-out dolls in postcard form.

Among the American makers of paper dolls were McLoughlin Brothers, Austin & Smith and R. A. Hobbs. A large number of the Raphael Tuck dolls, printed in Germany, were designed for sale in America and it is again now easier to find examples in the States. The firm was established in 1866 when the first member of the family came to England from East Prussia, but it is not known for sure when the first paper dolls were made. Most wore a curiously fanciful style of dress, that had little relation to the clothes worn at the time, but was peculiar to the firm. The majority of their dolls, by the early 20th century, were made in the image of lovely children and were provided not only with the idiosyncratic Tuck wardrobe, but also with pets, soft toys and in one case, a doll's pram. Removable shoes, an unusual addition to a paper doll were very occasionally provided, but as these were usually the first pieces to be lost by the child owner, complete sets are comparatively rare and much liked by collectors. In 1893, dolls with changeable heads were patented and could have either fair or dark hair, a few dolls of this type being provided with changeable gloves, even rarer than shoes. Some postcards were also sold showing Tuck paper dolls.

The firm of J. W. Spear also originated in Germany and dolls designed for the English market were printed at their works in Bavaria. 'Dolly's Wardrobe' was included in their range and consisted of a strong cardboard wardrobe containing three dolls and their clothes. Cheaper paper dolls were sold in transparent envelopes and included some 7,000 assorted designs. Their 'Doll Cut-Out Sheets' were printed on card and were identical to those sold in boxes but, unfortunately for the collector, were not marked, and can only now be identified by comparison with marked boxed sets. Spears 'Quick Change Dolly' possessed six different but equally attractive faces whose main differences lay in their hair colour.

Paper dolls are now among the most difficult to find in good condition as, apart from their fragility, there were so many small items of dress that were lost during play. Others made in fairly limited numbers are virtually unattributable, as the original boxes are lost. If an uncut sheet, perhaps from a magazine, is found, it should be left in this state, despite the temptation to cut out and assemble the figures, as their condition is more likely to remain good while in sheet form and another collector would obviously prefer to buy the doll in an uncut state. An interesting collection, closely reflecting the changes of fashion, could be formed of between-the-wars dolls, perhaps found

in ladies' journals. Even the rock-and-roll style dolls of the 50s are now quite difficult to locate, while in another five years mini-skirted paper dolls will also be difficult to find. I was recently delighted to find a wartime propaganda booklet that provided girls with dressing dolls in W.A.A.F., Land Army, A.T.S., Wrens and the National Fire Service uniforms. The booklet was entitled 'Dolly Joins the Forces' and describes how difficult it was for a girl to make up her mind which of the services to choose. 'With all these lovely uniforms to choose from, Dolly dreams and dreams, but she just cannot make up her mind. Perhaps you can decide for her.' The costumes were economically printed on cheap paper and the whole booklet forms a very descriptive period piece.

The German vision of a perfect child centred on a much less pampered type than the pale drawing room inhabitants portrayed by the French: with rosy cheeks, smiling faces and an altogether more healthy air, the German dolls epitomized the greater freedom that children were gaining by the end of the 19th century. In comparison with the total number manufactured, a far smaller percentage of closed-mouth dolls seem to have been produced by the German makers, mainly, it would appear, because the German industry only came into full production of child dolls at the end of the century, when the closed-mouth doll was already outmoded. Thuringia and Bavaria were the traditional dollmaking centres and it has been estimated that about half the world's total output of dolls at this time originated in Germany. The government encouraged this industry and gave assistance to schools, set up to teach doll design. The dollmaking companies were much less exclusive than the French, and work was often contracted out to other firms in order to produce a really economical item. The Simon & Halbig porcelain factory, for instance, provided heads for firms which assembled and costumed dolls. Similarly, the Heubach company, which created a vast range of ornamental items, provided fine-quality dolls' heads that were often added by doll assemblers to bodies of much lesser quality. Rauenstein, Limbach

Above:
A German bisque-shoulder-headed sailor girl with a swivel neck, the shoulder plate marked 'D Made in Germany 8'. The doll has plaster pate, sleeping blue eyes, the original mohair wig, and a pink fabric body with composition lower arms and legs. Tunbridge Wells Museum.

Above left:
A German shoulder-headed doll, 23 inches in height, marked 'A.M.370' for Armand Marseille. She has brown sleeping eyes, bisque lower arms and a leather body with fabric lower legs. She wears a red paisley dress. Author's collection.

and Armand Marseille were all porcelain factories to whom dolls were
only one line of production, French factories of course frequently
carrying out the whole dollmaking process themselves.

Early German bébés were given leather bodies and their shoulder
heads were sometimes provided with a swivel neck in imitation of the
French dolls, Simon & Halbig in particular making closed-mouth
dolls of this type, whose quality is excellent. The majority of German
bodies, however, were made with little attempt at realism and have
elongated torsos with peculiarly articulated legs. In better examples,
the actual finish of the leather bodies is good and their very oddity of
construction gives the figure the charm of a well constructed craft
object. Various economies were attempted, such as the substitution
of black fabric for leather on the lower legs which would, in any case,
be covered by the stockings. Those with bisque lower arms are now
preferred by collectors, though it is doubtful that they were more
expensive when new. Although dolls of this type tend to be particularly
associated with the 19th century, it should be remembered that similar
dolls were sold in the 1920s.

A bisque-headed girl made by
Kammer & Reinhardt, with simple
peg-jointed limbs, sleeping eyes,
mohair wig and open mouth. 8 inches
tall. Collection Mrs Jan Olsen.

The rapid increase in the number of new doll collectors during the
last few years has meant that the price of German dolls has risen
rapidly, and what are basically very common dolls are overpriced in
comparison with the much rarer French or early wooden figures. Many
of these new collectors are German and Dutch, and sensibly ignore the
prejudices of English and American collectors, judging a doll on its
own particular merit rather than its scarcity value.

Attribution of acquisitions becomes much easier after 1890, as that
year saw the introduction of the tariff laws that made it necessary to
mark goods with the country of origin. Before that time, though some
makers incised their names or trademarks on dolls, the country of
origin was not often added. It also became more common to mark
heads boldly with the name of the manufacturer, so that attribution
is usually simple with the aid of a book of doll marks. As there were so
many German factories which occasionally produced doll's heads,
individual examples sometimes occur that cannot be identified, and
in this respect an encyclopedia of china marks rather than a book
purely relating to dolls can be useful.

The firm of Kämmer & Reinhardt, established in 1886, produced
some of the most interesting and collectable of German dolls. The
actual K. & R. trademark was not used until 1895, which is an obvious
aid in dating. Originally the dolls were designed by Kämmer but, as he
died in 1901, the most interesting items created were made after his
death when Karl Krauser, who had worked for the old man, took over
the design side of the concern, the commercial side of the firm being
controlled by Reinhardt. The bisque heads were made to the specifications of Kämmer & Reinhardt by Simon & Halbig.

The girl dolls are characterized by the excellent quality of their
bodies and their attractive shaping. At the base of the socket heads
there is a figure which the change to metric measurement in England
made clear, as it gives the height of the doll in centimetres. This is an
aid for the new collector in determining whether a particular head
actually belongs to the body, as a marriage is unlikely to produce an
exact height match.

The company was interested in the introduction of new eye mechan-
isms, including one that enabled the doll to be laid down with the
sleeping eyes in the open position. This locking device is usually
encountered in the '117' in the 'Naughty' range, introduced in 1919,
and described in the firm's 1927 catalogue: 'Naughty Dolly. By means
of a simple device a pin falls automatically when the head of the whole
doll is turned to the right, preventing the eye from closing, even when
the doll is laid down. Not until the doll is turned to the left does the
pin return to its original position, when it again falls asleep and is no
longer "Naughty" but good.'

Collectors often consider K. & R. as the premier German dollmaker
because of the good quality of the complete doll and the attention to
such details as the tasteful packaging of wares. A large number were
sold dressed only in a simple chemise, shoes and socks, though, for
instance in the 1927 catalogue, a string of beads and a huge bow of
ribbon in the hair were added. At that time many dolls were still sold
with the long ringlets associated with a much earlier period, though
others sported very up-to-date bobbed hair. Shoulder heads were also
offered in this catalogue and despite the fact that more realistic dolls
were, by this time, widely available, major sales obviously centred
around the sweet-faced representations. Replacement heads, as well
as a very large variety of wigs, were advertised and the dolls' hospital
supplies were extensive, these being claimed as 'Our best and often our
biggest customers'. The company also supplied dolls' accessories such
as shoes, feeding bottles, dummies and pram toys.

After buying Simon & Halbig heads for some years, K. & R. eventu-

Left:
German open-mouth doll with fixed blue eyes, pierced ears and a gusseted pink leather body. The head swivels in the shoulder plate, and is marked 'Made in Germany. 255dep'. The dress is made of chiffon and lace, with a boned bodice. 20 inches tall. Tunbridge Wells Museum.

Above:
The frequency with which the British Royal children wore Highland dress encouraged the German dollmakers to create similarly dressed dolls. This 7-inch example has a white bisque head moulded with ornate plumes. The legs, with their ribbed and tasselled socks, are specially moulded for this particular doll.

Opposite:
One of the rarest dolls made by Jumeau is the so-called Long Faced bébé with fixed eyes. This example has the original mohair wig and cork pate, applied ears and a two-tone mouth. The jointed body with fixed wrists is marked 'Jumeau Medaille d'Or'. Doll in Wonderland, Brighton.

ally took over this firm as well as that of Heinrich Handwerk, a company that had, almost exclusively, produced heads in the sweet child image. Dolls of the shoulder headed type and marked only with the S. & H. symbol are usually of good quality and made with the most beautiful expressions. A large number of closed-mouth unmarked German shoulder heads are seen whose resemblance to the work of this company is great, both in the quality of the bisque and in the modelling, and dealers often refer to these as 'Simon and Halbig type'. Their early models were very much in the French doll idiom, with large eyes and pierced ears, some even possessing swivel necks. As the standard was so high, several French makers were prepared to utilize these heads and S. & H. marked examples are found both on French automata and sometimes also on dolls with marked Jumeau bodies. The Edison phonograph doll is another which made use of heads of this type.

46

Coloured dolls made by Simon & Halbig are particularly effective, as the tinting of the bisque was so skilful. Oriental, Polynesian and negro heads were produced, and all effectively costumed. Roullet et Décamps used a Simon & Halbig head on their key-wound walking doll, whose mechanical sections are covered with leather, a doll that is a particular favourite with collectors, despite the fact that few still work correctly.

The majority of new collectors purchase a doll made by Armand Marseille, a company that, despite its French name, worked in Köppelsdorf from 1865. Their output was huge, and because of their availability are still comparatively cheap, despite the fact that they are often more attractive than the rarer dolls. The '390' mould, which is the most frequently found, has the soft and gentle child's face associated with pictures in 19th-century children's books, which never fails to appeal to the casual buyer. The '370' shoulder head is found on a variety of bodies, from those of cheap cotton with composition arms to well-made leather with riveted joints. The company also sold dolls that were the cheapest on the market, an economy that is all too evident in some of the jointed compositions, whose bodies were just roughly shaped and stapled pasteboard.

The commonly found '390' head varies considerably in quality, both of colouring and finish, and has to be valued accordingly. A number were provided with eyebrows of mohair, inserted through a slit cut on the brow line: not a particularly successful method, as the mohair often became threadbare. Possibly their most beautiful 390 is that with a fired-on, rich, brown colour. Cheaper dolls were often sprayed black, which gives a rather flat and lifeless effect. Heads marked 'Floradora' are found in even greater number in America than in England and are usually mounted on cheap bodies with unusually long legs, often made of almost unshaped dowel sections. The original costume normally consisted only of a cheap muslin chemise, but fortunately mothers redressed them before they were given as presents and they are sometimes found with clothes rivalling those of far more expensive dolls.

Above left:
A bisque-headed German jointed girl, with sleeping blue eyes and an open mouth, made by the Heubach factory at Kopplesdorf. The hair wig is a replacement, but the blue embroidered dress is original. 20 inches tall. Antiques of Childhood, London.

Above:
All-bisque dolls whose heads do not swivel are known as stiff-necks. This closed-mouth example is 5 inches tall with brown fixed eyes and effectively painted lashes. Marked '307/ 9 4 '. The ribbed socks are yellow, and the shoes are brown. Author's collection.

Opposite:
A jointed French bébé marked 'R.D', with the plump face and heavy brows and lips particularly typical of Rabery et Delphieu. 30 inches tall. Collection Mrs Jan Olsen.

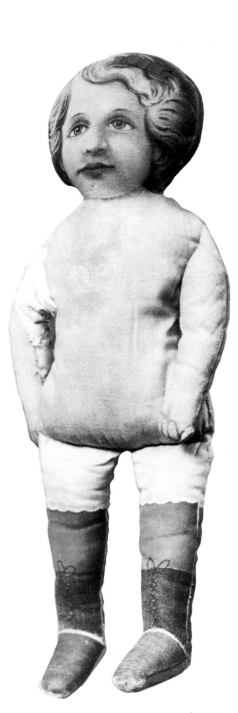

Printed cloth doll marked on the bottom of the left foot 'Art Fabric Mills, New York . . . Pat Feb 13th 1900'. The original child owner wrote 'Jane' in crayon on the back. 17½ inches tall. Blanding House Museum, Wisconsin.

Among the other producers of German bébés were Heubach of Thuringia, Ernst Heubach of Köppelsdorf and Schoenau & Hoffmeister, whose dolls are marked 'S. & H' but with a five pointed star between these letters enclosing the further initials, P.B. These S.P.B.H. figures can be extremely attractive with their larger than usual eyes, though the colouring is sometimes too high for current taste. Another company creating dolls in a rather French idiom was that of Gebrüder Krauss, whose products are recognized by their heavy brows and features. The Kestner family began to manufacture dolls in the early 19th century and worked in wax and papier mâché, though it is for their bisques that they are particularly known. A number are found without the actual Kestner mark, but bearing numbers that come within the Kestner series and are attributed by number. Little effort was put into the manufacture of unusual dolls, as the company saw its function as a producer of pretty-faced girl dolls of general appeal. Another firm with a very long dollmaking tradition is that of Cuno and Otto Dressel, who again centred their work on rather idealized children, usually with kid or leathercloth bodies.

The mass-produced German dolls were extremely cheap and the French makers had little chance of competing in the general market, as parents obviously chose dolls that were attractive but inexpensive. As the German industry boomed in the early years of the 20th century, the French declined, and although some setback was suffered by the Germans during the 1914–18 war, when the export of such frivolous items was interrupted, trade channels were soon re-established. With the development of unbreakable materials, china dolls, so easily smashed, were becoming less popular in the 1920s.

One of the most suitable materials for the creation of a toy was fabric, but this method was at first mainly associated with a home-made item, that despite holding great appeal for the child owner, was of little interest to the collector except as a primitive craft object. The creation of a more attractive rag doll was not accomplished until American manufacturers were able to explore the potential of the new cheap colour printing processes developed in the 1880s. Laurence & Co. of Boston were cloth distributors and printers rather than dollmakers but made some of the earliest dolls that could be bought by the yard from drapery shops all over the country.

Celia and Charity Smith were engaged in the designing of dolls from 1892, their patterns being produced, in the main, by the Arnold Print Works of Massachusetts, one of the largest manufacturers of prints and dress fabrics in the States. Their trademark, which include their date of establishment in a circle, was printed on the fabric. Among the most attractive of their dolls is Topsy, a coloured doll wearing a long pink dress with neatly buttoned cuffs, all of which, being printed, would remain in perfect order until the doll was worn away. Originally, this was printed on a yard of fabric and cost 10 cents, a white version of the same figure also being made. The product could only be purchased from a shop and not direct from the manufacturer. In comparison, the Art Fabric Mills of New York, on receipt of 50 cents, would post a printed doll to its customers. The best known product of the Art Fabric Mills is 'The Life Size Doll. Made so that Baby's clothes will now fit Dollie', patented in 1900 and made of heavy sateen decorated with oil colour.

Various methods of creating a more interesting rag doll were attempted such as 'upside down' or 'turnover' dolls whose unwanted heads were covered by a skirt, or 'turnabouts' whose unwanted faces were covered with a cap or hat. Another rag doll was given a sewn-on face that could, when dirty, be unpicked to reveal a clean one underneath. Photographic prints were also applied to faces once the process became sufficiently inexpensive to be used in this way.

In England, the printed rag doll is primarily associated with Dean's Rag Book Company, many of whose designs, introduced before the First World War, were still in production in the 1930s. Their 'Life Size Baby Doll' cost 1/6d and was printed on a thirty-inch square of fabric, the spaces being filled in with three small figures including Lucy Lockett. The firm claimed to use the 'most delicate and artistic colours', a claim that is most fully justified. While researching at Dean's I looked through piles of these old uncut fabric sheets whose most remarkable feature was the softness of the colours used, colours that could only be achieved today by the addition of the most expensive refinements to existing machinery.

Dean's 'Big Baby' wore a printed chemise and liberty bodice, with knee-length buttoned knickers. Wood-wool or cork was recommended for stuffing so that the figure could be washed, this being an essential feature of the work of a firm whose slogan read 'Indestructability, Washability and Hygenic merit'. In 1910 'Betty Blue' was introduced. 'From the top of her head to the soles of her dainty brown shoes, Betty Blue is indeed a darling dolly'. A smaller version of Betty Blue was known as Curly Locks. Their 'AI' label was used on fabric dolls for the first time in 1923 and 'The doll with a disc' series was introduced in the same year. As the imported German dolls were often meanly dressed, a great deal of effort was put into detailed costuming, particularly in the case of the pressed felt 'Posie Dolls', probably made as competition for the Italian Lencis. The Posy range wear costumes based on the colours and shapes of various flowers.

I was surprised to discover when studying Chad Valley catalogues that printed rag dolls were also made by this firm in 1923 and marketed under the registered trademark 'Aerolite'. Such printed dolls are not usually associated with this firm and their quality can only be judged by the printed illustrations that show 'Peggy' in a cloche hat and striped socks and 'Sonia' in a freely adapted German or Swiss costume. Peter Pan, Pixie and Red Cloud was also included in this series.

A very much played with Bruckner Topsy Turvey doll measuring some 12 inches, with the original costume. It is an American-made fabric doll, marked on the lower neck 'Pat d, July 9, 1901'. Blanding House Museum, Wisconsin.

A marked Simon & Halbig doll impressed '1079', with flirting eyes and a voice box in the torso. The walking mechanism is concealed under leather knickers. Author's collection.

Opposite:
Not all the dolls made by Fernand Gaultier are as attractive as this example, with its large fixed brown eyes and jointed body with fixed wrists. 16 inches tall. Collection Mrs Jan Olsen.

The Chad Valley company was established at the end of the Napoleonic wars by Antony Bunn Johnson and was engaged in printing, bookbinding and stationery until 1897 when Joseph and Alfred J. Johnson moved the company to a new factory in the village of Harborne, at that time outside the city of Birmingham. A small stream, the Chad, flowed nearby, so the new factory was named The Chad Valley Works. Despite recent changes in ownership, this firm is still engaged in the production of toys, though the making of dolls is now largely discontinued, and the 1976 catalogue only includes Barbapapa and Barbamama from a BBC television series and Molly Moppet and Dolly Denim, all made very much in the cartoon manner. In the years between the wars a very wide range of pressed felt-faced dolls was created, one of the most effective being a 22 inch Peter Pan, dressed in green and brown felt. 'La Petite Caresse', a range of chubby girls stuffed

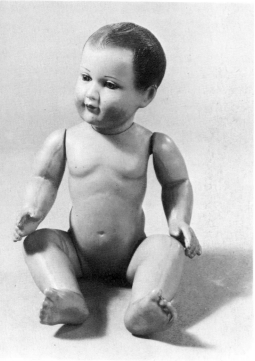

with Aerolite or kapok were also sold in felt costumes, decorated in this case with appliquéd felt flowers, and in four sizes from 12 to 18½ inches. A mama voice box could be inserted in the largest size at special request.

The 'Bambina' series, sold in 1927, were packed in a patent 'Bye-Bye' bed box, a sales ploy used at about the same time by Dean's. Bambinas ranged from 14½ to 18½ inches and were dressed either in knitted fur-trimmed suits or in felt dresses with art deco applied felt designs, the fabric used for the pressed faces being described as 'washable imitation Felt Cloth'. It was of this material that their well-known Princess Elizabeth doll was made.

Fashionably dressed 'Carina' dolls were sold from 1931 and were given economically created suits by the device of making the legs of the same coloured fabric as the coats. A cheaper version was made in 1933 with calico limbs, but 'Dressed with the care that typifies all Chad Valley dolls, may be had with painted or closing eyes, the latter being extra'. These were sold in sprigged voile, coloured or white organdie or the usual felt and wearing a wide-brimmed bonnet or a variation of a cloche hat. Some of the costumes were so heavily embellished by 1935 that they became amusingly vulgar with be-frilled taffeta dresses and hats, all very much in the contemporary Hollywood manner.

As late as 1948 similar dolls were still produced with 'Arms and legs made of coloured velvet–all models fitted with real leather shoes'. A label was tied to the wrist printed with the 'Chad Valley Seal of Purity'. One doll, with curly blonde hair, a gold and silver hair band, silk party dress and velvet cloak is so typically 30s in design that it is difficult to believe that it is appearing in a catalogue of the 40s. I have noticed the temptation among collectors to date many Chad Valleys as much earlier than their actual date because of this rather outmoded look, that is so often seen in the dolls made after the war, when it was difficult to obtain materials. Even in 1954, some felt-faced dolls were still made, including a Highland Lassie and Susan, who wore denim dungarees and carried gardening equipment.

Similar pressed felt-faced dolls were made by Nora Wellings, who had herself worked for a time as a designer at the Chad Valley factory in Wellington. Many Nora Wellings were costumed as particular characters, but among her prettier representations was Bo Peep in a pink taffeta dress and carrying a toy lamb. The majority of this maker's dolls still carry their firmly sewn on labels but there is often difficulty in attributing unmarked fabric-faced girl dolls, as there was so much similarity between the various makers, some Dean's, for instance, very closely resembling Nora Wellings.

Although rag was one of the cheapest indistructible materials, it had obvious disadvantages, not least the fact that very precise modelling, even over a base material, was not always possible. Discolouration of the surface also occurred when the head was washed too frequently. Consequently research continued in the attempt to develop a substance that looked as lovely as tinted bisque but also held great strength. Gutta percha had a rather short-lived popularity among the French makers, but few examples have survived. During the same period, rubber heads were produced, especially in America, but as this material perished, few can now be found, though it was used both by Steiner and Bru in the manufacture of complete bébés. In Germany Kämmer & Reinhardt produced some rubber-headed dolls, but there was much more general interest in the use of a man-made material known as celluloid, a substance invented in England in the mid-19th century. The main problem for the makers in utilizing this material was its glossy surface and the fact that discolouration occurred when it was exposed to the sun. Though various makers claimed to have overcome these problems, they are all too often apparent when examples are found. Early celluloids were purely imitative and the shoulder heads were attached to leather or leathercloth bodies. They were at first more expensive than bisque and used on good quality bodies and given abundant wigs.

The most frequently found celluloids are those bearing the 'Turtle' mark of the Rheinische Gummi und Celluloid Fabrik, established in the 1870s. This company usually supplied the heads for Kämmer & Reinhardt, some of which were almost identical with the bisque moulds. As celluloid is so easily damaged, it is now quite difficult to understand why the material was thought such an important advance, the all-celluloid dolls in particular being extremely fragile. Better examples mounted on well-made bodies are now collected, as they are still considerably cheaper than the bisques and are within the price range of many new collectors. One of the most desirable celluloids is that with five interchangeable heads, including one of a cat. An example of this particular doll is on view at the Bethnal Green Museum. Black celluloids have also remained in a more collectable state, as the colour was not so affected by light.

In their original condition, metal heads must have proved a more effective form of competition, as they could be pushed back into shape if dented. The fact that this process usually left a slight scar would have concerned a child less than a doll that was broken. In Germany in the 1880s sheet metal, brass, zinc and tinplate were all used in manufacture, but are difficult to attribute as the majority carry only a number. Shoulder heads of metal as well as socket heads were made well into the 1930s and frequently, when a bisque was smashed it was replaced with one of tin, so that it is now difficult to be sure whether or not a particular head is original. 'Minerva' marked dolls are the most often found in Britain, and were produced in Germany by A. Vischer, Buschow & Beck also using this name on their metal heads. In 1912 Minerva dolls that shed real tears were advertised though I know of no actual examples.

In America, The Metal Doll Company, run by Vincent Lake, made all-metal ball jointed dolls with snap-on interchangeable wigs, while a walking metal figure was produced by the Amor Metal Toy Stamping Company of New Jersey. In France Päen Frères used metal heads on bébés in the 1880s. Examples in good condition are well worth buying as they, like celluloids, soon became disfigured but are of interest in that they illustrate the makers' search for a child-proof material.

Below:
An unmarked metal shoulder-headed doll, 15 inches tall, with metal lower arms and legs, and a leathercloth body. Author's collection.

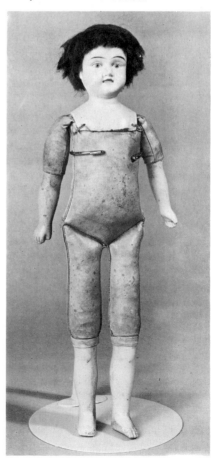

A number of variations on the basic papier mâché mixture were evolved in the attempt to make an unbreakable head, Parsons Jackson in the USA describing their material in glowing terms: 'Will never break, crack, surface chip or peel.' Composition heads were made as alternatives to china by such firms as Armand Marseille and, though despised by collectors just a few years ago, they are now bought, particularly in the States where the doll enthusiast casts a much wider net. Most of the composition mixtures were based on a combination of wood fibre and various binding agents. In England, the older dollmakers still refer to such heads as 'wood flours'. Most of the experiments with the indestructible substances were carried out in America, though both Bru and S.F.B.J. had used a material known as Fibrolaque. Solomon Hoffman was making 'Can't Break Em' dolls in 1892 while the Ideal Novelty Company claimed that their products could be dropped on stone floors without coming to harm. Adtocolite, a material that eventually cracked very badly, was unfortunately used by several makers, whose dolls are now far too ugly to be included in any but the most esoteric of collections.

At Christmas 1925 EffanBee, an American company, advertised 'Rosemary — the doll with the Golden Heart'. This was a sleeping doll with a voice box whose sales were aided by a necklace in little girl size,

Right:
'First Love' a vinyl 'pose and stay' idealized baby, whose available costumes include knitted separates, a romper suit and a sleepsuit. Pedigree Dolls, Canterbury.

Below:
Unmarked 8-inch tin mechanical boy in a grey suit with a blue hat and bow. When the key is wound the figure tilts from the hips and the arms swing above the head. Tunbridge Wells Museum.

Opposite:
Poured-wax doll with unusual teeth and fixed glass eyes, dressed in an original Lord Fauntleroy suit. Blaise Castle House Museum, Bristol.

bearing the firm's slogan on a heart-shaped pendant. A miniature version of this was also worn by the doll. Several other makers created composition figures in direct imitation of the traditional bisques, some even making composition shoulder heads to be attached to a fabric body.

In England, Dean's did not introduce compositions until the 1930s and their main concentration was upon the costuming, rather than the creation of an interesting doll. This company sold composition heads loose for home assembly at this time, a type of market in which the Germans had long since lost interest.

Latex foam was made in the 1930s by Latex Processes of Guernsey, though it did not become popular as a dollmaking material until the 1950s, the first plastic dolls being made in the German Democratic Republic in 1948. Firms such as Pedigree in England continued to use a wood flour mixture for heads until several years after the war, dollmaking being very difficult at this time, as materials had to be purchased long in advance on a quota system. One of the firm's managers remembered how vast quanities of identical dress material lay around for years, but was decorated in different ways, with lace and ribbons, each season in an attempt to make it look different.

Just after the war there were two distinct types of doll in demand in England: those with a hard head, made of cellulose acetate and mounted on a soft body, and a soft type that was latex dipped and filled with kapok, dolls of this type being known as Beauty Skin dolls. This type made an ideal take-to-bed toy but had a fatal disadvantage in the fact that the outer plastic split, and also became very discoloured, so that it is now almost impossible to find examples. Though most of my own childhood dolls are still in existence, the Beauty Skin doll had a very short life. Pedigree sold a large number of mechanical walking figures in the 50s that worked by means of a bar from neck to legs, but it was too expensive a construction to have any lasting appeal. It was at this time that nylon hair began to be used extensively in the British doll industry, replacing the traditional mohair.

To me, dolls made after 1930 are items of curiosity rather than collector's objects, but the price of old dolls is now sufficiently high to have forced many people into the collecting of dolls in general rather than those with any antique interest, and examples even from this recent period are bought. One of the best methods of dating such acquisitions is by reference to film star annuals of the time, as the dollmakers closely followed the shape of the fashionable face, and though a child-like doll was the aim, it was a child whose appearance was modelled on adult ideals of beauty as seen on the screen.

Left:
A felt-faced Chad Valley 'Bambina' in absolutely original condition with glass eyes and velvet cloth body. The costume is also made of felt. On the left foot is a label, 'Chad Valley Bambina (Regd and patent)', and on other foot 'Hygienic toys Chad Valley Co. Made in England'. Private collection (Jane Owen).

Opposite:
Chad Valley 'Bambina' in original felt costume, with mohair wig and glass eyes. The body is velvet, with the characteristic piped felt decoration of the shoes. The doll has the Chad Valley button on its left side, and a label under each foot. Antiques of Childhood, London.

Realism
and Caricature

In the early years of the 20th century there was considerable interest in the psychology of childhood, and the child's emotional involvement with his toys. It was felt that the beautiful walking and talking bébés were too perfect, and left no room for the play of the child's imagination. Manufacturers looked again at the idealized children they had created and felt that radical changes were needed. This change in attitude was at first apparent in Munich, but soon spread to Berlin and Dresden. It was, at first, manifest in the reactionary creation of toys that were so completely abstract in quality that they had little meaning for the children they were intended to stimulate, and therefore when, in 1904, the Dresden handicraft workshops asked for new designs, it was stipulated that they should be in the traditional manner.

The best known of designers to work in the new manner was Marion Kaulitz, who created dolls with composition or occasionally, fabric heads. The actual modelling of the heads was the work of Paul Vogel-sanger and the toys are often referred to as Munich Art Dolls. Examples are not easy to find, though one from 'Doll in Wonderland', Brighton, is illustrated. They were costumed in clear, bright colours, as it was felt that these would have the greatest appeal for a child. Max von Boehn describes how their first real success was achieved in 1909 at an exhibition organized in the warehouse of Hermann Tietz, where the name of Marion Kaulitz was heard for the first time as a doll artist. He describes her dolls as 'Full of individuality and character and yet always remaining childish, so true hearted and bright, so charmingly pert and rakish.' This designer, of Anglo-German parentage, usually marked the dolls, whose faces she herself painted, on the neck. The costumes were also to her own specifications. It is difficult at this distance in time to understand why these dolls were so revolutionary, as the modelling is not of any marked quality and one basic head often sufficed for several characters by the simple addition of different wigs. Their charming waif-like innocence is appreciated by collectors, but their real importance lies in the fact that they heralded a new style of dollmaking that worked towards the portrayal of a true-to-life child rather than a beautiful vision. The term 'character dolls' began to be used in this context from 1910.

The success of the Munich exhibition inspired the Berliners to stage their own displays and in 1912 an artist was discovered 'Whose name, both in Germany and outside, is immediately called to mind whenever German dolls are spoken of – Käthe Krüse.' Von Boehn recounts how

The first character doll made by Kammer & Reinhardt was called Baby. This example is marked '28 K & R 100'. The painted eyes and open-closed mouth, together with the realistic modelling of the features, made a great impact on the toy trade when first introduced. Author's collection.

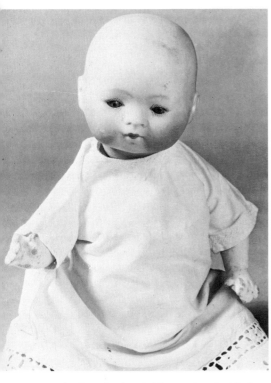

A closed-mouth bisque-headed baby with blue sleeping eyes and a composition bent-limb body, marked '1924–1'. 13 inches tall. Author's collection.

at first she used raw potatoes for the heads of the dolls she made for her own children. In 1923 she explained that her dolls were created because of her desire to give the child an illusion of holding a real baby in its arms, an idea originally thought of by her sculptor father. She felt that the love of a child for its doll was a type of womanly bliss 'Tantamount to education in maternal feeling', and possibly as an expression of this very personal emotion she actually represented her own children in doll form.

The concept that a small girl should nurse and care for a doll in preparation for her adult role is no longer feasible, and much of the over-stressed emotion which Käthe Krüse poured into her advertisements and statements is, to modern taste, slightly distasteful. The creation of an imitation baby, rather than a play doll is seen particularly in a version that was sand filled to simulate the weight of an actual child when nursed. Two baby dolls of this type were made, one with the eyes open and the other, much rarer, with painted sleeping eyes. This doll was not produced in large numbers, probably because its seven pound weight made it burdensome to a small girl, and it is therefore much liked by collectors. The modelling of the sand babies' heads, always set to the right, is effective, especially when photographed, as the slightly brash colouring is modified. Constructionally, the design of the body, that was made of cotton and padded with cotton wool, is realistic in movement as most of the weight was centred in the head, this particular doll reputedly being made in the likeness of her eldest child.

When she began to make dolls, her dissatisfaction with the result of her experiments caused her to work for four years before she allowed their public display in a Berlin department store. The dolls were all made with muslin heads that were stiffened, painted, and sprayed with fixative so that they were washable. The collector is aided in her identification of this dollmaker's work by the fact that, in her own words, 'Each doll carries my name and number on the sole of the left foot.' She acknowledged her indebtedness to the artistic suggestions of her sculptor husband, who is also thought to have helped in the creation of a completely professional object that could be commercially produced: a production that began just before the First World War.

A workshop was set up in Bad Kosen near Nuremberg, and her dolls won prizes at several world exhibitions. Those produced in the largest number were toddler type figures with thigh joints, whose hair was either painted, with the effectiveness which is a particular feature of all her work, or given wigs. The costumes were those of ordinary children of the period, and must have helped in their identification with their toy. In 1934 figures for shop window display were also made. Contemporaries regarded her creations as 'art dolls' rather than the exaggerated characters that were then popular, and she worked completely in accord with the taste of the more discerning parent, who required a figure with a gentle suggestion of personality, rather than the often crude statements made in bisque.

Realism in the creation of bisque baby doll heads was attempted by Fritz Bartenstein of Thuringia in the 1880s, who made several versions of two-faced dolls representing crying or laughing infants. He also made similar dolls in composition and waxed composition, though these have not survived in such good condition as the bisque. Occasionally, a poured-wax that appears almost a portrait of a particular baby is discovered, while in my own collection is a composition baby made in the 1880s whose head could only be described as that of a character doll, a term generally found in use after 1910. It should not therefore be thought that the idea of a realistic baby doll was a concept entirely fresh in the early 20th century; it was rather a popularization of an idea that had found occasional expression throughout the Victorian period.

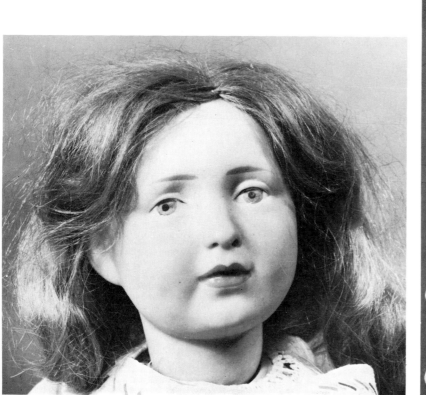

Peculiar to the 20th century was the expressed consciousness of the manufacturers in their attempt to produce a doll with realism: a consciousness that was fanned by the opinions of psychologists and educationalists regarding the patterns of a child's play and its importance in character formation. A much heavier approach begins to be seen in the advertisements of dollmakers, who became rather pompous regarding the artistic merit of their productions, rarely claiming that a figure was made purely for idle amusement.

Kämmer & Reinhardt of Walterhausen began to take a much more serious interest in the making of realistic bisque dolls after the great stir aroused by the exhibition of the work of Marion Kaulitz. This firm began to use the term 'Character Dolls' from around 1909, their most popular creation being 'Baby' or 'The first character doll', popularly known to collectors as 'The Kaiser Baby' as the result of an incorrect tradition claiming that the head was a portrait of the infant Kaiser. This doll was made with complete realism of feature and with the arms both modelled in different positions, making possible the crawling pose in which it was represented in the firm's catalogue. The coloured version of this doll is much rarer than the white, and is popular with collectors because of its skilful soft tinting.

The new character models were displayed for the first time at the Munich Exposition in 1909, though the initial response to 'Baby' from the retailers was rather slow. Their nervousness was overcome after the clever sales ploy of including a few samples in ordinary consignments, so that the customers were themselves made to judge the doll. This baby doll, with its engaging realism, was so different to the usual sweet-faced girls that small local shops regularly offered, that it became almost unexpectedly popular, and encouraged the firm to introduce 'Hans and Gretchen' in 1910, for which Reinhardt's young nephew posed. They were costumed in the more rational form of children's dress popular at the time, but now, all too commonly, are redressed by collectors, who fail to appreciate the interest of such contemporary costume. It was felt by the company that sales of character dolls would have risen even higher if it had been possible to provide them with sleeping eyes, a device that was difficult because of the very detailed modelling.

Above:
Painted composition-headed child with a mohair wig and a body of jointed wood and composition. It was made by Marion Kaulitz of Munich, who revolutionized the world of dollmaking with the realism of her work. Doll in Wonderland, Brighton.

Above left:
German bisque-headed character doll incised 'K & R 109' for Kämmer & Reinhardt. A boy and a girl version of this doll were made. The girl is called Elsie, and has painted eyes, a closed mouth and a composition body. Doll in Wonderland, Brighton.

Kämmer & Reinhardt characters are the collector's attribution dream, as they were not only marked clearly but were also sometimes given names, No 101 for instance being called Peter, a model that was very occasionally made with sleeping eyes. Number 114 popularly described as 'Pouty' by collectors has a most appealing, slightly sulky face mounted on a jointed body. Their most commonly found baby doll, that is sometimes classed as a character, is the 126, usually found with flirting eyes, i.e. eyes that move from side to side. The maker's details on German dolls are usually incised at the back of the head, but a straight-legged version of this doll which I owned recently was also marked around the top of the head where the cardboard cone is glued; in this case the date 28.2.28 was incised. This standing version of what was originally a bent-limb baby was announced in their 1927 catalogue, and was sold in a wide variety of outfits from long traditional baby gowns to the most up-to-date costumes of the 20s. One very rare 126 lowers and lifts its arms, gestures that are activated by a mechanical movement in the torso.

The fashion for character dolls was relatively short-lived, which is why the jointed versions in particular are so difficult to find. By the mid-twenties the K. & R. catalogue was again mainly occupied by girl dolls, though some characters, notably a negro girl and the character boy 115, were still offered. Some of the dolls were made in celluloid, and though the material responded to fine modelling even more than bisque, these are not highly popular, as the celluloid has often discoloured badly. The 1927 catalogue ceased to offer 'Baby', though the less interesting baby dolls continued in production until the mid-thirties.

Seeing the success of K. & R. in the marketing of more adventurous dolls, other firms began creating characters of their own, though with the exception of Heubach, in nothing like as wide a range as those made by Simon & Halbig for K. & R. The German makers were much more prepared than the French in the 20th century to experiment with new ideas, the French contribution to the development of character dolls

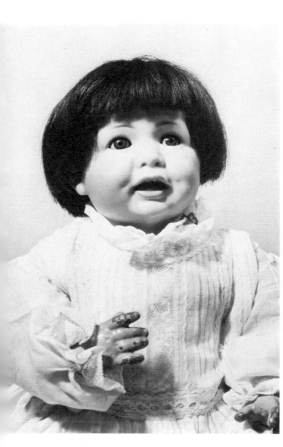

Above:
Bisque-headed character baby on a bent-limb body and with an open-closed mouth and blue eyes. Marked 'K & R 116A Simon & Halbig'. 15½ inches tall. Joy Stanford Collection.

Right:
Large numbers of dolls were costumed in variations of the popular sailor suit. This 18-inch jointed doll with sleeping brown eyes and a voice box in the torso wears an original costume, and is marked 'Made in Germany.J.D.K. 260' for Kestner. Author's collection.

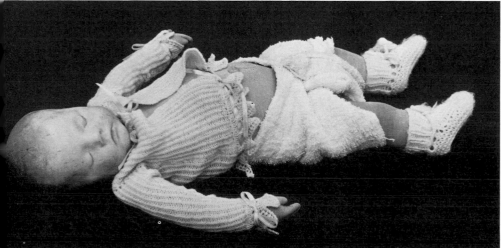

Left:
A sand-weighted doll by Kathe Kruse with a painted head and padded stockinette body. The navel is sewn on. This sleeping version of the doll is much rarer than the awake baby. Bethnal Green Museum, London.

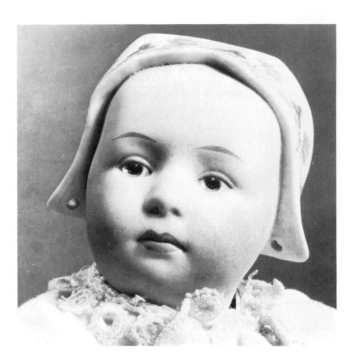

being of the most minimal kind. Early Kestner baby character heads, with dimpled cheeks and open/closed mouths are sometimes found on rather strangely shaped leather bodies, with composition lower legs, and arms that are very much an adaptation of the traditional leather girl-type bodies. Such bodies were combined very unsatisfactorily with ordinary socket heads, and new collectors often think that these are replacements. This type of transitional body, though unsatisfactory on aesthetic grounds, is liked by collectors as it marks a definite stage in development. Bent-limb baby bodies, that were so much more satisfactory, begin to be mentioned from about 1904, and were very well established by 1910. They were of a shape that was economical to produce, and the stringing process was much quicker than that necessitated by the many parts of a ball-jointed doll. Some manufacturers were reluctant to completely abandon ball joints, and they are sometimes seen at the top of arms on Jutta babies, while Armand Marseille made a very fat toddler baby with the usual bent baby arms and body but with very thick double-jointed legs.

Although Armand Marseille made characters, they are comparatively rare. A jointed boy with intaglio eyes, closed mouth and lightly moulded hair is effective, though nearly always found in very small sizes. A slightly smiling boy, No 500, is found on several bodies and was also made in a shoulder headed version with a cheap cloth body. Their basic baby dolls are made with a certain degree of realism, and are certainly not as idealized as their girl dolls. The 640 is a sweet-faced smiling girl with intaglio eyes, while another baby was given a specific name, 'Baby Betty', incised on the head. Their coloured dolls often merely involved tinting the basic 390 or 1894 head a rich brown, though an Indian with a frowning expression was specially modelled. Coloured baby dolls representing Chinese and black babies were simply effected from the basic open- or closed-mouth dream babies. Though probably perfectly satisfactory to the original owners, the Armand Marseille black dolls look particularly weak when compared to the heavily modelled version made by Simon & Halbig, with its definite negroid features, or to their Indian, modelled also with exciting sculptural strength.

The early 20th century was a period of quite rapid innovation and it was only a short time before the manufacturers needed to introduce yet another type of doll and, for a short while, realism was abandoned in favour of caricature. It is difficult to be precise about the date when

Above:
An unmarked Indian girl of German origin with an open mouth with teeth and a brown jointed body. The head is modelled with some realism and effectively tinted a soft brown. Author's collection.

Above left:
Bisque-headed German character doll, made by Gebruder Heubach, and known as Baby Stuart. It is marked with a sunburst and an entwined 'GH'. The fixed moulded bonnet is decorated with painted pink roses and has holes at either side for a ribbon. The eyes are blue intaglio. Doll in Wonderland, Brighton.

Above right:
An all-bisque caricature child with an amusing expression, made of self-tinted pink bisque. The doll, unmarked but of German origin, has intaglio eyes and brown-painted hair, and is 4 inches tall. Author's collection.

Right:
A black bisque-headed baby with fired-on tinting, brown sleeping eyes and an open mouth with two lower teeth. Marked 'A.M. 351 3K Germany' for Armand Marseille. The doll, which is 13½ inches tall, wears a cream silk suit. Author's collection.

Far right:
German bisque-headed character head on a jointed composition body, with open-closed mouth, moulded hair and blue intaglio eyes. The head is incised '531'. Doll in Wonderland, Brighton.

Goo-goos or Googlies were first introduced but in 1908 manufacturers were finding it necessary to explain how such eyes worked in the pages of trade magazines. Armand Marseille made several versions, including some with a 'Mohawk' hairstyle and others with a quiff. Some were given intaglio eyes, while others were of glass. Such caricatures were the ultimate in the creation of dolls with whimsical individuality, and though hardly lovely they have an amusing charm that attracts adults as well as children.

Armand Marseille were completely aware, in company with other German firms, that the best sellers among their dolls were those representing pretty children, so they were careful of expending too much energy in the creation of characters whose appeal was mainly to parents of artistic inclination.

Much more effort was put into the creation of such dolls by Gebrüder Heubach of Lichte in Thuringia, a firm that almost specialized in the production of unusual characters. Regrettably, lovely heads are frequently mounted on the cheapest of fabric bodies that must have come from a very different source. The factory was established in the 1820s but attributable heads do not appear until after 1891, when marking became obligatory. Not only doll's heads but a vast range of ornamental ware and mantelpiece trivia were also made by this prolific

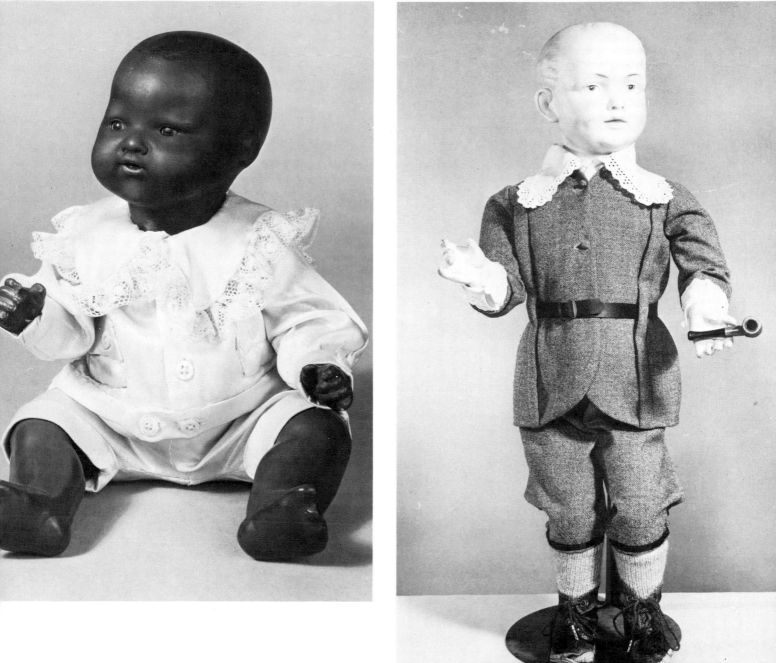

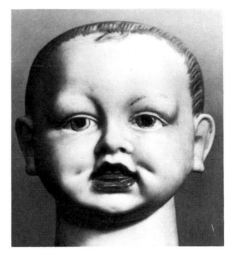

Unusual Goss bisque character head with open-closed mouth, painted eyes and a flange neck. Although the modelling is of a good standard, the decoration is poor. Marked 'Goss Copyright [indecipherable No's] W.H. Goss Stoke on Trent [indecipherable date]'. On either side a large 'G' and a '4'. Doll in Wonderland, Brighton.

firm. Doll collectors now often include their piano babies and figurines among their acquisitions, though they were originally made with the taste of adults rather than children in mind; these ornamental pieces having a sentimental appeal that is rarely found in their dolls. The bisque used for doll's heads is often self-coloured with a pink tint rather than the basic white body, surface coloured, that was popular with other makers. The mark on the heads either reads Heubach in a square or is in the form of a sunburst, the actual number of the mould being incised. Stamped small green figures are also characteristic of this maker.

The variety of character heads is surprisingly large, and some collectors specialize just in the work of this single maker whose production of interesting pieces was so great. Similarities can be seen between the heads of certain piano babies and those used on dolls, indicating the work of a particular artist. Eyes of smaller dolls are often of the intaglio type, that is, incised into the bisque, and painted white highlights were often added. A shoulder-headed and a socket-headed version of the same doll is sometimes seen, such as the so called 'smiling girl' marked Germany 1850. One of their most beautiful dolls is, fortunately, that most commonly found, representing a baby of about a year old with a much thinner face than that usually found on such dolls. A well-made heavy composition body is often found in conjunction with this head, which makes the figure an early acquisition in most collections.

One of the most effective Googly-eyed dolls made was that created by Heubach and marked Einco. This doll has a very round face and a closed mouth and was sometimes sold dressed in a wollen coat and a checked skirt. Another Googly has one eye in a winking position that is amusing for the collector of today, but must have been rather tiresome for the original child owner. Probably the rarest Heubach is the boy doll with painted bulging eyes and moulded hair, whose appearance is slightly alarming, as the expression is almost demented! This doll is of appeal to the collector because of its considerable rarity. Much more generally attractive is the black shoulder bisque with characteristic roughly modelled hair and sideways-glancing eyes, while the pensive faced girl with slightly pouting mouth and a mohair wig is also generally liked, and found either with sleeping or intaglio eyes.

'The Whistler' is a flange-headed doll, so called because the mouth is modelled in a whistling position and the body contains a bellows voice box that causes the doll to whistle when pressed. With little doubt, the most realistic of their characters is that representing a child in a particularly nasty temper, with the mouth twisted to one side in rage. One baby doll has a moulded bonnet that is decorated with flowers, another and much rarer version having a bisque bonnet that is removable. This must have caused many breakages, and the doll is consequently difficult to find. Yet another version has a fixed bonnet with holes for the insertion of ribbon.

Many of the Heubach products would have originally sold very cheaply, because of the stringent economy exercised in the body construction, but the appeal of the heads is such that this unevenness of quality becomes immaterial. As such a vast number of Heubach products are still available, including figures of animals and pincushion heads, it is little wonder that there is specialization. Despite the fact that some of the products, such as certain piano babies, are quite common, an artificially high price is commanded simply because they are included in doll collections, whereas a far superior bisque figurine without any connection with a known dollmaker can only command a fraction of the price. This is an example of a problem that often arises in doll collecting, where an object that might be considered of little worth in general antique terms has gained through some, often tenuous, association with the hobby.

Oriental babies were made by several German firms. This 9-inch baby doll in original costume, with brown sleeping eyes, is marked only with an impressed '4 Germany'. Author's collection.

Opposite:
A coffee-coloured Moroccan girl
with well-modelled black hair and
original costume. She has a sawdust-
filled cotton body, with brown-tinted
bisque arms and legs. Author's
collection.

Above:
A composition-headed girl
with inset glass eyes and bisque
lower arms, carrying a bisque-headed
baby. When the figure is wound by a
key which is fixed in position, the
figure rocks from side to side. 14
inches tall. Private collection (Martin
Olsen).

The tremendous variety of realistic characters made by the brothers Heubach is unsurpassed, either in number or variety, by any other dollmaker, and certainly far exceeds that produced by another firm of the same name with which it is sometimes confused. This firm, recorded as working in Köppelsdorf in the late 1880s is generally referred to as 'Heubach Köppelsdorf' as a means of distinction from the more important firm. A very wide variety of standard is seen in the heads made by Ernst Heubach, some are of the finest bisque and well finished, while others are decidedly poor. In comparison with Gebrüder Heubach, few interesting dolls were produced and their characters are only occasionally found. Their googly had a small round nose and a rather narrow, smiling mouth but is without much of the assured air of caricature that is associated, for instance, with the Einco doll, and is therefore less appealing. One of their best-liked characters is the negro baby with correctly modelled features, pierced ears with earrings and sleeping eyes. Another, much rarer, has a widely grinning open mouth with moulded teeth, in combination with sideways-glancing eyes. This doll was not only given earrings but a nose ring and neckband also. Their Indian boy (No 451) and Gypsy girl (No 452) in shades of brown, both have moulded hair and sleeping eyes.

German dolls are quite often found without the actual maker's name but with numbers incised and in such cases the dolls have to be given a tentative attribution by the fact that the particular number falls within a sequence regularly used by a firm. In this respect, a reliable book of dolls' marks is essential. As quality varies to such a great extent, the value of a doll, even made from a generally desirable mould, can be considerably less than, for instance, a price guide might suggest for a generally superior example. If good quality is combined with an interesting mould, then the doll is potentially collectable.

Although Simon & Halbig made a large number of characters for K. & R., comparatively few are found marked only with the S. & H. trade name. This firm concentrated mainly on idealized children and avoided the often grotesque features associated with the most extreme of character dolls. The general popularity of coloured dolls in the early 20th century was, however, pandered to, and besides the Indian and negro mentioned, a series of prettily tinted heads that were really just the standard white with added colour were produced. In comparison, the colour of their negro with slightly parted lips is at times very heavy, thus creating a doll that is not only rare but generally effective. The S. & H. 1488 is another of the firm's rare characters, though of a more winsome expression. Sleeping eyes and a closed mouth combine to create a softly expressive head. Several well tinted Burmese and Orientals were also made, and given appropriately constructed wigs and costumes that set off the quality of the heads. The smiling S. & H. 1388, with an open/closed mouth revealing moulded teeth has a peculiarly adult face, and yet was obviously made to represent a girl. An extremely effective character boy (No 153) was also produced, with painted eyes and moulded fair hair that has similarities with some of the Heubach modelling. Another exquisite doll is the closed-mouth negro girl with sleeping eyes and pierced ears (No 1358), which would almost come into the category of an idealized character doll.

The attraction in collecting German characters lies in the way in which, continually, new examples are found that have not previously occurred. On the day of writing for instance I examined a Bing negro baby of the most effective appearance, and was made very aware of the amount of activity, simply in the modelling, that must have taken place in the factories of the time. Recently, a number of indistinctly marked shoulder heads representing a smiling boy with moulded hair have appeared on the British market. They are sold either as loose heads or mounted on a variety of available bodies of the 20s and 30s. The quality

of the bisque is not good but even so, in a single week, they were offered in London from prices ranging from £40 to £130, being sold as genuine antiques. The new collector used only to worry about reproduction French dolls, but care has now to be exercised even in German products. The Americans in particular make large numbers of reproduction bisques which are usually incised as such on the head, though a few makers omit this helpful addition. Though many American collectors now enjoy reproductions, it is an aspect of doll collecting that is not popular in Europe and many collectors from this side of the Atlantic would be very upset to discover they had inadvertently purchased a fake.

A history of dollmaking dating back to the beginning of the 19th century is recorded for the Kestner company of Walterhausen. Early Kestners are unattributable, being made of wood or papier mâché, but after 1860 their porcelain factory was in operation. D. E. and E. Coleman comment that they were the only German dollmakers to create complete dolls as well as selling parts separately. Baby dolls are often marked only with the Kestner number, and are among the most frequently found characters, being made in a very wide range of sizes. Their Oriental baby (No 243) is liked by collectors even more than those made by A.M. which are really just their basic baby yellow tinted. The Kestner version has eyes that are cut in an upward slanting shape and the whole face is much flatter than the more European version. Their googly toddler with a ball-jointed composition body is also very popular.

An advertisement in a Sears Roebuck catalogue for 1910 stated 'Kestner is known for the excellence of manufacture, the fine quality features, and the general superiority of his dolls. His goods are the standard by which all others are judged. The heads are of absolutely the finest quality bisque.' In many respects these claims were correct, for though poor quality examples of most firm's work are occasionally found, a badly produced Kestner is a considerable rarity. Their basic baby dolls were occasionally given an imposed character by the addition of an incised Christian name, one baby with painted hair being marked 'Hilda.J.D.K.'

After the First World War the influence of the American market on the work of the German makers became important, as that continent provided a sales outlet that was both large and wealthy. It became quite common for the porcelain factories to produce dolls to American designer's specifications and among those made in this way by Kestner was Baby Bo Kaye, with moulded hair and a flange neck, that was designed by Joseph Kallus and copyrighted in 1926. Marked Kestner 'Century Doll Co' heads were also especially made for a firm based in New York.

In the early 20s, Grace Storey Putnam, an art teacher, decided to create a doll that was completely realistic and, after looking at many babies in the Los Angeles hospitals, she eventually found a three-day-old child whose features were perfect. The baby's head was originally modelled in wax and she was eventually able to persuade the Borgfeldt Doll Company to make the head in bisque, though the firm insisted that it should be given sleeping eyes. Photographs of the original wax model show the degree of modification the well-modelled head underwent before it became an acceptable doll, modifications that robbed the Bye-Lo Baby of much of its original character, by smoothing out wrinkles and, in fact, creating a head that is very like others of the period. This version was given a fabric body, though the all-bisque representation is now popular. A variety of German factories produced heads for the Bye-Lo Baby, including Kling and Alt, Beck and Gottschalck, though it was Kestner who made the attractive all-bisque with coloured shoes. Later dolls of this type were made in celluloid, composition and even rubber. It was dubbed the 'Million dollar baby' because of the queues that formed to buy it when it first appeared on the American market.

Another, much stranger doll of a rather grotesque appearance was designed by Rose O'Neill from drawings she had originally supplied to the *Ladies Home Journal* of 1909. Kewpies were originally created in bisque at the Kestner factory, though they were produced and distributed by Borgfeldt. The doll she designed in 1912 was in the form of a chubby child with its legs moulded together, arms outstretched, a quiff of hair, small sprouting wings on either side of the neck and webbed hands. The rather angelic effect of this design is shattered by the figure's impish features with sideways-glancing eyes, snub nose and roguishly smiling mouth. The Kewpies were made in very large numbers, and in a wide variety of sizes, some even being especially created to be worn as buttonholes! It has been estimated that over 5,000,000 Kewpies were sold, the Rose O'Neill signature being found across the sole of the foot. All-bisque versions with huge googly eyes were created as large as 17 inches high, though few of these have survived.

Below:
A wooden-headed baby doll with blue glass sleeping eyes and celluloid hands. It is very much in imitation of the Bye-Lo Baby, and is attributed to Schoenhut. It has the typical Bye-Lo type cloth body. Blanding House Museum, Wisconsin.

Right:
A group of Kewpies showing something of the variety designed by Rose O'Neill. On the left are bisque versions of a Kewpie traveller and the Huggers as well as a 7-inch standing doll. The large sitting doll is made of plaster, and that with a helmet is entirely moulded in bisque. The doll on the extreme right is celluloid. Blanding House Museum, Wisconsin.

116

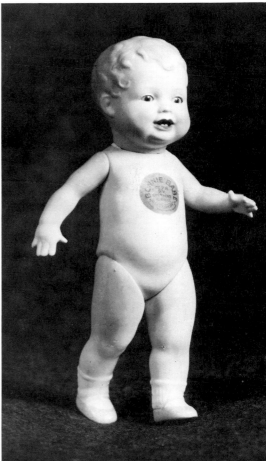

Many factories produced Kewpies, including the Fulper Pottery whose bisque was of reasonable quality but whose colour was too strong for an effective figure, though these are now much sought after, as examples of the work of a purely American factory. The name 'Fulper, Made in U.S.A' was incised down the back. Kewpies were made to represent a variety of characters and are seen as soldiers, seated in a chair playing the banjo, reading a book, or in pairs hugging one another. The Kewpie band included the Cook, the Gardener, the Carpenter, the Life Preserver and the Instructor. Scootles, another doll character designed by Rose O'Neill, also appeared in her cartoons and he was made as a bisque doll, too. So great was their popularity that they were copied in Japan, those impressed 'Nippon' sold simultaneously with the genuine Rose O'Neill versions. There is now great interest, especially in America, in the collecting of these figures, though they are obviously not found in anything like this wide variety in Britain.

It is considered that the all-bisque character girl named 'Didi' was also made to the specification of an American designer, in this case, Jeanne I. Orsini, by the firm of Kestner, as the head contains a wooden bar that is typical of Kestner's work. This doll represents a widely smiling girl, hand raised, index finger pointing and the thumb bent over, making an extremely difficult casting problem for the manufacturer. Like many of the Kewpies, this doll was originally sold with a paper sticker attached to the torso. It is to the Kestner company that a wide variety of good quality all-bisques are attributed, especially those with ribbed socks, but as the majority are unmarked some care has to be exercised.

A large number of smaller German companies produced character dolls, including Recknagel whose heads are often remarkable for the poor quality of the bisque, though the basic modelling is good. Dolls marked R.A. are usually attributed to this company. Some charming, pensive-faced characters were made by Kley and Hahn, while the Catterfelder Püppenfabrik created very Germanic looking characters, the girls wearing earphone type plaits over the ears, their character babies being remarkable for the fierceness of their expressions! The work of the Limbach factory was marked with an impressed clover mark; few characters were made but a girl doll with large, almost googly type eyes is an exception. This firm made the doll designed by the American designer Georgene Averill in 1926 and known as Bonnie Babe. This head represented a chubby-faced child with moulded, slightly curling hair and a few baby teeth.

Of lasting interest to collectors are the two- and three-faced dolls, all representing very different characters, made by Carl Bergner of Sonneberg. The basic idea was to represent a child in several moods, the crying face for instance, having moulded tears. The heads were attached to the bodies by a pin, which was turned by a knob that protruded from the top of the head. One three-faced example showed a white sleeping child, a brown smiling child and a black crying child, giving the young owner a choice of nationality as well as expression. A bent-limb character was also made by this company, though here the two-sided head was simply turned to the required expression and presumably a bonnet of some kind was originally supplied to cover the unwanted face. This was a particularly unsatisfactory method as, when viewed from the side, the shape is quite frightening. A similar type of doll, but in much poorer bisque, was also made by Max Schelhorn.

The Bruno Schmidt closed-mouth girl with painted eyes (527 B.S.W.), though usually classed as a character, is really so attractive as to verge on idealism. This company, which made several character dolls, worked in Walterhausen in the early 20th century. Another Schmidt, Franz, also produced character dolls.

In the work of Schoenau and Hoffmeister, a wide variety of standard is seen again, even in a single mould, so that one example might be quite lovely while another is of the meanest kind and mounted on a cheap cardboard type body. Their later dolls were very poorly dressed when sold, almost as though the makers of bisque dolls lost interest in this aspect of presentation, just at the time that the makers of rag dolls, for instance, began to exploit the possibilities of up-to-date costumes. This firm produced some named dolls such as Hanna, a baby that was made in both white and light brown, while their oriental girl with very exaggeratedly upswept brows is particularly attractive.

Both Hermann and Edmund Steiner made dolls in the early 20th century in Sonneberg that have little to differentiate them from the products of dozens of other factories, with the notable exception of an unusual Googly made by Hermann, with pupils that move around within the eyeball, a head that can be also recognized among other googlies by the very heavy lips.

The inventiveness of the German producers of dolls seems to have been exhausted by the late twenties and the impetus for the design of really exciting dolls came, to an increasing extent, from America. For a short time, during and just after the First World War, a few bisques were made in England by firms that usually produced household crockery.

The British government felt that it would be bad for wartime morale if china dolls, traditionally obtained from Germany, ceased to appear in the shops and firms were encouraged to make heads. Though reluctant to attempt this skilled trade, several firms did succeed in creating dolls, notably the Willow Pottery, Mayer & Sherratt, whose products were marked Melba, and Hancocks, some of whose dolls were only marked 'English Make B.3'. Mary Hillier, in an article in *Spinning Wheel*, recounted how John Sneed and G. L. Nunn, who represented a German dollmaker in England, produced their own doll during the war in Liverpool, which they described as the Nonsuch. The doll was given an open mouth with teeth and had dimpled cheeks. The bisque, in common with most of the other heads made in England, was of poor quality. The Goss Pottery also made some doll's heads, but though the bisque is of the fine quality associated with this firm, the decoration is usually poor. The dolls are consequently more prized by Goss collectors than those who search for lovely dolls. The majority attempt to represent sweet-faced children, but an interesting character from the factory is illustrated. Examples as large as 36 inches are found and eyes could be either fixed or sleeping. As they were relatively expensive to produce, dollmaking ceased after the war.

The difficulty in obtaining bisque dolls from Germany during the First World War also encouraged an American company to create heads of bisque and in 1918 the Fulper Pottery of New Jersey began manufacture, the pottery itself having been established since 1805. The bulk of the dolls were again of the sweet-faced type, but an interesting girl with moulded hair and sideways-glancing eyes that has a resemblance to some of the Heubach characters was also made. Besides the all-bisque Kewpie already mentioned, they also made a rather less appealing 'Peterkin' with a smiling mouth and raised eyebrows. The products of the Fulper Pottery are so popular among American collectors that they are now virtually unobtainable.

The Schoenhut company produced dolls in America for a much longer period and, as their dolls were exported, they are still obtainable in Europe. Albert Schoenhut, a descendant of a line of German toymakers, settled in Philadelphia at the age of 17 and began to create toys, probably the most successful of which was a circus that included a number of doll-like figures with effective jointing. The Schoenhut play doll, with metal jointing, was not marketed until 1911 and was given a head of basswood that was roughly machine carved and then put under pressure in hot moulds that burned away any roughness. The jointing of the 'All Wood Perfection Art Dolls' was really quite remarkable as it was so complex. No cord or elastic was used but only metal springs, so there could be no parts that broke loose in play. They were sold with either moulded hair or wigs.

Early dolls were sculpted by Graziano to represent realistic children between the age of eight and ten years. Two holes in the feet meant that the doll could be pegged to a metal stand in several positions. After 1916 Harry Schoenhut himself designed the dolls, and among the baby dolls was one suspiciously resembling the Bye-Lo Baby. Probably their most collectable doll is the Mannikin, made completely of wood and given additional jointing at the waist rather in the manner of the finest Parisiennes. The doll took the form of a young man, some 19 inches high, representing either football or baseball players.

Several collectable figures were made, including a Walkable Doll with an arrangement of wires that enabled it to walk when the arm was held. In order to create a more economical product, some dolls were made in 1924 with elastic instead of metal articulation. Their last dolls were most depressing, as the economy had plumbed the lowest depths, and the 'Schoenhut stuffed dolls with mama voices' and hollow wooden heads represent the end of a fine dollmaking tradition. The Schoenhut

Hand-carved all-wooden boy doll with painted hair and fixed glass eyes. The head swivels in the wooden torso, and the stringing is elastic. Doll in Wonderland, Brighton.

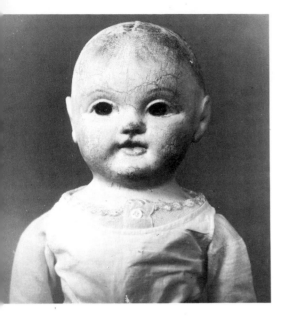

Philadelphia babies with moulded and painted rag features were distributed by J. B. Sheppard and Co., and are now very occasionally found. This example has brown eyes and the original black high-buttoned shoes. 21 inches tall. Blanding House Museum, Wisconsin.

dolls 'Made of all wood from Head to Foot and painted in Enamel oil colours, can be washed with a fine sponge or a soft cloth.' Unfortunately many children took these claims too literally and washed their dolls with great enthusiasm, so that faces are now often so rubbed as to be unattractive to all but the most dedicated. Even when examples in relatively untampered-with condition are found, time seems to have exaggerated the colouring and the general effect, though interesting, is hardly beautiful.

American designers of the early 20th century were not attempting to satisfy such a wide market as the Germans, and were consequently able to create more adventurous figures that were of immediate appeal to the native child. Instead of attempting to satisfy a variety of children, a group with a common background was now supplied, and characters from novels, films and even comic strips with immediate relevance were made in doll form.

One of the oldest American dollmakers was the firm of Horsman, that had begun in the 1860s as doll distributors. New developments were quickly embraced and the firm was among the first to produce rag dolls with printed photographic faces. Probably the best known product was the 'Can't Break Em' heads of composition that were sold after 1909, sometimes in the form of character dolls such as Baby Bumps, resembling K. & R.'s 'Baby', and the Campbell Kids, as seen in the Soup advertisements. Among other advertising dolls was 'Fairy' for Fairy soap and 'Jap Rose Kids' of Kirk soap. A very wide variety of baby dolls were made and the firm even co-operated with the Fulper Pottery in the creation of bisque heads just after the First World War.

The Ideal Toy Company, established in 1902 made, in addition to their well-known Shirley Temple, Baby Betty, Baby Talc and the engaging Flossie Flirt. Fleischaker & Baum, established in 1910 and using the trade name EffanBee, made Baby Grumpy in 1914 with an exaggerated frown and the small shoulder plate that characterized dolls of this period. Their Baby Dainty, made after 1912, had a stuffed cloth torso and composition arms and legs. This combination of stuffed body sections and composition limbs gives many a rather ungainly effect when undressed, but is typical of the period, when new constructions, not always successful, were undergoing continual experiment. Their 'Doll with a golden heart', wearing a heart-shaped pendant, was introduced about 1923. Few of this firm's dolls would be included in a collection of beautiful dolls, but they are of interest in historical development as typical of the experimentation of the period.

Among the designers whose ideas are evidenced in the evolution of the American doll is Joseph Kallus, president of the Cameo Doll Company, established in 1922. He is known to have worked with Rose O'Neill in the modelling of her Kewpies and his company has manufactured these in a variety of materials to the present time. One of his most attractive designs in the eyes of European collectors, still rather blind to the charms of composition dolls, is Baby Bo Kaye, made in bisque by Kestner. The composition version of this doll made by Cameo is, however, much more common. Another of his designs, created both in bisque and composition, was the strange waif-like creature, Little Annie Rooney, made in the mid-twenties to represent a film character played by Mary Pickford. 'Margie, the doll that is different – she balances herself in any position or pose' and made of wood pulp, was given a separate section for the neck to allow for realism in movement. The arms and legs were also jointed and the feet made very large to enable a variety of poses to be achieved. They were marked by a heart-shaped label reading 'Margie'. Dorothy S. Coleman, in an article in *Spinning Wheel*, commented that this doll was also distributed in England but examples are now only rarely found. Possibly the most distasteful doll he created was Betty Boop, copy-

Cloth doll with lithographed features on a mask-type face. There are similarities to the Columbian babies of a similar construction. The clothes are original except for the apron. 15 inches tall. Blanding House Museum, Wisconsin.

righted in 1932 and made to represent the cartoon character. This is again a cleverly jointed doll as the feet were modelled wearing high-heeled shoes. Betty Boop has small round high breasts and huge round eyes. The hair is the most idiosyncratic feature, as it is composed of a series of what can only be described as knobbles! Simply because the doll is so completely grotesque, it is much liked by collectors of recent dolls. 'Joy', a jointed child, sometimes with a hole through a moulded lock of hair for a ribbon, is much softer in appearance, and more akin to the German products of the 20s, with round, sideways-glancing eyes and a smiling face.

Madame Alexander [Beatrice Behrman], was of Russo-Austrian descent and was brought up in New York surrounded by the dolls her parents repaired in their dolls' hospital. She began to model dolls herself in 1915, possibly because of the doll shortage occasioned by the war. The Alexander Doll Company made a vast number of dolls in a variety of materials, the first creation being a muslin Red Cross nurse. Among the dolls most liked by collectors are the four sisters from *Little Women*, made first in 1933 and the characters from the novels of Charles Dickens. The pressed rag faces of the early dolls were finished by Madame Alexander herself. Luella Hart points out that one of her dolls, actually representing *The Little Colonel* in Annie F. Johnson's book, is often mistaken for a Shirley Temple, who played this role in a film. Madame Alexander did not patent a Shirley Temple, though she did produce Jane Withers, Scarlett o'Hara, and the Dionne Quintuplets. Sometimes, dolls made originally with pressed fabric faces were later made of plastic; many have composition heads. Much of the charm of her creations lies in their costuming, as there is frequently little characterization or even positive modelling in the faces. Proof of their appeal for several generations of American children lies in their great following, culminating in the Madame Alexander Fan Club.

123

Aluminium-headed double-jointed girl with a brown hair wig and a wooden body. The hands and feet are also aluminium. The head is marked '20 ✡ U.S. Pat.', and the doll was made by Giebler Falk Aluminium Co. 20 inches tall. Blanding House Museum, Wisconsin.

Opposite:
Felt dolls are often spoiled by their poor condition, but this example, marked 'Lenci' on the foot, is as fresh as new, as is the felt romper suit and cap. Both the joined second and third fingers and the sideways-glancing painted eyes are typical of this firm. Private collection (Jane Owen).

The character dolls created by Dewees Cochran were specifically made to reflect the six basic types of American children. Her portrait doll, made of a casting compound, was sold through a Madison Avenue shop, and her first clients were the two daughters of the Irving Berlins. The hand-modelled 'Look Alike' dolls sold for $85 each and started a vogue among New York parents who wanted their children to be perpetuated in this way. From these genuine portraits, which she usually developed from photographs of children, were evolved the commercially produced 'Look Alike' heads, first made in 1936. Four of the first group were marketed by EffanBee and sold as 'Portrait Dolls'; they achieved great success, as they were the first completely realistic dolls to be made in America, though their buyers were among the more discerning public, a public that was similar to that supplied by Käthe Krüse in Germany. She made few dolls during the war, as latex was needed as a war material, but afterwards she established Dewees Cochran Dolls as a company. Among her most famous creations was Cindy, made of latex in 1947, but due to a disagreement with the maker she withdrew from the arrangement and Cindy was altered. Dewees Cochran's original Cindy represented an innocent girl of twelve, very much a schoolgirl and not at all like the rather brash American Cindy. The originals are obviously collectable and, fortunately, are marked 'Dewees Cochran Dolls' on the torso.

In 1952 she introduced her 'Grow Up Dolls', with the girls shown at five stages from 5 to 20 and the boys in three stages from 5 to 23. Amusing names differentiated the characters such an Angela Appleseed and Jefferson Jones. The dolls created by Dewees Cochran are unusual among American dolls of the period as they represented real children rather than the almost caricature-like figures designed by other commercial companies. In the 'Look Alikes', whose features were to be appropriately coloured by the buyer in imitation of a specific child, she probably achieved the ultimate in a commercially produced character doll.

At present, the doll scene in America is remarkable for the large number of people who are designing and making their own dolls at home, not only of resin materials but of bisque, wood and even wax. As old dolls increase in price, many collectors are beginning to appreciate the work of present-day makers and are buying examples of modern figures, so that an almost separate field of collecting is developing, alongside that related to antique dolls.

Another traditional American dollmaking material was rag, used commercially in 1885 by a group of ladies who were attempting to raise funds for church missionaries. The dolls are known as Beecher Missionary Babies and were made either of pink or black stockinette, with painted features and woollen hair. The term Philadelphia Baby is used to refer to dolls made of a type of knitted material but with a muslin-covered painted face. They are similar to Chase dolls but without an elbow joint and were originally sold wearing boots. It is thought that they were made for sale in a Philadelphia department store, that of J. B. Sheperd. Mothers' Congress dolls are similarly made, but with some shaping of the heads by means of seams, a design that was patented in 1900 by Madge Lansing Mead. As the two distinct types originated in the same area they are often grouped together and described as Philadelphia Babies.

Martha Chase of Rhode Island created a much greater number of dolls that appear in many American collections. Originally her stockinette baby doll was made for the amusement of her own children, but a small factory soon developed. A mask face was used and stockinette was stretched over it to give a softer finish. After a coat of size the heads were painted, in a decidedly primitive manner in oil colours, the texture of the hair being suggested by the use of very thick paint

scumbled over the surface. Only the parts of the dolls that would be visible when costumed were painted and the body parts were made of sateen. The fact that the dolls could be bathed was widely advertised and they were sold with a Chase trademark. A variety of figures, including some characters from Dickens and *Alice in Wonderland*, were made but the collector is now most likely to find the basic play doll with fair hair. After the Second World War, the Chase Hospital dolls, for use in teaching hospitals, were developed.

In the early years of the 20th century, a very large number of printed fabric dolls were made as colour printing on fabric had become attractively inexpensive. 'Dolly Dimple' was made as an advertisement for self-raising flour – 'The Heart of the Grain plus the Art of the Brain'. Two grades of flour were made and sold in sacks on which different dolls were printed. 'Dolly Dimple Self-Raising Flour is put up in the red Doll, red stitch cambric sac' or 'Dolly Dimple Highest patent flour put up in a blue stitch, blue doll cambric sac'. The doll's name was stamped on the printed combinations. The Art Fabric Company of New York made a life-size doll in heavy sateen 'By means of a patent Gussett the feet protrude in front, enabling the doll to stand alone'. This company printed rag dolls in sheet form between 1905 and 1910.

There was also considerable English involvement in the creation of rag dolls that, because of their softness, made such attractive toys. The first rag dolls made by Chad Valley, rather sad objects with little shape, were sold *circa* 1920. These were stockinette figures that were given pretentious names such as Lady Betty, Zoë and Irish Molly. Out of a range of twelve, only three represented boys. The dolls were sold wearing hand-woven wigs that could be brushed and combed, and the clothes were removable. A cheaper series, without hand-woven wigs, represented such characters as a Nurse, a Chef, a Pierrot, a Pierrette, a Welsh Girl and Poppy. An even smaller version cost 48 shillings a dozen and included a footballer, Boy Blue, and Miss Muffett. A range of fluffy stockinette dolls was also offered in 1920 wearing winter sports costumes. 'Printed Hygenic down-stuffed dolls representing a Pixie or Red Cloud in ornate printed Indian Costume or Sonia in Swiss dress', cost 18 shillings a dozen, and bore the brand mark 'Aerolite' referring to the material with which they were filled. They were sold from 1923.

In the same year a quite terrifying Mephistopheles, with huge horns, long whiskers, outstretched arms and a long forked tail appeared in the catalogue. This stag-beetle-like creature measured $10\frac{1}{2}$ inches; dressed in Turkey red cloth, it could be purchased for 3/6d. The dolls were described as thoroughly well sewn to keep their shape well. The range also included Tinkle Bell, with bells at her fingers and toes.

'La Petite Caresse', a series of dolls with curls of 'real hair' and hand-coloured faces were dressed in velveteen snow suits decorated with white fur. They measured from 11 to 18 inches high but were probably popular with children because of their softness, despite their crudity of construction. 'Bambina' dolls that carried a tie-on label at the wrist besides the usual sewn-on foot label wore fashionable clothes of the early 20s including one in a smart pram suit. Their 22-inch Peter Pan, dressed in brown and green felt, is seen in the 1926 catalogues where La Petite Caresse dolls, dressed in felt dresses with appliqué flowers are now mentioned as being filled with kapok as well as Aerolite.

Probably their most famous dolls are the Mabel Lucie Attwell range seen in their catalogues from 1927 onwards. These dolls were made in three sizes: $14\frac{1}{2}$, 16, and $18\frac{1}{2}$ inches. 'Personally designed by Miss Mabel Lucie Attwell, these delightful hand-painted felt and velvet dolls faithfully reproduce the inimitable features of her well-known draw-

Chad Valley 'Bambina' designed by Mabel Lucie Attwell. The doll has a felt face, glass eyes and a body of velvet cloth. The grey metal button that was fixed to the side of the Chad Valley toys can be seen, as can the Bambina label on one foot. On the other foot is the label 'Hygienic Toys Chad Valley Made in England'. Private collection (Jane Owen).

ings of children.' Each was originally packed in a patent Bed Bye box. Sixteen variously-dressed dolls were offered, all with the sideways-glancing eyes and smiling mouths associated with this artist. One black doll wearing dungarees with a check patch at the knee was included. Few boy dolls were created by the majority of dollmakers but in this range of sixteen, there were nine, including one as a soldier, and another in the dress of a Victorian gentleman with a top hat and tailed coat. The remainder wore the short fashionable outfits of the time. Most of the wigs were very curly, but one boy in a romper suit had short straight hair with a fringe.

The 1927 catalogue also illustrated a doll dressed in felt decorated with appliquéd spots and carrying a rattle that was 'Personally selected and purchased at the British Industries Fair by Her Majesty the Queen' (Mary). Amusing A.A. and R.A.C. Road Scout Mascots were introduced in 1930 that claimed 'Official approval'. The A.A. doll was very fierce with bulging eyes and a small black moustache, rather in the manner of a miniature Hitler. It was dressed in felt breeches and the arm was fixed in a saluting position. The R.A.C. doll is much less impressive and has a milder face. His jacket is open at the neck to reveal the shirt and tie, whereas the A.A. uniform is buttoned to the high collar. Once introduced, such dolls continued to appear in catalogues for some time. In 1930 'The Chad Valley Niggers' measuring 12 or 14 inches high, were made, and closely resemble some of the Nora Wellings dolls as their mouths are in a tooth-showing smiling position. Rajah and Nabob were splendidly dressed in robes, turbans, and earrings and were modelled in a sitting position, while the other four in the range all stood. Of these only one was a girl and she predictably wore beads and a raffia skirt.

The Mabel Lucie Attwell range was reduced by 1931, only ten of the original selection being illustrated, though a figure named 'Snookums' with a smiling mouth revealing one centre tooth was introduced. A number of other ranges were introduced in 1930, including the Carina Dolls, dressed in fashionable outfits, and Caresse Imps. In the 1933–34 catalogue a new line of 'Special character dolls' was offered; these appear to have sold well as individual examples are often found. A label was hung on each doll's wrist, being the Chad Valley 'Seal of Purity'. The dolls were described as 'Of superior quality with velveteen limbs, fully jointed and with "Chad Valley" fabric heads. The costumes are excellently made, great care being paid to correctness of detail.' They were all 19 inches high and represented a Highlander in full dress uniform, a Grenadier, a huntsman, a Colleen, a nurse, a policeman and a Scotch girl. The huntsman was given an adult's face while the Colleen and the Nurse shared a face, as did the remainder of the boy dolls.

A range of velveteen-limbed dolls, wearing the huge hats so fashionable in the mid 30s, was also produced in 1934 with either fabric mask faces or with 'hard to break' heads. These were also available with painted or closing eyes, the latter costing extra. In 1935 'Nursery Rhyme Character Dolls' were made. 'With this dainty range of dolls we believe that a very real gap in the doll kingdom will be filled. The characters are just as the kiddies see them in the pages of their favourite story book. Each model is approximately 14 inches high, made with the Chad Valley mask and velveteen limbs. The faces were given some individual expression and the costumes appear well made: Miss Muffett looks suitably horrified at the big black spider on her lap and throws her arms in the air, Mary Mary carries flowers in one hand and a basket in the other. Jack Horner has a pie, Boy Blue a horn, Bo-Peep a crook, Mary a lamb. Simple Simon was obviously something of a problem but was provided with a whip and sand bucket. Most of the doll lines such as the Nigger Boys, introduced several years before, were still made in chocolate-coloured velveteen and bear a close resemblance to those later marketed by Nora Wellings, who worked as a designer for Chad Valley before she set up her own factory. The sailor dolls that are often associated with Nora Wellings were also made by Chad Valley and Dean's Rag Book Company, and a positive attribution can only be given when a doll of this kind is marked.

The Chad Valley catalogues show soldier dolls ranging in size from 8 to $13\frac{1}{2}$ inches, and costumed in red jackets and black plush bearskins. Velveteen pixies and gnomes were also made. In 1939, with the impending war encouraging the sale of militaristic toys, the 'Four Services' dolls were introduced. A sailor, a soldier, an airman and a marine were packed together in a box, though complete sets are very rarely seen, as their production was soon halted when the factory was used for the war effort. Another line introduced in that year, and consequently made only in a small number, was matched pairs of dolls in boxes; that illustrated in their catalogue represented a pirate and his girl friend. The series also included a Dutch boy and girl, Bo Peep and Boy Blue. They were of an even more exaggeratedly doll-like form than usual, with heads that are bigger in proportion to the height of the body than was previously seen in the work of the firm. During the war, toy production almost ceased, as the factory worked on government contracts, and the 1947 catalogue is a much more economical publication.

Several of the dolls made before the war again appear, but in a limited range, though still carrying the Hygenic Seal. Moveable arms and legs were used on all the dolls, and it was claimed that the wigs could be combed. Schoolgirls carrying felt satchels appear to have provided a popular line. Many of the dolls appearing in the 1948 catalogue are decidedly old fashioned, and it is little wonder that they are often dated some ten years earlier than their actual manufacture. Dolls 18 inches tall cost £3, while the smallest sizes were £1. A character boy named 'Jeremy', with velveteen limbs and sideways-glancing eyes wore a simple smock with shorts and measured 14 inches.

Rubber dolls were first made by Chad Valley in 1947. Unjointed baby dolls wore a nappy, but the jointed ones wore a silk dress as well. Prices ranged from £10. 11s a dozen to £5. 18s. In 1948, rubber-skinned dolls filled with kapok were offered at £1 for the 17-inch size, and indicated how soon after its introduction plastic could undercut the hand-made rag dolls in price. Nevertheless, the company continued to make both felt and plush dolls until 1954, when their current range included a girl gardener, a Highland Lassie, a Guardsman, and a young rider in jodhpurs, hard hat and waistcoat. Though the company had marketed a 'Superior Series' of art dolls in 1934 it was considered necessary to promote anew what was an outdated dollmaking method and they were described as 'A refreshing alternative to the thousands of plastic dolls now on the market. For beauty of features and dressing our dolls are unsurpassed. They last a lifetime. Many 25-year old ones are returned to us for refurbishing so they may be passed on to the next generation.' Most of the fabric dolls were by this stage under 12 inches high and still included 'Dutch' and 'Darkie' dolls, the 'Bambina' series and 'Jeremy'. After this date the manufacture of fabric dolls appears to have ceased, and though the current range of soft toys is quite delightful, the only dolls are the Barbapapa series with round eyes and noses.

Another British company whose dolls were exported both to Europe and America was Dean's Rag Book Company of Rye, established in 1903. Their printed fabric dolls are easily recognizable, as the maker's name was included in the design. A 'Life Size Baby Doll' was printed on a sheet 30 inches square with small dolls occupying the spaces that would otherwise be wasted. Like Chad Valley, Dean's

Stockinette child with applied ears and painted eyes, stamped on the torso 'Patented Sept. 26, ? ?'. The upper left leg is stamped 'Mrs. S. S. Smith manufacturer and dealer in the Alabama Indestructible Doll, Roanoke, Ala.' The clothing is not original, and there has been some restoration to the face. This type of doll is known as an Alabama Baby. 22 inches tall. Blanding House Museum, Wisconsin.

Sawdust-filled printed cloth girl attributed to E. I. Horsman & Co. 1903–1917. This print is known as Daisy Darling. Blanding House Museum, Wisconsin.

stressed the quality of 'Indestructability, Washability and Hygenic Merit'. From around 1906 printed clothes were sometimes included on the cut-out sheets but separate printed sheets of clothes were only available after 1925. Catalogues were printed in English, French, and German. Several sets were issued including characters from *Alice in Wonderland* and there was a Mr Puck and his family.

A number of new dolls were introduced in the year before the outbreak of the First World War including black dolls, made of a soft woolly cloth and with big googly eyes, Red Riding Hood, Master Sprite–a goblin with a long beard, and Cheeky Imp. The company was much influenced by the continental appreciation of character dolls and the 'Wiedersheim' series based on the drawings of Grace Wiedersheim, and with typical googly eyes, were made as a fabric answer to those in bisque. 'Peggy and Teddy' with eyes of this type were made as a matching pair.

After the war, the more serious attitude to dolls that had begun in Germany was continued in England and Dean's commented 'We shudder to think what might happen if the news got about that a doll was promoted for sheer idle amusement.' Tru-shu feet that were large and enabled the dolls to stand were introduced in 1920, and their Tru-To-Life rag dolls were advertised as the finest representation of the human face. Tru-To-Lifes were made at first either as cut-out sheets or in a commercially assembled form. The 'Cowham Kiddies', designed by Hilda Cowham, and given names like Captivating Cora, appeared in this range. Some of the Cowham Kiddies were even made with their eyes printed asleep.

Dean's felt dressed Posy Dolls were an apparent answer to the products of Lenci in Italy, and are similar in concept, as the outfits were created with an equal attention to detail. The Posy dolls, however, were all given costumes that were based on flower shapes and colours. Their sideways-glancing eyes were a popular decorative device of the period and seen also in the work of Lenci, Chad Valley and Nora Wellings. Velvet-faced dolls were produced by Dean's after 1926 and are again frequently confused with the products of Chad Valley or even Nora Wellings if the sewn-on labels are missing. Dancing pairs made to move amusingly on a revolving gramophone record were made in 1928, but do not appear to have been popular toys, as those discovered are often in almost unplayed-with condition. Dean's as well as Schoenhut had designs on the successful American Bye-Lo Baby and produced their own By-Lo-Baby!

Nora Wellings, after working as a designer at Chad Valley for seven years, established her own factory at the Victoria Toy Works in Wellington in 1926. The business side of the concern was managed by her brother Leonard. Many of her dolls were especially made as mascots to be sold on board the great ocean liners on the Atlantic lines and this accounts for the number found in American collections. Both pressed felt and velveteen-faced dolls were made and she stressed that all her dolls were marked with her sewn-on label. A variety of character dolls representing personalities as diverse as 'Mary' who 'had a little lamb' and 'Britannia', with shield and flowing robes, were made though the most commonly found are the chocolate-coloured South Sea Islanders and the sailor boys.

Though occasional art dolls were made, the character doll was very much a fashion of the past by the 1940s, when the majority resembled highly painted women rather than children. The doll designers of today consider that a character such as the Kämmer & Reinhardt 'Baby' would be virtually impossible to market, as the public still demands a more idealized treatment and would find the dolls' realism distasteful. Pedigree Dolls of Canterbury have introduced a new baby doll this year (1976) that is named 'First Love'. The doll, which can

A pressed-velvet-faced black doll with glass eyes, a mohair wig and original beads. Although it is un-marked, it was almost certainly designed by Nora Wellings. Antiques of Childhood, London.

assume a number of positions, is designed by Peter Nevett, who made a study of dozens of basic baby types from photographs and then evolved an idealized head that was of general appeal. The doll is described in their catalogue as 'The most beautiful baby ever. The ultimate in posing, unique natural pose head.' Because of the modern child's love of appropriate accessories, the doll is provided with a bath and a push chair as well as several well-made outfits. This creation of a baby doll that is completely idealized is almost bound to appeal to a public tired of the crude realities of life. A similar escapism is seen in their range of sweet-faced 'Victorian Dolls', costumed in simplified 19th-century dress made of satins and ginghams, and given names such as Emma and Charlotte. 'Gives dolls a new direction. Old England re-lived.'

Folk Dolls and Figures of Magical Significance

The use of images in magical rites, folk customs and superstition is a theme that recurs throughout the history of mankind and is evidenced in both civilized and under-developed countries. Even in 18th-century England, when educated people prided themselves on their rational thought, chapbooks on sale in the streets still held illustrations in which a black devil, with wings, breasts, horns and long ears, was shown distributing doll-like images to eager witches who grasped them greedily. Maggie, in George Eliot's *Mill on the Floss*, thought to be largely autobiographical, kept a fetish that was punished for all her childish misfortunes. 'This was the trunk of a large wooden doll, which once stared with the roundest of eyes above the reddest of cheeks, but was now entirely defaced by a long career of vicarious suffering. Three nails driven into her head commemorated as many crises in Maggie's nine years of earthly struggle.' During the Boer War an image of Paul Kruger was set up in a London street and for a few pence, passers-by could vent their emotions by driving yet another nail into the figure, a fate that was also suffered in the last war by images of Hitler!

The earliest images used for mystical rites are generally considered to be fertility symbols. The oldest statues in human form date from the Aurignacian civilization, and the fact that these figures were modelled with detailed legs and only a suggestion of arms is an indication of the sexual connotation. There is a scarcity of any male figures before the First Iron Age, and those in female form are almost all believed to have aided procreation in some way. The rather doll-like paddle figures of Egypt date from around 2000 BC; they were made of flat lengths of wood cut into a simplified human shape and painted with bright geometric designs. These figures were often included in doll collections, as their hair, made of clay knotted on to cord, and their small size suggested some kind of toy. The painting of what were later discovered to be fertility emblems on the reverse side established their true function. The Egyptians also made use of small figures known as Ushabti or 'Answerers' in their tombs after it was decided that the walling up of wives and servants should cease. The Ushabti, made of wood, alabaster, clay or stone were dedicated to the god Osiris and were believed to completely impersonate the servants of the dead man and serve all his wants in the afterlife: the more important the man, the greater was the number of figures included. Early examples closely resemble mummies, but there is more realism in later types, where extra detail is given to the hands, which are crossed. Eventually, an almost factory-

like production of Ushabti was established and the high artistic standard seen in early examples could not be maintained.

In early European civilization, as in primitive African tradition, it is often difficult to establish the point at which a small figure ceases to be a plaything and becomes a votive symbol. The small jointed dolls of bone, ivory or clay, discovered in the remains of Greek and Roman civilization, have only survived because they were dedicated to the gods by girls when they reached womanhood. In the culture of India, an identical figure could be a doll or a votive offering, depending purely on the intention of its owner.

The word for doll in both the Korean and the Chinese languages has the same derivation as the term for an idol or a fetish. Gustav Schlegal observed that in China small girls did not play with dolls, as they were thought to possess magical power, so that their use as toys has only developed in recent decades. Archaeologists have discovered in China doll-like figures of clay and wood with moveable limbs that were substituted for the sacrifice of living relatives after the time of Confucius (551–478 BC). No house in China was without its altar of deities, made of substances appropriate to a man's station in life. The use of straw dolls dressed in blood-stained paper and, to incantations, pierced with needles, was a popular theme throughout Chinese society. A prince was charged as plotting against the Emperor for the use of a wooden doll dressed in paper and endowed with evil by a sorcerer. The use of figures in both Chinese wedding and funeral processions means that despite the lack of early dolls, a number of ceremonial examples still exist for collectors.

Above left:
The ancient tradition of rag-doll-making is shown by this extremely primitive 7-inch tall figure found in a tomb at Hawara, and dating from late 4th century AD. Ashmolean Museum, Oxford.

Above:
A faience ushabti figure of an Egyptian royal scribe. It is of unknown provenance, but dates from the XIX–XX Dynasty. Ashmolean Museum, Oxford.

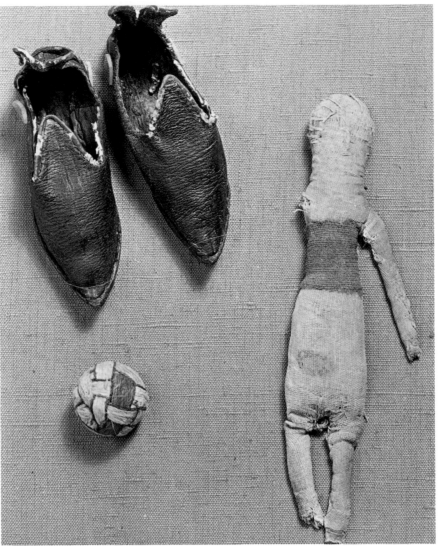

The Japanese culture has particular associations with dolls and their use is not as dark in character as that connected with the Chinese. The clay dolls said to bring good fortune, that were made in over a hundred regions, served several different purposes, as they could prevent illness and disaster and help provide good harvests. Such dolls were revered and handed down within families. Gosho dolls, brilliant white because of a coat of gofum, and in the form of babies with large heads, were originally given as good luck symbols among noblemen. Today new parents also sometimes receive them as tokens of good luck.

Superstitious rites, whereby a baby could be protected during the dangerous years of early infancy, are popular in most communities. Healing dolls, at first made of paper but later in the form of commercially produced figures of papier mâché, were used as an aid in sickness and called Hoko San or servant dolls. If put into the bed of a child suffering from an incurable illness the figure would attract the disease to itself; in the morning the doll would be thrown into the sea and the child would soon recover. Another doll-like image, the Amagatsu, was put near the heads of new-born babies as a protection from evil and in supplication to the gods. In rural areas of Japan today, many ailments are still attributed to evil spiritual elements that are believed to take possession of the human body and affect the personality.

The use of cheaply available straw and paper for the manufacturing of images was widespread in Japan. If a woman was betrayed, she could create a straw doll in the image of her faithless man, pierce it with needles and bury it where he slept. This type of action also enabled

revenge to be taken against a robber; a paper doll, hung upside down, represented the god of riches whose task it was to discover and punish the thief: the doll was hung upside down and fastened by the feet so that the god could not escape until his duty was performed. At the Shinto purification ceremony, feast towels, cut into human shape, were given to the bathers by the priest, to blot out the sins of the years.

Many different forms of Bodhidharma, the Indian priest who introduced Buddhism to China, exist. A version made in the Kansai district has unpainted eyes so that the pupils could be indicated when the owner petitioned the god. In India, dolls were rarely made purely for amusement and almost all represented some stage or story in the history of the country. Even the poorest of children could learn the traditions of their land by playing with these figures, made by the village potter. At the festival celebrating the birth of Krishna, the child god, a figure representing him is placed in a cradle and songs sung by the children gathered around. Doll-like figures made by the potter could have either a magical or a play use: if placed with reverence by an adult as a votive offering for a good harvest, the figure is endowed with magic, but exactly the same figure might be seen played with by a child

These dolls, of the Ibibio tribe of Eastern Nigeria, are carved in several stages. The completed doll is 9 inches in height. British Museum, London.

A Bantu doll representing an Afrikaans missionary and his wife.

135

Wooden doll of the Ashanti people of Ghana. Women, as well as children, carry such dolls as fertility fetishes; they are believed to ensure that the children will be well formed. The Art Institute of Chicago.

Left:
Hakata dolls in the process of manufacture. These dolls are made of clay and painted in delicate colours; their characters are based on old folksongs. Japan Tourist Office.

Above:
Extremely elegant Hakata doll. Hakata is the old name of part of the modern city of Fukuoka in Kyusu. Japan Tourist Office.

as a toy. Many of these doll-like forms have a long history, and the
Kalighat doll, for instance, is thought to have an Egyptian origin because of its mummy-like shape. Many of the clay dolls represent the
mother and child theme, and were sometimes made by the women
themselves who recounted their significance to the watching children
while they worked.

Traditional Indian dolls were made of papier mâché, rag and vegetable fibre, bronze, cowdung and pith as well as clay but unfortunately
many of these methods have almost died out, as the undiscerning
tourists prefer the rag dolls dressed in regional costumes of the country
rather than the brightly coloured, almost abstract forms that look so
unlike dolls to Europeans.

In Africa the gourd is often dressed in leaves and rags to represent
a person and exorcise the demons of sickness. In Nigeria, when the
death of a twin occurs, the mother or surviving twin must forever carry
its image and this has to be bathed and dressed alongside the living
twin, as the Yoruba tribe believe that the souls of twins are indivisible.
In the Lake Nyasa region of Central Africa a figure of wood and rags is
created when a tribesman dies and concealed in a small black box by
the witchdoctor, who in this way shuts up the spirit of the dead. The
chief centre of the fetish cult is found in the tribes of West and Central
Africa, and vast numbers of voodoo dolls are made to represent a
variety of jungle spirits. High profit, a good harvest, easy childbirth,
a good catch of fish and even the luring back of a faithless husband
could all be achieved by use of a fetish. A warrior might find it necessary to set out for battle armed with a whole variety of fetishes, one
guarding him against blows, another against arrows and yet more
against ill luck. Some of these figures, driven all over with splinters of
glass and nails and smeared with blood and oil are so repulsive that it
is mainly museums that wish to include them in their collections.

The dolls that aid women in the bearing of children are not in the
least frightening and must help many people. A barren woman of the
Atuto tribe need only carry a doll blessed by the village magician on her

Wooden model from the Torres Straits. This was a fertility symbol believed to give good garden produce. Cambridge Museum of Archaeology and Ethnology.

back to conceive. If for some reason the magic did not work she could, with no disrespect, give the figure to a child as a plaything. In some tribes a woman desirous of a male child will be given a boy doll to carry during pregnancy. A figure carved by the Biteke tribe can be seen at the Horniman Museum in London. The simply carved wooden figure becomes the property of the woman as soon as she becomes pregnant and a section is cut away from its stomach area. After the child is born, part of the afterbirth is mixed with ground cam-wood and packed into the prepared cavity, both the figure and the remains of the afterbirth then being buried in a corner of the hut to exert a protective influence over the child as he grows.

Many customs concerning dolls in Europe were also connected with fertility. A continental custom was to throw a small doll attached to a cord to a group of young women; if a child was not desired the woman who caught it had only to throw it back; if on the other hand a pregnancy was wanted she kept the charm. In 19th-century Brunswick, peasant women kept spinning wheels as their dowry. They were decorated with small male and female dolls made of plaited flax, whose purpose was to ensure a fruitful marriage.

Plato was fully cognizant of the use of wax images in wizardry and the use of such figures, usually with evil intent, is almost universal. It accounts in some measure for the suspicion that often surrounds figures made of this substance. Wax figures were very frequently used in connection with love magic, as an image that was first baptized and then melted inflamed the passion of the desired person. In 1469 the Duchess of Bedford, mother of the Queen, was accused of having ensured her daughter's marriage to Edward IV by witchcraft. A figure of a man-at-arms was produced and it was claimed that the model had been used by the Duchess to cast a spell. The English and Scottish witch trials are rich in references to waxen images, whose traditions are more associated with evil than with good, though the method of summoning a lover from afar by slowly burning his image does not appear over harmful. In comparison with the type of witchcraft-play indulged in by young girls, the witches' figures made of wax and containing nail clippings or hair from the accursed are much more sinister. A figure of this type was discovered in the bedroom of the sick Lord Derby in 1594 and burned in the hope of destroying the spell. Knowing himself to be bewitched, this expedient was not successful and he died. Both Popes and Kings were very conscious of the danger to their persons that could be effected by the use of image magic, and when it was discovered the perpetrators paid with their lives.

Wax images could also be used by priests in the exorcising of evil spirits. If it was thought an illness was caused by witchcraft in the Middle Ages, three masses were said over a wax doll by a priest on a feast day. The figure was then pierced in the spot where the invalid felt pain, which forced the witch to retract her spell. An effigy of a possessing devil could also be made by a priest and thrown into a fire with words of exorcism.

Scottish history reveals many ugly instances of image magic, but few as unpleasant as that directed towards the Laird of Parks male children in the 17th century. Five witches together modelled a figure of clay that had 'All the marks of a child such as head, eyes, nose . . . it wanted no mark of a child and the hands of it folded down by its sides.' Each day the witches damped the figure with water and then thrust it into the fire, 'Sometimes one part of it, sometimes another part of it until the child was dead.' Janet Breadheid was one of the witches and she told her accusers that after the death of one boy, the image would be kept in its own cradle and then six months after the birth of another male child they would again roast it at the fire until that child also was dead.

Above:
An African doll from the Sudan, with human hair, a wax face and bamboo legs. British Museum, London.

Right:
An early 20th-century composition-headed doll marked on the base 'Made in China'. The arms are of wire and the body is just a simple armature, but the doll is given interest by the embroidered costume. 8 inches tall. Private collection (Marian Wenzel).

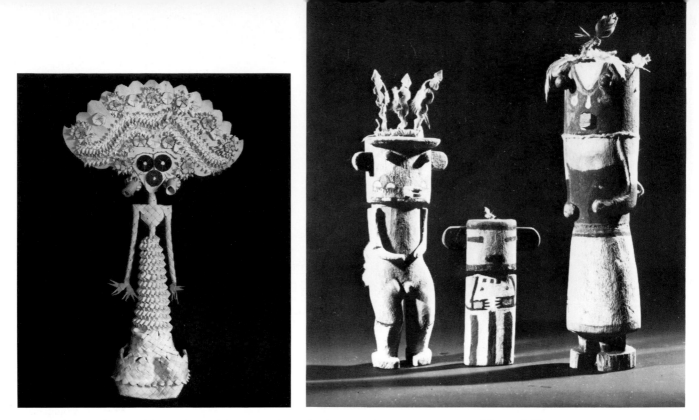

Another ugly manifestation of the practice of witchcraft in Scotland was the Corp Creadh, a small clay figure of a man that was pierced with pins so that the victim would suffer, the insertion of each pin being accompanied by a curse. If made of a hard substance, the Corp Creadh could be placed in a stream where it would slowly crumble away while the victim also wasted slowly away; if however a swift violent death was desired the image would be made of a very soft substance. The magic could be halted and the person saved if the Corp Creadh could be discovered. The use of a similar image is described in Hector Boece *Scotorum Historica*. In the 10th century King Duff fell victim to a mystery illness. Fortunately a woman was discovered making a wax 'picture' of the king by a fire and after its destruction he recovered quickly.

In a Hereford house, being redecorated in 1960, a small doll, believed to be 18th century and dressed in a gown of spotted fabric, was discovered concealed in the cellar. A piece of paper pinned to the skirt carried the name of Mary Ann Wand and the inscription 'I cast this spell upon you with my whole heart, wishing you never rest nor eat nor sleep the restern part of your life. I hope your flesh will waste away and I hope you will never spend another penny I aught to have. Wishing this from my whole heart.'

The properties of the mandrake, a plant whose root was thought to resemble the human figure, were respected throughout Europe and in Eastern countries. The *Hortus Sanitatus* of 1491 shows the root as male and female figures with leaves growing up from the head. One of the German emperors owned a pair of mandrakes, both costumed in velvet cloaks. The mandrake was washed in wine and dressed after being pulled from the ground attached to the tail of a black dog, as no man could himself pull the shrieking root from the earth without suffering death. The Hungarian gipsies made use of anything with churchyard associations for their image magic, including the burned clothes of dead people and pieces of coffin wood.

Much of the lore associated with image magic in Europe was carried to America by the early settlers. In New England at the Salem witchcraft trials, Bridget Bishop, a malicious woman with a long-standing reputation for witchcraft, was said to have employed doll-like figures in her practices. Two workmen testified to have discovered in the cellar wall of a house she had lived in, 'Several puppets made up

Above left:
Balinese corn dolly, made in the likeness of a goddess. These female figures are made at each harvest, and kept until the next one to ensure a good crop. Horniman Museum, London.

Above:
North American Indian kachina dolls, representing lightning, corn and snow. Every natural power and living thing is believed to have a kachina, or spirit, and dancers impersonate them at festivals. After the ceremonies, the dolls are taken home. British Museum, London.

Opposite top:
A parian-ware doll dressed in the national costume of Norway. London Museum.

Opposite bottom:
Mexican figure of a fisherwoman with her catch, made of plaited palm leaves. Like the corn dollies, these were made to increase prosperity and good fortune.

of rags and hogs bristles, with headless pins in them with the points outwards.' This concealing of the image in the wall is still a technique of modern witches.

Among the most collectable of figures associated with magic are those of the Hopi and Zuni Indians which, after use by tribesmen in their ritual dances, are given to their children as toys; in this way an appreciation of the meaning of the various characters is developed in the early years of life. Originally, the images were not allowed to leave the villages, but the Hopi Indians now make large numbers purely for sale to tourists. The products of the Zuni Indians, who were originally much stricter about the use to which the figures were put after the ceremonies, are still difficult to find. The images, carved from dry cottonwood root, painted in brilliant colours and decorated with feathers and beads, are made in imitation of the masks worn by tribesmen in their impersonation of the Kachinas. These supernatural beings, including Nuvak, the god of Spring, who ensures light snow so as not to damage young plants, and Owa and Owa Mana who send warm rain and winds, are impersonated annually in the tribal dances held in underground caves.

It is thought that cornhusk dolls were played with as traditional toys by Indian children: when the early settlers arrived, these basic dolls became a shared interest with the European children who often painted theirs with simple features. In many Indian tribes, this addition might be considered to have endowed the doll with a soul and would have been avoided. These figures were fully accepted by parents from all social classes, and even the children of strict Puritans who would have frowned on commercially made dolls because of their essential frivolity, were happy to allow their children to play with these simple toys. In North America, these cornhusk figures are known as Shuck dolls. The use of straw as a dollmaking material is especially popular in South America, where extra detail is often given with dyed raffia.

The corn doll is seen in a variety of forms in most cultures and though sometimes a toy, it usually has ancient ritualistic traditions. Basically, the doll represents a horn of plenty, and figures are often made purely in the form of a sheaf of wheat, symbolizing the corn goddess Ceres. In England, the Ivy Girl of Kent was a fairly accurately made female figure decorated with straw braids. The doll was dressed in woman's clothes which, in the early 19th century were, for the sake of economy, sometimes made of paper. A large number of corn dollies are now made purely as souvenirs and are quite small, but a correct doll, made for harvest celebrations, should be the height of a sheaf of corn. The Whalton Kern Babby used to be costumed and carried to the parish church on a pole. It remained in the church until replaced by a new Babby the following year. This was a simplification of the old tradition of an effigy of Mother Earth which would be carried to the harvest field and brought home, gaily decorated, with the last load. A particularly fine example of a corn doll from Montenegro, decorated with scraps of lace and beads, and measuring the height of a sheaf of corn, can be seen at the Horniman Museum in London. There are various European traditions associated with figures of straw, such as the custom in Baden Sauerland and in Lower Austria in the 19th century when an ugly straw doll was carried out of the villages and then buried in the snow or in a dung heap. In Silesia in the same period, on mid-Lent Sundays, a figure of straw was carried in procession, beaten, burned, and then thrown into the water. The ugly associations of dolls made of straw or corn are not often seen in Britain, though in Ireland the tradition of the Corp Creadh was followed in the shape of images made from a sheaf of wheat, twisted into the resemblance of the human figure. A straw heart was made and pins run into the stems of corn.

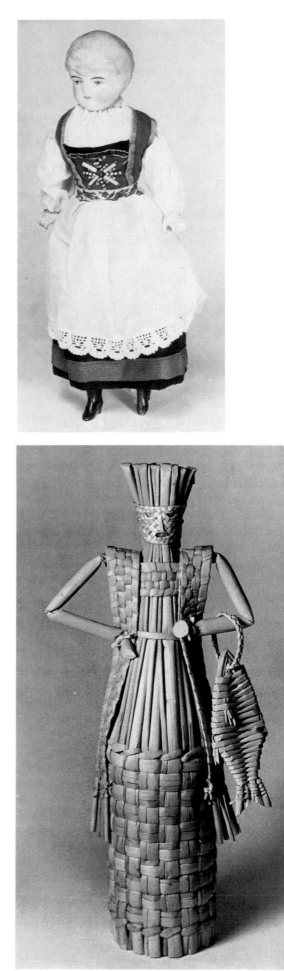

The figure would then be burned in the name of the devil near the victim's home and then buried in wet or dry soil depending on the speed of death required; as recently as 1895 the Corp Creadh was blamed for a death.

The happy May Day rites also frequently included a doll-like figure that would be gaily decorated and placed in a bower on a cart or carried to the celebrations fixed to a pole and surrounded with a hoop of flowers. Ordinary play dolls were often used for this purpose, as is seen in contemporary illustrations and accounts.

Costume dolls are collected by many people who like to return home with some holiday souvenir as it is still possible to amass a huge collection at a low cost. Unfortunately, many of the regional dolls are now made so completely with the intention of selling to the more undiscerning tourist that they retain very little of the authentic costume, and plastic and nylon 'silks' and lace are often combined to create objects that have lost almost all of their native associations. Souvenir dolls have been especially made since the 18th century and

Above:
A porcelain-headed fortune-telling doll with leather arms. The skirt is made of sheets of variously coloured paper, on which are written prophecies for the future. National Museum of Finland, Helsinki.

Right:
Group of Eskimo dolls dressed in sealskin, with wooden faces and bodies of rawhide. They are particularly effective figures, as all the materials used in their construction are indigenous. Metropolitan Toronto and Region Conservation Authority.

pairs of wax-headed figures dressed in various Dutch peasant costumes and of a high quality were probably made to be sold to young people on the Grand Tour. A number of papier-mâché dolls dating to the mid-19th century and dressed in the costumes of various Swiss and Austrian regions were also almost certainly made as a form of souvenir. The Breton fishergirls, with terracotta limbs or bodies of ungussetted leather, were made as gifts in the second half of the 19th century, though by this time a deterioration in the standard of costuming can be seen; clothes are frequently not removable and though the heads of the dolls are often of good quality, the general effect is that of a low-priced object. Much better quality clothes are sometimes seen on a range of French celluloid dolls made in the early 20th century and costumed in effective Swiss and Breton dress. A whole range of dolls with pressed-felt and papier-mâché faces was made between the wars to be sold dressed in the costumes of Finland, Austria, and Czechoslovakia, though unfortunately many of the makers used felt much too lavishly, as of course edges do not need finishing on this amenable but inaccurate material. During the First World War shops in Paris and New York sold Polish relief-fund dolls dressed in native costumes. Collectors of antique dolls often avoid those dressed in regional costumes, as fashionable dress of various periods is preferred, making the former a very possible field for the new collector.

Those intending to collect recently made dolls should look for examples in which natural materials are still used; both the Indians and the Eskimo, for instance, still make effective dolls of leather and fur, while rag dolls can be found in Scotland and in Wales dressed in local flannel and wool. Traditional, wooden dolls can be obtained from Russian and Polish gift shops, while many of the modern Japanese dolls are still highly decorative and made to an acceptable standard. If chosen with care, a group of modern dolls can exhibit a whole range of dollmaking methods and styles and the tawdry effect, often seen in a group of dolls bought without consideration, can be completely avoided.

Dutch and German Cabinet Houses

A simple two-roomed Nuremberg cabinet house dating from the second half of the 17th century. The scale of the rooms makes it possible to see the cooking area of the kitchen clearly. In the foreground is the spit with the date '1550' scratched on the foot. The man doll appears to be wax over plaster, and the small doll on a cushion is wax. The plates standing on a ledge of the panelling are blue and white, while the large stove in the corner of the upper room is of the green glazed type so typical of early German interiors. Germanisches Nationalmuseum, Nürnberg.

Simple dolls' rooms and their furnishings were played with by children from the Greek and Roman civilizations, and small objects of clay and bronze, believed to be toys, have survived. The Egyptians made such vast quantities of models for use in the afterlife, even providing one with a garden with a pond that could be filled with water, that it is extremely difficult to differentiate between toys and models. It seems likely that such miniatures continued to be played with through the centuries but the first recorded structure of a form we could accept as a doll's house was bought in 1558 by Albrecht V of Bavaria for his small daughter. One wonders if the Duke bought this house with something like the intention of fathers of today, who buy their sons expensive model railways, as it was kept safely in his own Art Chamber. Regrettably, this house is only known through a contemporary account but it contained several interesting features, including a bathroom on the first floor and a kitchen and dancing room on the second. There was also a sewing room and the bedroom contained correctly made beds, with curtains and hangings embroidered in gold.

Another early German house, known only from references and an existing woodcut, is that assembled by Anna Köferlin, a burger's wife of Nürnberg, in 1631. The woodcut shows a very large house, with the circular paned windows found in later houses and there cut from tin, together with a wealth of surface ornamentation. The people looking at the house seem tiny in comparison with its vast proportions. The house contained not only a music room and library but also an armoury. Anna Köferlin is herself of interest to collectors, as she was the first dolls' house enthusiast to put her creation on view to the public—at a small fee! She informed viewers of the pedagogic intention of the building in a pamphlet which she issued. 'It will give you a good lesson, so that when you go back home, or when God gives you your own home, you will be able to order your bodies and lives, and organise the duties of your household correctly.' Very early in the history of the dolls' house we are thus able to distinguish a dual purpose, part collectors' cabinet, part a vehicle of household instruction for the young.

Early in the history of the doll's house, the activities of connoisseurs and art dealers are also in evidence, as in 1617, Philip Hainhofer, a collector and dealer, supplied an art cabinet representing a farmyard to Duke Phillip II of Pomerania. This model was made by Mathias Kager and the animals were carved by Johann Schwegler. This recording of the makers' names indicated the importance with which

Below:
Detail of the painted side of a Nuremberg house dating from the end of the 17th century. The windows are all made of cut tin, and the painted decoration is in grey, white and orange. Germanisches Nationalmuseum, Nürnberg.

Above:
An interesting walnut cabinet house dating from around 1700. Both the upper floor and the cellar are in the original state, but the furnishings of the central room were mainly added in the 19th century. This house was originally owned by the Wengen family of Basel, and contains a silver dish made by a Basel goldsmith, Peter Biermann, dated 1709. Historisches Museum, Basel.

such constructions were regarded. Hainhofer also supplied the town of Augsburg with a costly art cabinet as a gift for the Swedish king, Gustavus Adolphus, in 1632, and this was given the extravagant addition of mechanical dancing dolls.

In 1572, the small Princess of Saxony had received a toy kitchen that included 71 dishes, 40 meat plates, 36 spoons, and 28 egg-cups, all of pewter. In addition to furniture of all descriptions, there was also a poultry run. Among the interesting small furnishings were a cradle, a barber's bowl and several inkstands. These items are listed here to show the wealth of equipment with which the German toy kitchens were provided even at this early date.

Fourteen different guilds were said, by the end of the 17th century, to contribute to dolls' houses, and Christoff Weigel commented in 1698, 'There is hardly a trade in which the things usually made big are not often copied on a small scale as toys. This applies specially to dolls' houses which contain everything necessary for a household's pride and ornament, daintily made and sometimes precious.' The grip of the various trade guilds was of course strong in Germany, so that a craftsman could only sell items made in his particular skill. These strict

rules were later to prove some hindrance to the toy trade and were relaxed.

Paul von Stetten commented in the mid-18th century, 'As to the education of girls, I must make mention of the toys with which many played until they became brides, namely the so-called doll's houses. In these everything which belonged to a house and its management was reproduced in small and some went to such lengths of sumptuousness that the cost of such a property would run to 1,000 gulden and more.'

We are fortunate that several of the highly treasured early dolls' houses remain and can be seen at the Germanisches Nationalmuseum, Nürnberg. The earliest house at the museum dates to 1600 and represents a three-storey Nürnberg town house, though unfortunately the contents were restored in the mid-18th century. The house, despite its large size, is made from wood only about half an inch thick and could not have withstood much transportation. The roof contains two windows on either side of a decorative arched centre, but it is the inside of this house that is the most interesting, as the intention was so obviously adult-directed. A staircase and various landings divide the main rooms and it is the decoration of the walls of this area that is so intriguing. On the upper landing, a hunting frieze is painted just below ceiling level, while on either side of the doors figures in 17th-century costume, representing halberdiers, stand, presumably on guard. On another wall is painted a lady wearing a ruff, a figure very reminiscent of the dummy boards seen in actual houses of this period in England.

The bedroom walls are also decorated with a frieze, but this time of formalized swags of fruit and flowers. Over the first-floor doorways stags are painted in a resting position – only the bodies are painted, as the heads are fully carved and are fixed to the bodies at the neck; an unsatisfactory, if now amusing, artistic device not previously seen in a doll's house. On this floor the guarding halberdiers are also painted. Some of the reception-room ceilings are painted with geometric designs, while the swagged friezes also appear in several rooms. The kitchen is packed with wall shelves, some with cut-out notches so that pans could be positioned on narrow shelves with their very long handles pointing down. Away from the cooking area and free from splashes of grease, are the shelves for the more important serving dishes. Some of these shelves were individually shaped to display single prestige pieces.

Above left:
The courtyard of the late 17th-century house showing a painted scene in the background of a formal garden. Although there is a strange miscellany of items, the pierced-work hanging lantern is particularly notable. Germanisches National-museum, Nürnberg.

Above:
An interesting group of wax dolls from the late 17th-century Nürnberg house, two of which have the legs and round bases moulded together. All are of the black-bead-eyed type. The simple chairs are upholstered in velvet, there is a green earthenware stove, and the hanging shelves are ivory. The impressive-looking portraits are simply painted on card. Germanisches Nationalmuseum, Nürnberg.

A cabinet house which dates from 1660, although parts were restored in the 18th century. The galleried courtyard with its highly decorated cisterns is an unusual feature, as are the murals of guards and animals on the walls. In the gallery a series of paintings illustrate the dalliance of a monk and a nun. Germanisches Nationalmuseum, Nürnberg.

The very adult intention of the house is underlined by the painted couples seated at table in what would have been the great hall on the ground floor. One fetchingly costumed lady very purposefully holds the obviously straying hands of the gentleman seated next to her, and the rather bawdy air of the complete group was obviously not intended for the education of a child in her womanly duties! On the floor of this room is an unusual trapdoor leading to the cellars that form the base of the house. On the right of the ground floor is a galleried area that appears to represent an outdoor scene, as it is from here that the water for the house is obtained from an ornate cistern. Another series of paintings is used to decorate the upper gallery. We see a nun singing while a monk watches with interest. In the next picture, her dress front lowered to show vast breasts, the nun is being caressed by the monk. They are discovered by a watchman! The last picture shows them both doing penance. . .

Another Nürnberg cabinet dating to the second half of the 17th century is very much simpler and consists only of a simple box shape containing a large-scale living room above a kitchen and was obviously intended purely for the display of its contents. The kitchen is of the typical Nürnberg plan, with shelves on the left and a large square oven in one corner with an arched storage area for the fuel. Over the cooking area there is always a canopy to carry away the smoke. The canopies are invariably attractive, as shelves were constructed around them for the storage of equipment. This cabinet contains several of the black, painted boards on which various vegetables or items of clothing were drawn, so that the housekeeper could indicate to her illiterate servants the tasks of the day by a simple cross alongside the relevant sketch. In the kitchen is also a mechanical spit with the date 1550 scratched on the foot. Many of the pewter plates with which such cabinets were plentifully supplied carry touch marks, which makes their accurate dating possible. The scale of this particular cabinet is so large that even the silver hallmarks can be seen.

In the living room a tiny wax doll, surely originally intended as a pincushion, is lavishly costumed in gold braid and lace, while a rather sinister wax-over-plaster gentleman sits at a table. These strangely assorted characters sit in a well-panelled room, with blue and white plates of fine quality on a plate rack at ceiling level. On a wall is a particularly fine cistern with a working tap, a refinement not seen in British doll's houses until nearly two centuries later. A lace pillow, with its necessary bobbins, stands on the floor. The table with its round stretcher is a fine miniature piece and is set for a simple meal. As with so many early cabinets, later generations were unable to resist adding a few appropriate pieces and here a type of chap book, dated 1725, is seen hanging from a cupboard.

Another house dating to the end of the 17th century is of interest, as it contains on the ground floor a small room known as the *Gewölbe* where goods were unloaded and stacked around so that they could be sold. Actual trade was apparently carried on in such vaults in town houses and this room with its blue-painted storage cupboard is obviously fitted for the purpose. On either side of the central cupboard are stacked racks of paper labelled as writing paper and consisting of several colours in different sizes. All these back shelves are occupied by paper, far too much for the use of one household, and this was probably the trade of the merchant owner. Around the other walls are unlabelled drawers, though one area was reserved for the storage of especially made miniature chests. Before the chests stands a set of graduated weights on their own stand. In a rack there is flax for tinder boxes. From the ceiling hang sponges and boards and a fine carved and gilded swan that was probably a trade sign. A wax lady doll, whose fair wig is plaited in several layers around her face, stands in this room.

Above:
A small Nuremberg dolls' house, probably of the type that children were allowed to play with. It opens at the front to reveal four rooms. The circular cut-metal windows are typical of the early Nuremberg houses. Bethnal Green Museum, London.

Opposite:
Interior of the Stromer cabinet house with the date '1639', probably that of its completion. Germanisches Nationalmuseum, Nürnberg.

Part of the nursery area of the small-scale lower rooms in the Stromer house. The unoccupied baby's cradle is neatly tied across with ribbon. Miniature baby walkers, such as this one in the middle of the room, are seen in many early continental houses—they were obviously an essential piece of nursery equipment. Germanisches Nationalmuseum, Nürnberg.

Right:
The drawing room of Margaretha de Ruyters' house has a fine painted ceiling and silk-hung walls, and the fire basket and andirons are both made of silver. The wax lady doll wears a rich gold lace petticoat; even the sleeves of the costume are decorated with small bows. Rijksmuseum, Amsterdam.

Below:
The bedroom of Margaretha de Ruyters' house. The walls are hung with red chintz with matching bed hangings. The ewer and basin are silver, and the small table is supported by a gilded putto. Rijksmuseum, Amsterdam.

This house has an extra point of interest in the tin gutter that leads to a drainpipe, primitively fashioned in the shape of a dragon's head, a detail vary rarely encountered even in houses as fine as these. The exterior of the house is painted and the sides are further decorated with grey, white and orange panels. The windows are unglazed, and of the typical round cut tin, such as those in the small Nürnberg house at the Bethnal Green Museum. Some of the furnishings are obviously commercial, such as a set of red and blue tin chairs with a matching table. A swinging cradle on a wooden stand with drawers in the base for clothes is particularly fine, and its intended occupant, in tight swaddling clothes, lies in the arms of its wax mother.

The dining room contains one of the heavily glazed earthenware stoves seen in almost every early German doll's house or set of rooms, and which are very much display models, as they have no moving parts. On the ground floor is a garden, and through an arch a much finer formal garden leads to a grand painted house in the distance. In the foreground of this partly painted area is a strange mixture of objects including a coach, chickens—and a splendid leopard! On a side shelf stands an enchanting miniature coach and horses, obviously intended as an outdoor toy for the supposed children of the house. Stables lead off the courtyard, and are occupied by two very well-fed carved wooden horses, surrounded by a variety of tools, baskets and tin lanterns. This house is also rich in doll inhabitants, all with black bead-like eyes. The construction of two of the wax dolls is unusual, as the lower legs are moulded in one with the round bases so that they could stand. The kitchen contains a table with matching bowls and a tureen, all made of pewter.

The kitchen of the Stromer house is unrivalled for its wealth of equipment in pewter, brass and copper. Note the painted detail of the canopy over the cooking area, and the doors in the base instead of the more usual arches. Germanisches Nationalmuseum, Nürnberg.

All the Nürnberg houses on display are of a very impressive size, obviously directed towards an adult, and the proportions of the rooms are also very much planned for an adult's convenience in viewing, as the scale is very much bigger than that encountered in the English baby houses. It is even larger than that of the Dutch cabinets. These Nürnberg houses were obviously prestige display pieces and their size would have defeated most children. The sensibilities of the adult viewer are also catered for by the old Nürnberg craftsmen, who felt that plain dividing boards at ceilings and walls were unsatisfactory, and frequently added a horizontal decorative painted board across the front of a room or an archway at ceiling level. The function of the railings in both the Kress and the Stromer houses again appears more decorative than essential, but makes these houses particularly memorable.

The Stromer house, with its date, 1639, painted on an attic window, is one of the most photographed German houses. It is made of pine and has painted mock windows at the sides, except at one point where, at ground level a pane, possibly of mica, is used. An exterior painted door leads to the stable and a man in a red shirt is painted as though about to enter. The construction of the interior is strange, as the scale changes so completely in the bottom section, where eight small rooms are snugly accommodated, and one cannot but wonder whether, as in one of the Dutch cabinet houses, two separate houses were skilfully amalgamated in 1639. The balustrading along the front of the house is very simply cut in outline, and is painted to simulate depth. The house is far more practical than the others on display, as it appears to lift apart in several sections and even the roof is removable.

Right:
It was customary in Holland for the mistress of the house to sit in the 'best kitchen'. In Petronella Oortman's house this contained a cupboard well stocked with the porcelain and silver which had formed part of her dowry—all the shelves are specially shaped for china display. The child's chair has a bell and there is a foot warmer in the foreground. Rijksmuseum, Amsterdam.

The hall outside the best kitchen of the Oortman house has an economical corner fireplace and an entrance to a cellar. On a shelf lies food ready for serving, and a bird cage hangs over the door. At the back is a privy with a wooden seat and brass taps on the cistern. Rijksmuseum, Amsterdam.

The decoration of much of the furniture was achieved by the application of lighter woods in carefully cut strips, which was probably easier than carving, but created a good effect. The panelling of the walls is very fine, and especially painted pictures fit neatly in intended positions, as in several of the English baby houses. The back wall of the upper hall is painted to resemble a wall hanging, with heavy painted folds. Particularly memorable among the furnishings is a fine parcel-gilt goblet on the table in an upstairs dining room. Several sets of playing cards lie around, rather as in Ann Sharp's house in England, indicating the popularity of the gaming table.

On one flight of stairs, a dog is painted on the wall, forever running up the stairs at the same point. The lovely rich mellow colour of this house makes it a particular favourite, as well as the unexpected incidental detail. The canopy over the kitchen fire, usually left plain, is here painted with flowers despite the fact that it can be scarcely seen under the wealth of pewter plates. This kitchen has an air of even greater order than that seen in the other houses and brass, tin, pewter, and copper, all made by specialist craftsmen, combine to create a lavish effect. Instead of the usual open arch under the fire, this house has closing doors. The clockwork jack is probably the finest that can be seen.

The gentleman's room on the left of the centre floor is appealing, as so few doll's houses contain rooms specially equipped for a man. This Nürnberger was supplied with a water container fixed to the wall that could be pivoted down into the bowl beneath, where he could wash with a sponge that hung from a ribbon.

On the bed a clean and most exquisitely stitched shirt is neatly laid out, together with a lace nightcap. From a brass peg on the wall hangs a barber's bowl. The night commode is of the simplest box type, but still contains its original earthenware chamber. The table is laid with blue and white tea bowls and saucers of a later date than the house, and exquisite cutlery with delicate ivory handles. On a table lies a letter.

In the lower part of the house are the small rooms, whose interesting contents can only be adequately viewed when kneeling on the floor, a lack of consideration for the adults' convenience not often seen in cabinet houses! The nursery is occupied by a painted wooden rocking horse of the very early style, with its legs painted on the curved base and a filigree silver cradle in which lies a wax baby doll with black painted eyes, the sole occupant of this huge house.

The stable, also in the lower area, contains besides two horses and a cow, a bed for the stable lad. A small room above the store room where kegs are ranged is presumably that of a manservant, as a razor, various working knives and a corkscrew lie around. Several of the other small rooms are used for storage and the imposing entrance to the house lies between the two groups of four rooms, with a staircase leading up to the main living areas.

The general arrangement of the Kress house, dating from the second half of the 17th century, is much more complex than that of the Stromer house, and the decorative balustrading that contributes so much to the period effect is here carved in the round. In some ways, this house is of more interest, as it still contains its original inhabitants, including a poured-wax, bent-limb baby with black painted hair. A glass bottle on a table contains a homunculus, also made of delicately worked glass and the only one ever seen in a doll's house, despite the fascination of the subject in the 17th and even 18th centuries. Another unusual touch is a lady doll, now in undress, with the items of her costume including a green corset and a muff laid out around the room.

The quality of the furnishings is as uneven, as in several of the cabinet houses, and here the long-case clock is of the crudest construction, though the stairs and the general interior detail is particularly fine. These contradictions indicate how a good craftsman was employed to build the house, but the contents were purchased almost piecemeal. In the dining room are two matching tables, inlaid with bone or ivory. On a wall is a painted sundial, dated 1785, again indicating a continuing family interest in the cabinet. A goblet such as those made in human size from a coconut is here made from a walnut set in silver. This type of interesting detail packs the German houses, so that each time a kitchen, for instance, is studied, fresh detail emerges, making their interest continual. This house stands on a much deeper base than the other Nürnberg houses and the room fronts are given arches to add to the decorative effect. Again, however, there are the small rooms of a different scale in the lower part. The gables on this house are removeable and are seen in various positions in different photographs, which has caused collectors studying doll's houses from pictures some confusion. The general scale of the Krauss house is more accurate than that seen in the other cabinets, and is reminiscent of the detailed correctness seen in the Dutch cabinets.

The Dutch involvement in the construction of large dolls' houses appears to have begun rather later than the German, and their much more elegant structures are very much descendents of the lovely col-

Below left:
The walls of the kitchen in Margaretha de Ruyters' house are papered and cream painted, and the fireplace is painted to give the marbled and tiled effect. Concealed in the cupboard behind the wax housekeeper is a privy. Rijksmuseum, Amsterdam.

Below:
The reception room in the Petronella Oortman house, with wall paintings by Nicolaas Piemont (1644–1709). The rosewood chairs are fine miniatures and have velvet-fringed seats. On the table lies an ivory pipe and a porcelain tea bowl. The bible on the stand is brass bound. Rijksmuseum, Amsterdam.

The urn of painted flowers on the chimney board indicates that it is now summer in the Petronella Oortman house; the fire dogs, peat buckets and other pieces of equipment are stored away in the loft. The continued chimneypiece is decorated with a painting of a cock by W. van Rooyen. Rijksmuseum, Amsterdam.

lectors' cabinets with small drawers and display areas that were a speciality of Antwerp and south Germany. The centre of these cabinets was sometimes made in the form of a chemist's shop or even as a display area for miniature china. Complete stage sets are seen in others. The craftsmanship of such cabinets can be superb, and in comparison even the finest of the doll's houses seems clumsy.

Margaretha de Ruyter's house is the oldest at the Rijkmuseum in Amsterdam. In 1673 she married a clergyman, Bernadus Somer, and an inventory of her possessions was made shortly after her death that mentions a 'walnut doll's house' and it is certainly this house that can now be seen. The cabinet itself, of inlaid walnut, stands on heavy barley-twist legs and simple partitions divide the rooms. In the house is a pincushion, commemorating the year 1676 when her father, Michiel Andriaanzoon, died. Inlaid walnut is also used for some of the floors, a touch giving the appearance of the structure greater unity.

No effort is made to suggest stairs, except in the attic, where plain wooden steps lead up to a storage area. It is in the decoration of this house, dating from the mid-17th century, that the main interest lies, and the structure is of added attractiveness as it exhibits something of the character of a play-house that is very obviously the outcome of adult intention. The main rooms on the first floor are furnished with great attention, even to the elegantly panelled and painted ceilings. The walls of the lying-in room are hung with red and gold printed fabric, while the same material is used for the bed hangings and the counterpane. The chimneypieces are probably the least satisfactory aspect, as they are crudely made in comparison to the general quality: that in the lying-in room has a painting in the centre panel above and in the grate is a lovely silver fire back and a pair of silver fire dogs. A nurse sits by the fire nursing a baby that is swaddled to a board with silk and ribbon, while the mother lies in bed—a bed that, like so many seen in 17th- and 18th-century houses, is roughly made of unpolished wood and obviously never intended for view. Several chairs with barley-twist legs complete the furnishings, together with a fine miniature cabinet, with the overlarge lock often seen on small models of this type, decorated with inlaid oyster-shell pattern.

The drawing-room walls are also hung with fabric, but this time of a soft green faded silk. The notable piece of furniture in this room is a fully stocked linen press. A set of carved ivory hanging shelves, almost impossible to hang straight, gives, just fleetingly, the impression of a playhouse, quickly dispelled by the perfection of the ivory chairs. A ground floor salon is a little disappointing, for here the walls are simply whitewashed, though the room contains some fine examples of miniature porcelain, such as two barber's bowls that hang on the wall on either side of a cupboard that is itself filled with miniature glass, both white and clear. On a table is a particularly good red stoneware teapot about $\frac{3}{4}$ inch high, together with ivory pipes and some glass tea bowls. The carpet in this room is represented by painted paper.

The superbly panelled bedroom in the Oortman house, with its ceiling painting by Jan Voorhout (1647–1723) of Moses with the Tablets of the Law. The draped bed fits into a recess in the panelling, and has cupboards on either side. The dressing table has a beautifully embroidered linen cover. Rijksmuseum, Amsterdam.

A wire mousetrap, complete with its captive mouse, lies on the cream and black tiled storeroom floor. Jars, some covered with leather, contain, for instance, oil of cedar. On the top shelf white metal plates hold, among other things, a boar's head. From the palings separating the storerooms hang dried fish and bunches of grapes. In the kitchen, a rack holds wooden plates painted to resemble Delft china. Wooden foot-warmers lie in front of the chairs in the kitchen as in the other rooms, a piece of equipment absent in the Nürnberg houses. The kitchen is provided with a sink and a copper. A cupboard contains a privy with a wooden lid. In several rooms, besides the kitchen, can be seen examples of the very delicate canework that was used to make, among other things, carrying boards for babies. Turned white wood ware is also in evidence in the more utilitarian rooms, a type that continued to be used in dolls' houses until the First World War and is still made.

This cabinet house on a heavy walnut stand dates from the last quarter of the 17th century, and belonged to Margaretha de Ruyter. The laundry room on the top floor is typical of Dutch houses of the period. Rijksmuseum, Amsterdam.

Above:
The massive walnut cabinet utilized by Sara Ploos van Amstel. Gemeentemuseum, The Hague.

Above:
The laundry room of Sara Ploos van Amstel's house, showing a variety of finely made baskets, including one in the foreground which was intended for carrying a baby. On the left is a particularly fine mangle. The palings at the rear are a feature of several Dutch houses. Gemeentemuseum, The Hague.

Right:
The kitchen of Sara Ploos van Amstel's cabinet house, with a wealth of pewter and brass. Most of the furnishings came from the third cabinet that was purchased. The wax serving maids are dressed in chintz caracots with white caps and aprons. Gemeentemuseum, The Hague.

The top floor houses the whitewashed nursery, with its badly made chimneypiece, made attractive by the lace and braid decoration and the mock Delft tiles, that are simply painted. The simply constructed bed is also made splendid by its drapery, and the silk pineapple-shaped tassels with which it is surmounted. A child doll leads a baby in a walker that is made of cane wound round with pink silk and gold thread with wheels made of circles of wood, again silk-wound. Possibly this piece was made by Margaretha herself—it is certainly home-made, as were many of the other furnishings, from scraps of dress materials. In a wicker cradle, another baby lies asleep.

In the laundry room miniature pieces of costume hang on the line while other beautifully stitched linen, and blankets with binding of silk ribbon, lie in piles on wooden benches.

The dolls contained in this house are of considerable interest, as they indicate the standard that was possible in the 17th century. Their construction, of wire bound with silk, is very reminiscent of that used for crib figures, and causes me to wonder how frequently such dolls are misclassified as crèche when found out of their setting. The heads are made of wax modelled with great individuality and the lower parts of the arms and legs are also made of this substance. In nearly every case, one hand is modelled in an open position, so an object could be carried, while the other is shown closed. The skilful characterization means that the nurse has a coarse, peasant-like face, while that of the lady is long, narrow and patrician. A small boy doll plays with a kite and an old man, wearing a hat and smock, works in a storeroom in the loft.

Margaretha de Ruyter's house has something of the atmosphere of a play-house because of the number of items that are obviously made by an amateur and the scale, in several cases, would not have satisfied the taste of an adult. The commemorative pincushion, dated 1676, three years after her marriage to Bernadus Somer, indicates that she continued to busy herself with the contents of the cabinet after her marriage.

The other house exhibited at the Rijksmuseum is much more positively a cabinet piece, and for that reason is a little cool in comparison. This house has an interesting history, and was popularly associated for many years with stories concerning a house that was especially commissioned by Peter the Great but not purchased as the cost was considered too high. The museum itself does not regard these stories with any seriousness, and it is thought that the house was made for Petronella Oortman, who married Johannes Brandt in 1686. A touch of distinction is the fact that a painting of the cabinet can also be seen, the work of Jacob Appel (1680–1751), which shows the detail of the interior, either at the time of construction or shortly after. From the painting it can be seen that dolls were once part of the contents of the house: some of them with hair dressed in the popular *fontange*. The various rooms are numbered in the painting, which gives more the appearance of a plan than an artistic rendering, as the painter has made no attempt to suggest perspective and the complete floors as well as the

The music room of Sara Ploos van Amstel's cabinet house is particularly well equipped, though the painted walls are typical of a period earlier than the date of assembly. The furniture is of mixed Dutch and English styles. Gemeentemuseum, The Hague.

ceilings can be seen completely in each room. From the painting it is also seen that glass panes originally protected the valuable contents, contents that were further shielded by curtains that could be closed when the cabinet was not on view.

The cabinet itself is of massive and costly proportions, and lavishly veneered with tortoiseshell. The woodwork, chimneypieces and panelling of the interior are of the very highest workmanship, and it is obvious that no expense was spared in the creation of a finely scaled model house. Despite the elegant appearance, it was necessary to include the storage and work rooms upon which a well-organized Dutch home depended, and at the top of the cabinet is a well-equipped

The porcelain room of the house created by Sara Ploos van Amstel. This section, where a mixture of blue and white porcelain and glass pieces are shown, was originally part of another house. Gemeentemuseum, The Hague.

General interior of Sarah Ploos van Amstel's cabinet house, showing the garden and the skill with which the lower walls were amalgamated. However, much of Sarah's energy was lost before she reached the bedrooms, or perhaps she, like many viewers of today, found the low ceilings discouraging. Gemeentemuseum, The Hague.

laundry. From its ceiling hangs a line filled with minutely knitted stockings and articles of clothing. On a trestle table lie two exquisite brass coal irons. The realism of the interior is maintained by the simple roof beams and the two rooms that lead off the work room and provide the servants' accommodation. In these partly obscured rooms are chintz-hung four-poster beds, a rush-seated chair and a chamber pot. The detail of the doors and their fanlights is perfect, even in these lesser rooms.

The nursery has simple whitewashed walls but a fine painted ceiling and decorative windows at the rear, painted with birds and flowers in a somewhat Chinoiserie manner. On the walls hang a few simple paintings in the manner of C. Dusart: one forms part of the continued chimneypiece, as it is positioned over the marble fireplace. A table was draped with a silk cloth to create a dressing table on which is placed a candlestick and a jewel box. The chairs are of the simple rush-seated kind, but made more elegant by the addition of silk cushions. On the floor stands a baby's cradle, with that practical continental addition of a curtain that could be drawn forward to protect the child or to persuade him that it is time for sleep!

Landscapes by Nicholaas Piemont (1644–1709) decorate the main reception room on the first floor where a flower-painted chimney board covering the grate shows that it is summer. Again it is the splendidly carved chimneypiece that dominates the room together with its integral bird painting by W. van Rooyen. The most exquisite rosewood furniture is accompanied by a stand with a brass-bound bible and a table bearing ivory pipes and a porcelain tea bowl. Rosewood is also used for the panelling of the main bedroom, that contains an interesting bed enclosed in the panelling, with a wardrobe built-in on one side and a linen cupboard with monogrammed contents on the other. Over this fireplace is a painting by J. Voorhout, and near the fire an equipage of silver composed of a brazier with a kettle and an urn, both made by the Amsterdam silversmith Christiaan Waarenberg. The house was equipped for a large family; another cradle can be seen in this room, as well as a wicker child's chair.

On the ground floor the entrance hall, with its pink marble floor, contains a large built-in china cupboard with a wide range of miniature porcelain. Over one door, bottles hang from a rack, together with a tiny figure made of wire. Food is laid out ready for serving on a shelf that runs along one side. Leading off this service area is a very skilfully constructed cellar, made to look as though it leads down to an even lower level. A fireplace is built across the corner of the hall, cleverly utilizing the remaining space.

The tapestry room, also on the ground floor, houses a black and gold lacquer cabinet in which a collection of shells is displayed, and a blue silk-covered day bed with a bolster. A lace pillow, scissors and a workbox indicate that the room was often used by a lady. A door leads off to an apparent library, which also adds considerably to the realism.

The kitchens of dolls' houses are always among the most interesting of the rooms, and in a Dutch house this area was often divided into the 'best' kitchen – which contained fine pieces of equipment brought with the wife as her dowry, and the more practical kitchen where the servants worked. The best kitchen is here dominated by a magnificent painted cupboard, with shelves especially shaped for the display of china. In this cupboard, obviously the bride's great delight, are rummers, tea caddies, blue and white porcelain and, obviously a much later addition, a few transfer-printed pieces. The chairs are of rush, but have velvet cushions, again indicating that this room is for the housewife herself. There is another fine miniature child's chair in this room, with a door at the front and a brass bell, attached to a rod for the baby's amusement.

This cabinet house is the most exquisitely constructed and planned doll's house in the world: the perfection of its detail and the wealth of its equipage makes the enthusiast very aware of the superiority of Dutch 17th-century craftsmen over the German and English doll's house makers even of the 18th century.

The cabinet house at the Hague, dating from the mid-18th century, is of great interest, as it was so fully documented by its original owner, Sara Rothe, the wife of Jacob Ploos van Amstel. At the death of Sara in 1760, an inventory of her possessions was made, and this included 'A cabinet of art Curios with all those household articles appertaining to the same.' This 18th-century Dutch lady provided a great service to collectors by keeping quite precise notes of the contents of the house. In 1743 she attended an auction at the Keizerskroom in Amsterdam,

where she bought three cabinets with all their contents, one of which dated from the 17th century. In October of the same year, she decided to amalgamate the contents of the three houses into a cabinet of walnut, on which she spent 230 florins. This is the handsome cabinet, standing on massive bun feet, that we see today. It is unlikely that this cabinet was especially made for her, otherwise the crazily curved ceilings in the very low upper bedrooms would have been avoided. It seems probable that she chose a good standard design, of the type intended as a piece of household furniture, and this of course accounts for the large drawers in the lower part.

The central section of the base of the cupboard was selected as her garden, and the floor was painted to resemble bricks. Through a painted archway at the back, and in a decidedly amateurish *trompe l'oeil*, a distant view of the garden is seen. Although the general effect of this area is attractive, the quality of the painting is poor and Master Buttener, who was paid 18 florins for his artistic effort, is unlikely to have made any other mark on posterity.

On the right of the garden is the kitchen, with the usual large prestige cupboard, in which is displayed a miniature barber's bowl, a teapot and strainer in silver, and a variety of silver and porcelain items. Blue and white porcelain plates are also displayed on a delft rack, while other equipment includes a china colander and a waffle iron. The foot-warmer here retains its original ivory or bone vessel, a detail that is usually lost. A papier-mâché tea set in red and grey, ivory-handled knives in a cutlery box, plaster miniature fruit and a tiny slipware candlestick and tazza in Whieldon-type ware all delight the collector of miniatures. Sara had little problem herself in equipping this kitchen, as the one she had bought fitted almost exactly into the space available, though she did not use the silverware and replaced it with utensils made of iron.

The lying-in room is also on the ground floor, and this too came from one of the older structures. The original was surely a house of magnificence, as the detail is so much greater, with opening doors, a fine chimneypiece and an elaborately painted ceiling. The original room was hung with gilt paper 'which I have had removed and let the same be hung with rose red moire.' This room, where the recently confined woman displays her baby, is most effectively crowded with five dolls. The mother wears a blue dress and a shoulder cape, made by Sara and her cousin, who also sewed the flounces on the bed, though with some help from a seamstress.

Dominating the main entrance hall on the first floor is the large lantern which Sara purchased especially, like the pocket watch that forms the face of the long case clock. But a weak feature of this area is the needlepoint runner she made herself.

Extravagant displays of fine Chinese porcelain were the delight of the Dutch burgers in the 18th century, and the porcelain room in this cabinet house is deservedly popular today. In one of the older houses there was a small china room and Sara's carpenter, Jan Meyjer, was instructed to fit this into her cabinet and enclose it in a wooden frame of a more up-to-date style. Though he made a brave attempt to integrate the structure, the effect is somewhat strange, as the area resembles a proscenium arch. The small shelves are packed with Chinese porcelain, known in Holland as *Kraak* china after the Portuguese carracks that carried it. A number of the very small pieces in this area are in fact glass, though decorated to resemble porcelain. A painted canvas was used in this room to imitate a carpet, on which stands a well-made table with barley-twist legs.

The music-room walls were painted with landscapes, on which pictures were hung and the ceiling as well as the carpet was here painted on canvas. A strange mixture of Dutch and rather frivolous

French-inspired furniture, much of which is out of scale, is seen in this room, though the effect in a dolls' house context is satisfactory. The usual miscellany of silver pieces is accompanied by a very lovely Nevers glass blackamoor, which stands on a cupboard, while on a table in the foreground is an inkwell and a sander in gold. A clavichord is not quite up to the standard of the other furnishings, and matches a gold and blue baby chair in the nursery, both in colour and decoration, and it seems probable that these were toy pieces of the period. In this room, as in most of the others, the doors were not made to open.

Sara appears to have lost interest in the project after furnishing the two floors, or perhaps she too found the low bedrooms in which nothing could be seen without the aid of steps discouraging, and her notebook lists of purchases were discontinued. Her carpenter did succeed in creating chimneypieces that conformed to the strange shape of the rooms, and items of furniture were obtained for the nursery and storeroom but, having accommodated the more interesting sections of the old cabinets, Sara Ploos van Amstel obviously felt her project was complete.

The splendid cabinet house that was made for Petronella Oortman, who married Johannes Brandt in 1686. The exterior is decorated with marquetry of pewter on tortoiseshell. The initials 'B.O.' appear on the sides of the house and in carved rosewood on the hall lintel inside. Rijksmuseum, Amsterdam.

English Baby Houses

The Dutch and German craze for the assembling of small objects in collector's cabinets in the form of dolls' houses had, by the early 18th century, spread to England, and finely proportioned houses, known as baby houses, were created; occasionally, it would appear, more for the amusement of adults than children. The lovely model at Nostell Priory was decorated by two women mainly for their own pleasure, and it is also difficult to imagine unsupervised children playing with a baby house like that found at Uppark. Even when a house was originally intended as a plaything, such as that which once belonged to Ann Sharp, the owner added to its contents when she was of adult age. It is difficult to ascertain whether any of the baby houses ever graced a drawing room in the Continental manner, and in fact this seems unlikely, as the only contemporary references tend to place the dolls' houses very much in the context of childhood. It seems that, despite the obvious enjoyment that ladies of the period derived from equipping the houses, they were a little coy about what might be construed as a childish occupation. No such qualms appear to have bothered their Dutch contemporaries!

It is likely that the majority were intended for the carefully supervised play of children, an intention that gives the English houses more appeal than the Dutch to many collectors, who find the less careful regard to scale attractive. Maria Edgeworth in her *Practical Education*, published in 1801, commented on the fact that 'A completely furnished baby house proves as tiresome to a child as a furnished seat to a young nobleman,' an observation indicative of the fact that the houses were intended to be furnished by their child owners. Prints of the period show children with commercially produced furniture that could be purchased from toy shops and in, for instance, Ann Sharp's house, several of the play furnishings still retain their original prices.

That exquisite polished oak baby house on its integral stand, the Westbrook house, was made as early as 1705 as a parting gift from the tradesmen of the Isle of Dogs, to Elizabeth, the young daughter of John Westbrook of Essex. The contemporary furnishings and dolls were most carefully tended by its owner, despite the fact that its primary purpose was as a plaything. When Horace Walpole sent a gift of shells to the five-year-old Lady Anne Fitzpatrick in 1772, he suggested that they 'Might find grace and room, both in your baby house and sight.' There is also that tantalizing letter written by Walpole to Mann in 1750 in which he refers to the Prince 'Building baby houses at Kew.'

The well-proportioned façade of the so-called Norwich house, painted to represent bricks. This type of house was probably a toy in the practical sense, as although well-constructed, it is much less splendid than the large baby houses. Strangers Hall, Norwich.

A particularly charming small baby house of the type that would have been owned by children of moderate means. The quality is uneven: the polished mahogany door with its drop brass handle is of good work-manship, but the dormer windows are crudely made, and the glass is painted. The sides and backs of the house are plain. The house is painted to resemble stone, and is mid-18th century. Bethnal Green Museum.

Right:
Ann Sharp's baby house can at present only be viewed complete in this old photograph. The uneven quality of the furnishings can be seen in the contents, which mainly date from the early years of the 18th century. Ann was given this house by Queen Anne. Strangers Hall, Norwich.

Above:
A painting of Ann Sharp herself, unsigned, but attributed to J. Richardson (1165–1745). Private collection (Captain Bulwer Long).

Bernard Hughes, in an article in *Country Life*, tells us that the Prince had become attracted to this hobby when visiting the Brunswick court, where the Dowager Duchess, the Princess Augusta Dorothea, was occupied in representing the whole court in miniature.

The many small skills involved in doll costuming, the working of carpets and embroidery of bed hangings would have held great appeal for the gentlewomen of the period, whose craftwork in shells, mica and hair still entrances collectors, and some of the houses have the appearance of being used as a vehicle for the display of these skills. We should, however, tread very carefully, when suggesting that English baby houses, like the Dutch cabinets, were mainly adult conceits, as when evidence exists, it more frequently points to the child's involvement.

Furniture makers and architects whose names are revered such as Vanbrugh, Chippendale and Adam, are linked by family traditions with various baby houses, some even being suggested as working plans for full-sized homes. The examination of authentic architect's models, such as that in the Bodleian Library, Oxford, created by Nicholas Hawksmoor in preparation for the building of the Radcliffe Camera, shows clearly the difference between a model and a play house. Other architect's models are small, with roofs that lift off to show the carefully scaled arrangement of the rooms and corridors beneath, while, in turn, the upper floor also pivots or lifts away to show the ground floor, always from above and completely unsuitable for furnishing. In a painting of the family of Thomas Hope, completed in 1802 by Benjamin West, an exquisitely proportioned architect's model is shown in the background standing on its own perfectly made pedestal, a construction far too small in scale ever to have held furnishings. Baby houses certainly appear to have derived their inspiration from the full-sized homes of their owners, as in the case of Nostell Priory, but their use as any sort of architect's model is unfeasible.

Several of the English baby houses still stand in the homes of their original owners, and the casual viewer finds it very easy to see similarities between furnishings in the actual house and those in miniature, though closer examination often reveals only the characteristics of the period. Thomas Chippendale's name is traditionally associated with the miniatures in Nostell Priory, though his involvement in the furnishing of the mansion itself did not begin until 1766. As Chippendale was born some thirty miles away, at Otley, in 1718, it has tempted generations to think that at least a portion of the undocumented period of his life might have been spent in creating some of the dolls' house furnishings. Chippendale certainly appears to have benefited by many commissions from North-country patrons, but at present there is no proof to substantiate his involvement in the baby house, merely a romantic tradition that appeals to collectors.

The fitted interior of Edmund Joy's house showing the wallpaper, which can be seen through the windows from the outside. The height of the house to the top of the lantern is 6 feet 6 inches. The central section appears to be intended for hanging a child's clothes, with shelves and drawers for books. Bethnal Green Museum, London.

Cabinet makers and interior decorators of the 18th century were not above an involvement in what might now be considered beneath the dignity of fine craftsmen, and many trivial commissions were accepted. Thomas Bromwich of The Golden Lyon, Ludgate Hill, sold wallpapers, chintzes and window blinds, supplying Walpole in particular with furnishings for Strawberry Hill, yet he was quite prepared to paper a doll's house; the back of one of his bills showing an account for 'Lining a Baby house with various fine papers.'

Surviving baby houses are almost without exception of fine quality, poorer examples of less obvious worth presumably being discarded by their owners. Even the smaller houses, such as that in the Norwich museum, exhibit such skill of construction that families must have treated them with respect despite their outdated appearance. The early 18th-century house in Strangers Hall, Norwich, is typical of the smaller, well-made houses of the period, having brass carrying handles on either side to assist the servants in moving it about the

Above:
A doll labelled 'William Rochett' by
Ann Sharp (the label is still in place)
stands beside a wheeled linen horse
that once stood on the ground floor.
The doll is poured wax with inset
blue glass eyes, and has an unusual
slightly open mouth showing the
tongue. Strangers Hall, Norwich.

Above right:
Also from Ann Sharp's house is
Lady Jemima Johnson, a carved
wooden doll dressed in embroidered
silk. She stands at an alabaster table
with matching tea bowls and saucers.
Strangers Hall, Norwich.

Top left:
A group of items from the display
shelf at the top of Ann Sharp's house.
The wheeled toy is the only example
as yet known. It shows a gentleman
sitting by a pool against a rocky
landscape; the carving of the figure
is probably Bavarian. Strangers Hall,
Norwich.

Left:
A group of objects from the display
shelf in Ann Sharp's house, including
a model theatre, a straw-work box,
some German carved figures and
items in wood and ivory. Strangers
Hall, Norwich.

house. Not all baby houses, even in the smaller sizes, have these
handles, but when present their design is often of help in dating. In
this example the coigning on the façade is particularly well painted to
simulate depth, a detail that did not often concern doll's house makers.
Typically 18th century is the lock that protected the contents either
from younger brothers and sisters, or from the careless play of the
young owner herself when the children's nurse was absent. This house
boasts not only a locking façade but also, and obviously for play, a
locking front door. Despite the fine quality of the construction, the
window frames are a little disappointing, as they are simply glued to the
glass and not correctly made. This rather shoddy treatment of windows
is encountered on occasion even in the finest of baby houses, as the
insertion of minute panes of glass would have tried the patience of
even the finest craftsman. Here the twelve-paned windows are suggested by simply-cut card or fine wood which was painted.

Like many 18th-century houses that have continued as playthings
for decades, the contents of the house exhibit a miscellany of styles and
periods, from late 19th-century Kate Greenaway prints to an entrancing working jack in the kitchen, the most effective, as it holds the oldest
furnishings, of all the rooms. These include a miniature brass range
with water tank and hot water tap which, though probably much later
than the house, is a good model. As is so often the case, the only remaining original fittings appear to be the spit rack and the built-in dresser
without which few 18th-century houses were made. The blue and
white transfer-printed service on the dresser was made by Rogers in
the early 19th century and is of a design known as 'Monopteris'. This
house is discussed first as it is more typical of the majority of houses
made in the period than the prestige pieces such as that at Uppark.

It is regrettable that the baby house that retained more of its original
atmosphere than perhaps any other cannot at present be viewed
complete, and the only record of its original state is in photographs
taken before the last war. Ann Sharp's house has long been the starting
point for those wishing to trace the evolution of the English baby
house and to examine the empty frame of the house, its top sawn away,

167

and its fascinating contents piled in boxes, was, to the doll's house
enthusiast, like visiting the burned-out shell of a once loved home.
Presumably, by reference to the old photograph, the contents can one
day be reassembled in something like the order in which Ann Sharp
left them, but it is saddening to be made aware of the casualness with
which some museums still regard playthings of the past, even, as in this
case, when the importance is known.

Ann Sharp was one of the fourteen children of John, Archbishop
of York, and was presented with the baby house by her godmother
Princess Anne, later to become Queen, whose miniature once hung
in the house. Ann Sharp was born in 1691 and, at the age of twenty-
one married Heneage Dering, the Dean of Ripon. She died in 1771.
The family notes that still accompany the house suggest an uneventful
life and her sole claim to fame rests in the house which she carefully
arranged herself, labelling each of the 'inhabitants' with its name, and,
frequently, its station in the household.

Basically, this house is of a simple cupboard shape to which later
glass-fronted doors were added. It is constructed, like the majority of
baby houses, of pine, though the exterior has been repainted several
times. The chimneypieces are of the simplest construction, being mere
pieces of picture moulding, painted in imitation of marble. Some of
the chimneypieces are on the back walls and others in corners. The
doors are roughly cut out and papered to match the walls, a device
used in actual houses of the period in order to make the doors less
conspicuous. As in the Dutch houses, the main staircase and hall are
situated on the first floor, but in this case the stairs are cut in the
crudest manner though the hall floor was papered to resemble tiles.
It is this very crudity of construction which gives the house its appearance of great age though, logically, one wonders why Queen Anne did
not order a more finely made object for her godchild.

Few traces of the original furnishings still remain in the house; in
the hall hangs a red lacquered corner cupboard, while the backs and
canopies of the beds are still attached to the walls, their silk curtains
hanging in the empty rooms. Even the inside lining of the bed canopy
was especially embroidered rather than, as is often the case, pieces of

odd material being used. One bedroom has a lightly embossed paper, while that in the room originally the parlour was once gilded, and what appears to be an excise mark or even a maker's mark can still be seen printed on the bottom edge. If an excise mark, then this paper was printed after 1714 when such marking became law. The ground floor, the traditional area for kitchens, servants' quarters, and store rooms in houses of this type, has white painted walls, on one of which is painted a huntsman. An additional shelf at roof level provided display space for the miscellaneous array of objects of curiosity so loved by ladies of the period.

The contents of the house, now in boxes, include the charming dolls that Ann labelled so carefully, such as 'William Rochett, the heir', who is dressed in a suit of pale blue silk. This doll is unusual for the period, as it has blue eyes with pupils and a mouth modelled in an open-closed position with the tip of the tongue showing. Several of the other dolls are modelled only to the waist, and the lower parts are made of rolled up playing cards. A baby in a cradle, sometimes described as wax, is in fact just a rough piece of wood wrapped around with baby clothes. 'Fanny Lang, Childers Maid' has an interesting carved head that is artistically painted while a small wax doll is also merely a torso fixed to card. So many of these do not appear to be fragments of damaged dolls, and this suggests that some were sold in this way to be made up as required at home. Both wood and wax dolls in this house are found with the same construction. The variety of standard seen in this family of dolls is also fascinating, as 'Mrs Lennox', for instance, has a simple head almost like a late 19th-century wooden top, her skittle-shaped body ending in straight wooden legs, wrapped about with fabric. 'Lady Jemima Johnson' is a very cross-faced individual, her wooden head carved with skill to create an elderly and fierce expression. Even if this house contained only dolls, it would be of great importance in showing the variety available around 1700.

In the original setting, one of the rooms on the top floor had the most sinister atmosphere, as from the ceiling hung a large glass ball, containing a carved cedar and lime wood chandelier, with sconces for eighteen candles. In fact, an adult 'toy' of the period and not intended for a baby house, but hung in front of a wax portrait of Mother Shipton the Yorkshire witch, and seen in the gloom of the house, it reflected the more sinister aspects of life in the period. In the same room stood another adult toy, one of the alabaster sets on a matching table, the whole decorated with green painted leaves. It was in this eerie room, with a monkey on a chair and a birdcage in a dark alcove, that young William Rochett was placed by Ann.

In another room, and of great interest as it is the only example known, is a small card dolls' house, complete with its original furnishings, the whole construction made of painted playing cards. The style of the furnishings would suggest a date considerably later than the main doll's house and, as the drawing room contains furniture in the whimsical Gothick taste, its date must be after 1750. A bedroom contains a four-poster bed draped with silk that was neatly sewn in place and a few simply made chairs. The drawing-room has a drop-leaf table and a Gothick style long case clock. The walls are decorated by poorly painted pictures of country houses. The kitchen has a card dresser with sketched-on plates and the splendid fireplace has a rather complicated hanging device, from which is incongruously suspended a tiny kettle. This small house beautifully illustrated the fusing of several styles in the 18th century, from the medieval-style kitchen fireplace to the whimsical mannered furniture of the Gothick taste.

The contents of Ann Sharp's house are endearing because so many of the pieces are home-made or bought from the cheapest range in toy shops. The furnishings date from the time when she was given the

A Leeds-ware serving plate with moulded oysters from Ann Sharp's house. This type of moulded border decoration is typical of Leeds, as is the soft cream colour and the very light body of the material. Strangers Hall, Norwich.

The red lacquer toy clock, marked 'Beesley, London' from Ann Sharp's house. The case is very crudely made, but looks impressive because of the extravagant metal face. The hands move together. Strangers Hall, Norwich.

Above:
The dining room of the baby house at
Uppark, showing the finely made
furniture and the salts—often utilized
as wine-coolers. The table is lavishly
equipped with silver. The two serving
men are fine-quality wooden dolls of
the period. National Trust.

Right:
The impressive façade of the Uppark
baby house showing the Feather-
stonhaugh coat-of-arms on the
decorated pediment. The front opens
in nine sections to reveal individual
rooms. National Trust.

house as a child, almost to the end of her life, as she appears to have added anything she considered vaguely suitable to the house. The majority of the chairs, made of walnut, are perhaps the most badly made in any baby house, while the fire baskets are made of the thinnest tin, glued to playing cards that act as fire backs. The majority of what could be described as the original furnishings are of this highly economical type. The rich effect is given by the gift-type objects that were included, such as several fine items in lignum vitae and ivory, that were especially marketed for the amusement of adults. A cellarette is made of this wood and contains 'bottles' of turned wood with ivory stoppers, a large cruet set, similarly made, has removable items. The most enchanting piece of lignum vitae is an urn, packed full of ivory and wood cooking utensils, in a number and variety to delight any collector of miniatures. A round cutlery box containing perfectly made ivory pieces still bears the original price of 20/9d on the base.

Several of the silver miniatures, including candlesticks and a pair of snuffers on a tray, hallmarked 1686, were again intended as adult gifts and placed in the baby house for display. A fine coffee pot is marked with the maker's initials 'M.D.' The shellwork boxes, possibly received as gifts, or even made by Ann herself, were also additions of her adult life, many women of the mid-century amusing themselves with this type of work. One is an interesting combination of shell craft and straw work not previously encountered.

As in the Dutch houses, the bed frames are roughly made, as they were to be draped. On the corners of the blankets are the embroidered 'clocks' seen on full-sized blankets of the period. A red lacquered set, which includes the hanging cupboard still in the hall, appears to be commercially made baby house furniture of a high standard. A gate-leg table has the price 5/5d written in pencil. The hanging clock with an embossed metal face is particularly effective, and this too bears an indecipherable price. On the face is the name of a clockmaker who worked in Dean Street in 1725. This object, despite its correct appearance, is obviously a toy, as the hands move together in the true fashion of a plaything. A small brown-painted table decorated with a picture of a girl meeting a soldier also appears to be a commercial piece.

Well-made panelling gives importance to the two upper floors of the Uppark baby house. In the housekeeper's room on the ground floor is an alabaster table with matching tea bowls and pot. National Trust.

The sinister wax portrait of Mother Shipton, the Yorkshire witch, which once hung in an upstairs room in Ann Sharp's house. The ornately carved chandelier was protected by a glass shade, which contributed to the air of mystery in this room. Strangers Hall, Norwich.

This mixture of toy and miniature, both home-made and commercial, contribute to an absolutely unique charm. While the beds, for instance, are very correctly embroidered and hung miniatures, the room that doubles as a stables and scullery contains a plump and delightful toy horse on wheels with a skin of ruched linen decorated with coloured paper and silk. Pictures thought appropriate include 'Christ Betrayed', and a man and woman in hectic combat, 'The Unhappy Marriage'. The kitchen, with its built-in shelves, again exhibits a fairy-tale scale, with fire irons nearly twice as tall as the maid and a huge tea caddy. The brass platewarmer in the kitchen is particularly fine, as it still pivots, whereas some of the silver versions are static. In the scullery a tin pig roasts on a spit while a pudding boils in a pot.

The miniature china in the house is of the finest order and includes several of the small oriental pieces that often ended up in baby houses when slightly damaged. There is also a fine creamware dish with moulded oysters on shells and a set of the characteristically lightweight Leeds plates with feather edging made after 1760. One serving plate has a lovely pierced-work edge. Originally some of these plates carried amusingly modelled wax food, including the essential boar's head. The miniature glass is also particularly fine, and includes a beautiful purple glass jug of the type described as Bristol and some fine milk glass spoons and flasks. Possibly the finest piece of glass seen in an English baby house is a delicate yellow and clear glass goblet with a spiral threaded stem. A candlestick is made of amber glass with a white candle and a red flame, all blown in fine detail and extremely lovely.

Though the house is obviously not as Ann left it as a child but, perhaps more interestingly, as she left it at the end of her life, it is the earliest baby house in existence and its present plight is most regrettable.

After the disturbingly strange atmosphere of Ann Sharp's house, with its very human sense of period, the elegant baby house at Uppark has a cooling effect. Here is a house cared for with sympathy by generations and now supervised by the National Trust which fully recognizes its importance. This splendid house, constructed by a fine cabinet-maker, was made for Sarah Lethieullier who later became the wife of Sir Matthew Fetherstonehaugh who purchased the estate of Uppark in 1747. He married Sarah the same year and she brought her doll's house, with her family coat of arms on the pediment, to her new home, where it has remained to the present.

Above:
The hall and staircase of the Nostell Priory house, showing the skill with which the panelling was constructed, and the slightly out-of-scale but well-made stairs. The serving man is wood and the lady is poured wax. Nostell Priory, Yorkshire.

Above left:
The house at Nostell Priory has one of the most splendidly decorated drawing rooms of any dolls' house, with painted walls, a gilt-enriched mahogany door and a fine grey marble chimneypiece. Nostell Priory, Yorkshire.

The bedroom of the Nostell Priory house, with chintz bed-hangings, a carved ivory chair, and a flower painting on a cupboard door in the panelling. The dolls are wax. The child is particularly interesting, as although quite authentic, it is unlike those usually associated with the period. Nostell Priory, Yorkshire.

172

The interior of the Nostell Priory
house, showing the elegant proportions of the rooms and the richness
of the decoration. In the kitchen
stands a carved wooden cook.
Nostell Priory, Yorkshire.

When closed, the baby house has an impressive Palladian façade, three stories high, and resting on an arched stand containing cupboards. It is believed that the house was made about 1730. The front opens in nine sections so that the rooms can be viewed separately. On the parapet seven rather over-large statues stand perilously, a regretable touch, as they seem both out of scale and character with the cool perfection of the house. Pine is again used for the construction, and all the detail on the pillars is carved. The house is now painted a soft grey. Window frames, though finely mitred and constructed, are again placed on an unbroken sheet of glass though in this case the sash windows do open.

Inside, all the rooms are correctly panelled and pictures were especially painted to fit snugly into this panelling as in Uppark itself. The bedroom chimneypieces are a little disappointing, as they are so simply made, but the splendidly draped beds more than compensate. The silk-draped dressing tables, so easily made at home, are seen here as in other similar houses. The carved ivory cabriole legged chairs seen in the bedrooms are exquisitely made miniatures.

All the doors in the house are polished and unpainted, as was the fashion in actual houses, and each has its own brass model lock, cleaned with great care once a year by local Trust members. In the parlour, with its silver candle sconces bearing the Lethieullier arms, sit stately poured-wax dolls with the traditional black irisless eyes. The legs of the man doll are modelled in wax to above knee level, and his shoes were included in the mould. The ladies were also made with moulded painted boots and their heads are slightly turned. All wear fashionable wigs and the elegant dress of the period. In this room is a silver tea table on which stands a fine matching equipage.

The dining-room, with its well proportioned central display shelves, is extremely effective, as two wooden serving men await the diners. The chairs in this room are fine miniatures with cane seats, and detail on the cabriole legs not often encountered on miniature furniture; chairs that are in fact even finer than any seen in the Dutch cabinet houses. The gate-legged table is also extremely well constructed and bears an array of, admittedly out of scale, silver miniatures, including a Charles II tankard. A silver salt is utilized as a wine cooler, an adaptation that is found in several of the baby houses, and adds to the rich effect of gleaming metal, an effect further heightened by such details as the brass fire dogs and fenders.

As children were born so regularly in the 18th century, a lying-in room was a necessity in a dolls' house, and this example is made more interesting by its doll inhabitants—two wax babies lying together in a cradle, while their mother rests under a well quilted counterpane.

The equipment of the kitchen is also splendid, and includes rows of pewter plates, a rather out-of-scale iron with its heating brick still intact, an unusual chocolate-making machine and a lovely Leeds coffee pot. All the pieces in this room gleam with colour, and amply repay the care that is taken of them each year by local women who spring clean the baby house. Several of the pieces standing on the kitchen floor are miniature pieces rather than dolls' house furnishings, but the addition of such objects is within the 18th-century tradition and does not detract from the general effect.

In the housekeeper's room is an alabaster tea set on a matching table that obviously derives from the same source as that in Ann Sharp's house, though this is more finely decorated in blue and purple and consists of a tea caddy, sugar bowl and tazza, as well as tea bowls and saucers. Similar sets made on an even larger scale are found and were obviously made as 'toys' rather than baby-house furnishings. A flat topped piece of furniture that is possibly intended as a wine cooler is also made of alabaster and to the same, slightly unsuitable, scale.

When the house was peopled, it was decided that wood was quite
suitable for servants, while the family was made in wax, though not
in the exquisite detail seen in those in the Rijksmuseum. The allure of
the house at Uppark rests heavily on its precise air of stability: no
wind of change is stirring in the servants' quarters of this house, and
there is nothing to alter the ordered routine of life. We gaze at this
microcosm of assured life through a great void and perhaps envy its
serenity.

Even the perfection that is Uppark cannot, to my personal taste,
rival that most lovely of English baby houses found at Nostell Priory.
Even the craftsmanship of the Dutch cabinet houses is somewhat
diminished by this house, which retains the atmosphere of a toy while
exhibiting an amalgam of the skills of the period. The date of the construction is usually given as 1735, and it is thought that the house was
intended for the children of the 4th baronet who rebuilt Nostell Priory
itself. The baby house has an elaborate façade that is often said to be a
copy of the design for Nostell itself, as the Ionic pilasters and the elegant pediment are present on both. In fact the baby house bears only
what might be described as a doll's house builder's artist's impression
and there are almost as many differences as similarities between the
two.

Various stories also associate this house with the names of Chippendale and Adam but, like so many family stories regarding doll's houses,
the tradition rests on doubtful foundations. Nostell Priory as it now
stands was thought to be the work of James Paine but it is now considered to have been originally designed by Colonel James Moyser, an
amateur gentleman-architect in Lord Burlington's circle, the nineteen-
year-old Paine only being entrusted with the supervision of the building. Paine was later to make many alterations to Moyser's design and
he designed much of the beautiful interior. As Robert Adam did not
become involved with the mansion until after 1765, the dolls' house
can have no relation to his work. The date of the construction of the
baby house is also probably later than is usually believed, since Paine's
engraving of the Winn coat of arms, also seen on the pediment of the
baby house, was not designed until 1743 and this detail does not appear
to be a later addition.

The baby house was therefore probably made to the design of Paine
or an assistant working for him, and its furnishing was supervised by
Lady Winn and her sister Miss Fanshaw, as an original label fixed to
the floor of an upper room testifies. Fortunately, the decoration is still
in its original state and has that lovely original patina seen only on
houses whose exteriors have never been repainted. The house opens
by sliding the complete fronts to the side, so that a large area is needed
for its display. It is constructed of pine an inch thick and all the detail
is carved. The figures and urns that surmount this house are less
obtrusive than those at Uppark and are integrated into the general
design: they are, of course, not present on the actual house.

The interior is divided into nine rooms with a staircase leading down
to the lower hall. This staircase, though effective, is heavily made in
comparison with the remainder of the house, and the stairs themselves
are completely out of proportion, as are the banister rails. As in so many
baby houses, the stairs lead to a non-existent part of the house. All
the doors are very finely made and are pedimented; each is supplied
with brass locks that actually work.

In the kitchen is an arched fireplace with a steel fire basket and guard.
The spit rack is lightly varnished wood and matches that of the dresser
and ladle rail. In many houses the original spits are lost but here they
are still in place on the rack. The walls were painted to represent
stones, and around the triple arched fireplace wooden brick edging
was used. Near the fire stands the only original fabric dog seen in such

The library of Queen Mary's house with a ceiling by William Walcot. Cabinets contain 700 drawings and paintings by contemporary artists, and the books are written by authors such as J. M. Barrie and G. K. Chesterton. Royal Collection.

a house; an engaging, moth-eaten creature with large feet and something of the sheep in his lineage. An exquisitely made plate rack stands on the floor, and the dresser is equipped with fine silver plates. The cook is similar to some of the wooden dolls found in Ann Sharp's house and has a rough-textured painted face, quite unlike the usual English 18th-century dolls, but seen in no other country, and apparently commercially made. This particular doll is interesting, as one hand is modelled with a hole running through the clenched fist, a method also seen in the wax dolls in the Dutch houses and a device later continued in some porcelain dolls of the mid-19th century. A big wooden cutting block, similar to that made in full-size and designed for the mansion by Chippendale, is also found in the kitchen. The full-sized version indicates how, in the 18th century, a designer was prepared to turn his attention to the most mundane of objects. At the top of the kitchen dresser is a group of exquisite Chinese porcelain, including a fine caddy that must surely have originally graced one of the more important rooms.

The lower hall houses a well-made long-case clock, and especially painted pictures of game fit in panels over the doors. The hall floor is carved in imitation of tiles. The wainscot panelling is fine, contributing to the realism of the whole. Over the white marble chimneypiece hangs a badly painted picture of a spaniel, possibly a pet, and far below the standard of the other paintings. A hanging brass chandelier picks up the warm colours of the panelling and the gleam of the 'toy' silver displayed on a table.

There is a small parlour on the ground floor that contains one of the breathtaking carved miniature marble chimneypieces in grey, surmounted by a mirror and a painting, giving the effect of a continued

The Queen's bedroom in Queen Mary's dolls' house. Over the fireplace is a painting of the Duchess of Teck by Frank Salisbury. The ceiling is by Glyn Philpot and the carpet by the Stratford-on-Avon School of Needlework. Royal Collection.

chimneypiece. Beneath a wall mirror is a wall-mounted ormulu side table with a marble top. The extending gate-leg table carries some good glass, including what are probably Venetian pieces. An attractive blue decanter has a white stopper and each place-setting was provided with two glasses, one blue and the other white.

Decoratively, the drawing-room is the most spectacular ever seen in a baby house. The splendid grey marble chimneypiece is surmounted by a gilded bust that is reflected in a mirror, while above this the effect of a continued chimneypiece was achieved by carving leaves, flowers and an eagle on the wall. All the walls of this important room were decorated with painted pastoral scenes on a golden yellow background that gives a peculiarly lavish effect. Even the skirting boards, usually left plain, were here painted to match. On the mahogany door the carved details are picked out in gold, all contributing to the opulence of the effect. After the splendour of the decoration, the furnishings of the room pale into insignificance, but are in fact made in fine detail and consist of matching chairs and two settees with cabriole legs. The tea table is made of silver and is very similar to that at Uppark, as it holds a silver tea equipage. On either wall stand an Italianate chest and a heavily decorated cupboard containing drawers. This splendid room is as memorable to the doll's house collector as Chippendale's Chinoiserie state bedroom in the mansion itself is to the furniture enthusiast.

Carved ivory chairs, again rather similar to those encountered at Uppark, are found in a nursery which has a painted picture, forming a cupboard, above the corner chimneypiece. The walls of this room are painted in that soft green that was so popular in baby houses of the period. Unfortunately, an over-enthusiastic arranger has placed the woollen blankets with embroidered clocks on the floor as rugs, a misuse very jarring to the purist. Photographs taken some time ago show that this room was once occupied by a cradle, though this is no longer present and only a quilted baby basket remains. The wax girl doll is of particular interest, as such a degree of realism was given to the face which is extremely alert and expressive and would, if found

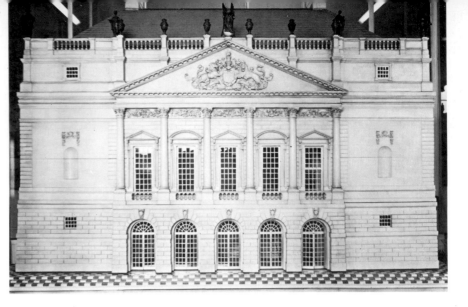

without its original 18th-century clothes, be dated as much later. The wax nurse has moulded hair and her dress is, economically, suspiciously similar to the curtain fabric.

The main bedroom contains a well-made kneehole desk with a dressing mirror standing on its surface. Lady Winn and Miss Fanshaw obviously enjoyed the embroidery and soft furnishings greatly, as fine fabrics are found in so many of these rooms and the quilts are correctly worked miniatures. The bedroom chimneypieces, though less spectacular than those in the reception rooms, are still fine, and one contains an amusing fire basket constructed from odds and ends of ivory, including an outline man that is used to decorate the fireback. The fire irons are well-made ivory miniatures.

A lady doll standing in the boudoir is of the beautiful wax patrician type seen only in the finest houses. All the dolls, from cook to lady of the house, are in original condition and perfectly compliment the furnishings, whose play use, because of this fine condition, was obviously so carefully supervised.

Interiors were very sparsely furnished in the 18th century; a room being frequently set around with chairs and with only a table in the centre. Dolls' houses of this period should similarly retain this look of spaciousness, despite the fact that such an arrangement is perhaps less immediately eye-catching. The Tate House at the Bethnal Green Museum, though well-made and of impressive size, fails in this respect as its contents have been added to down the years and what we now see is a traditional family dolls' house with evidence of each generation, as in a real home; a house whose contents reveal little of 18th-century life but delights hundreds of visitors who succumb to the attraction of the miniature.

As so little 18th-century miniature furniture remains, the collector who acquires an early house is also forced to add later pieces, as a completely unfurnished house always appears forlorn. It would seem preferable to add Victorian and Edwardian items rather than furnish with reproductions, so that a family house effect can be given if not a perfect period interior.

During the 19th century, the dolls' houses made in Europe became very much the province of children and it was not until the early 20th century that an association with adults again emerged. This revival of interest was due largely to the inspiration of Queen Mary who, because of her obvious enjoyment in restoring and furnishing dolls' houses, was presented with what can only be classed as a baby house of the most complicated type as a gift in 1924. A. C. Benson, who edited the book of the *Queens Doll's House*, observed that the purpose in the minds of those who designed, constructed, and furnished the house was 'To present to Her Majesty a little model of a House of the Twentieth Century, which should be fitted up with perfect fidelity,

Above:
Detail of the central Venetian window of the Tate baby house, showing that the sash windows still move. The bricks are painted, and in their original state. Access was obtained to individual rooms at the front, and each section locked. Bethnal Green Museum, London.

Above right:
The north front of the Queen's dolls' house, designed in the classical manner by Sir Edwin Lutyens. The walls lift upwards to reveal the interior. Royal Collection.

The east front of Queen Mary's dolls' house, showing the complex design of the interior and the basement garage with its splendid miniature vehicles. Royal Collection.

down to the smallest details, so as to represent as closely and minutely as possible a genuine and complete example of a domestic interior with all the household arrangements characteristic of daily life of the present time . . . the house thus represented is not a palace nor a ceremonious residence, but essentially a home, a family mansion belonging to a monarch.'

The design of the house was the work of Sir Edwin Lutyens and its building, equipping and furnishing took three years to assemble. The exterior is of wood, carved and painted to resemble Portland stone, the vases and statues on the parapet being the work of Sir George Frampton. Sir Laurence Weaver commented that 'The problem of revealing the inside of the house without treating any of the walls as a door was finally faced and solved. The walls and roof form an outer case which fits closely over the inner fabric and can be raised and lowered by a highly ingenious electrical contrivance which is, in effect, a lift. When therefore the exterior is wafted upwards by such invisible means, the interior stands revealed, and as every apartment is lit by an external window and only the back staircase has borrowed light, every corner of this house can be studied by the visitor.' In addition to such ingenuity, the base of the house contained the machinery, electrical transformer and the tank for bath waste. At the west end of the basement a flap lifts down to reveal a complete garage with small motor cars and an inspection pit!

The 18th-century tradition, by which each small object in a baby house was made, not by an all-purpose toy maker but by the craftsman to which the particular skill belonged was followed, so that for instance Wedgwood supplied a breakfast service in Old Lavender Ware and

The bedroom of the Tate house showing the fine proportions of the rooms. However, this also illustrates how many items were added later, so that the 18th-century atmosphere is largely lost. Bethnal Green Museum, London.

Broadwood the grand piano. Both the dinner service and the storage jars in the kitchen were made by Doulton, while a carpet was woven by the Stratford-on-Avon School of Weaving for Crippled Girls. Singer supplied a working sewing machine while Raphael Tuck provided the calendars, a fact to which this firm continually referred in the postcards they published of the contents of the house.

Lapis lazuli and marble were used with great extravagance for the floors of the reception areas and the roof was made from 3,800 tiny old Delabole slates. The King's and the Queen's rooms were decorated with great magnificence; the Queen's bed, for instance, is hung with specially woven blue and silver silk damask, with embroidered seed pearls decorating the quilted silk coverlet. Beside the bed, on a gilded cabinet, lies a book and a bunch of violets. The wardrobe is amboyna wood with carved limewood detail and is completely fitted with shelves and drawers. The handles and lock, which works, are of gold. In the Queen's bathroom is a bow-fronted chest on which stands a Fabergé Japanese tree set with diamonds.

The perfection of the house impressed thousands of people who visited the British Empire Exhibition where it was displayed, and inspired several women of the period to create model homes on a much less ambitious scale. Thamar (Tamara) Karsavina, the Russian ballerina, also owned a dolls' house which she furnished 'In the same manner as her own house, with the same touches of gilt and wine-coloured silk and formal decorativeness, and a tiny doll in a stiff pink silk gown, lying in an ornate French bed.' 'Yet,' wrote Ethel Mannin in *Young in the Twenties*, 'from delighted contemplation of the dolls house she will look up and speak of the essays of Lamb or the novels of Dostoievski.'

Despite the fact that many collectors consider Queen Mary's house over-contrived and completely foreign to the often haphazard arrangements which give baby houses their great charm, its creation led to the retention, creation and even restoration of many family dolls' houses that would otherwise have never survived. Exhibition houses were also made in this period by several newspapers, while a number of descriptive books popularized the Queen's house and its concept. Raphael Tuck created an album especially to house the set of forty-eight postcards of the house, which they sold at The British Empire Exhibition of 1924 and which can still occasionally be found complete.

Continental Dolls' Houses

There has been little interest shown by French and Italian museums in the subject of toys until comparatively recently, though no doubt with the increase in the number of collectors, more dolls' houses will be taken from reserve collections and more frequently exhibited. The Germans and Dutch have a traditional appreciation of miniature dwellings, and as the Germans in particular gained useful revenue in the 19th century from the flourishing toy trade, such items have earned their places, literally, in the museums.

We know from literary references of some of the lavish French houses that were the important gifts of princes but there is a large gap in the recorded development between the late 18th century and the period around 1870 when commercially made houses appear in some number; though dolls' houses must have continued to be made in the early 19th century, examples are almost impossible to locate, and it is the much later houses that are likely to come the way of the collector. One of the earliest known French houses was that bearing a date 1680 over the door and contained in a chest some six and a half feet long and three feet high, which was described by M. Claretie and was the property of a Strasbourg family. This house provided a picture of French middle-class life of the time and was peopled by dolls representing rather tough looking characters, not at all like the patrician ladies of the Dutch and German cabinet houses. The writer described the huge door with its heavy ironwork and a shuttered window from which visitors ringing at the bell that hung outside could be seen. The house stood in a cobbled courtyard in which was an apiary, a poultry yard and a sundial.

Monsieur Claretie also mentions the fine dolls' house that was owned by Marie Antoinette and was reputedly furnished with appropriate splendour. Her children also owned beautiful dolls' houses for which Louis XVI, himself a fine locksmith, provided some of the locks. One of these houses was said to contain a particularly lovely glass chandelier. Such references to actual dolls' houses are scarce, and far more commonly referred to are the model rooms which gave adults as well as children much pleasure, and which provided suitably frivolous gifts from one noble to another. A lying-in room was owned by the young sister of Louis XIII, who also owned another model room in which the scene where Judith murdered Holofernes was depicted.

Above:
This side view of the 17th-century Italian palace shows the exquisite carpentry of the windows. Museum of Industrial Art, Bologna.

Opposite:
Interior of a dolls' house of the 1890s, which belonged to the daughters of State Councillor M. Hallberg. National Museum of Finland, Helsinki.

Of great delight to generations of French children was *un petit ménage* which consisted of a box or container full of tiny objects often representing toy sets or cooking utensils. Similar gifts were given to Louis XIII when a child and catalogued by his chief physician Heroard. His boxes contained small pewter objects, dinner services and even fine Nevers glass toys, all items that could have perfectly suited the model rooms of the period.

D'Allemagne describes how, in 1675, a gilded room containing a four-poster bed was given to the Duc de Maine by Madame de Thianges: over its doorway was inscribed *La Chambre du Sublime*. The duke himself was depicted in a wax portrait figure seated next to Madame de la Rochefoucauld on a sofa. Other persons of note, such as La Fontaine, were also represented.

A dolls' room of great sumptuousness was owned by Madam de Maintenon when she was at the height of her power; a room which, later in life, she converted into a penitent's closet, furnished with a *prie-dieu* and a bed of bast as a sign of her repentance. In the house of Madame de Sevigné in Paris can be seen another model room in which a wax figure of Voltaire is seated at a writing table.

Mrs Neville Jackson, in *Toys of other Days*, written in 1908, commented that the dolls' houses made in France in the late 18th century came mainly from the Departments of Seine et Oise, Moselle and the Haut Rhine. Although most of the rooms referred to were intended primarily for display, there were play houses and rooms also available. Cardinal Richelieu as early as 1630 had presented the Princess d'Enghien with a model that was certainly intended as a toy: it depicted a mother lying in bed surrounded by nurse, maidservant, midwife, and grandmother. The Princess was told that she could dress and undress the dolls in the lying-in scene, but was not allowed to bath the baby.

Examples of fine Nevers glass are occasionally seen in Dutch cabinet houses and must have also found their way into such fine rooms as those described. This important glass-making skill was introduced to France when, as the result of the marriage between Ludovico Gonzaga and Henriette de Cleves, Ludovico became Duke of Nevers.

Italian glassmakers were brought from L'Altare to settle in Nevers, where glass continued to be made in the Italian manner until the 18th century. The small figures and toys that so delighted the young Dauphin, among many others, were made of blown and manipulated portions of glass rod. Figures made in this way were not confined to Nevers, but now tend to be so classified by collectors. The delicate glass threads from which the figures were made were wired with copper, except in a few instances where the work was unusually fine. Animal shapes are frequently hollow-blown, and thin glass threads, *verre frise*, form the applied decoration. This particular glass-making skill is more like lamp working, as rods of glass of different colours were softened and then wound over the metal armature. When the glass was sufficiently thick, it was reheated and then modelled to shape. Some complete groups of figures such as crêche settings were made in this way and are highly valued as objects of fine craftsmanship. The small toy pieces found in the better doll's houses are often mistakenly described as Nevers, and the description of the actual techniques used should help in correct attribution.

The popularity of trade and national exhibitions in the mid-19th century meant that more precise references to toys are found, and the published catalogues sometimes provided line drawings of exhibits. In 1844, at the Paris Exposition, a certain M. Kopp of the Rue du Temple, Paris, was mentioned in the '*citations favourables*' for a collection of toys and, above all, for his gay model of a dining room 'With sideboard and furnished table'. An honourable mention was also given to M. Colin who made 'playthings and households with care, which he exhibits as models'. A furnished kitchen and a dressing table were exhibited to show the perfection of the products of his factory. Other firms which made dolls' house furnishings in the 19th century included Merlin et Cie and Bane et Rossignol.

Many of the late 19th-century French houses have a whimsicality of design that makes a welcome change from the more sombre English and German houses. Collectors often attribute any house with fanciful decoration to France, but it should be remembered that many English houses that were commercially made exhibit a lighthearted touch.

Left:
The kitchen in the 17th-century Italian palace. The crude construction of this room is much more at variance with the reception areas than in any of the Northern houses. Museum of Industrial Art, Bologna.

Below:
A cardboard mill with moving figures and a sand-driven water wheel, made in the 18th century, but in 17th-century taste. This type of construction was particularly popular in France. Musée l'Histoire et de l'Education, Paris.

Right:
An 18th-century French nun's room with straw-work furniture. Note the relative comfort of the room and the number of icons. A weight-driven clock hangs from the wall. Musée des Arts Decoratifs, Paris.

Below:
A reception room in a mid-19th-century house, furnished in a typically French manner but with a mixture of German and French items. Musée des Arts Decoratifs, Paris.

Some help in the attribution of a house is given by carefully measuring
the essential rooms and proportions, to discover whether the craftsman was working in inches or centimetres. I have found this method of
help in confirming a suspicion that a particular house is of continental
origin, though it obviously can only be used in conjunction with other
factors. The furnishings of such houses, even when completely
original, are usually of little help in deciding a country of origin, as such
vast quantities of toys were exported from Germany, and to a much
lesser degree, France. Although in their own time dolls' houses were
made in the main for home sale because of their size, there is now so
much movement of objects in the antiques trade that a house bought in
the flea market in Paris on Friday might have been sold from a house
in Liverpool on the previous day.

The majority of the commercially made houses of undisputable
French origin are made of a peculiarly light wood, which means that
quite large houses can be moved easily. The two French houses in my
own collection, despite the apparent thickness of the wood, are feather
light. As the complete surface is painted or papered it is almost impossible, without damaging the object, to discover the actual wood
used but it was certainly ideal for the purpose as a perfectly strong and
rigid construction was possible. A few of these commercial houses
have engaging tower-like sections; others have working lifts while the
decorative balconies and verandas were almost an essential! The
example of a French house of this period at the Musée des Arts
Decoratifs, Paris, is a notable exception from these generalizations, as
its lower windows are protected by sinister bars and its façade is
uncompromisingly substantial. The wide front entrance, with the
panelled double doors, so often encountered in French houses, is,
however, much more typical.

A whole range of houses that were exported in some quantity was
made by an as yet unknown firm in the late 19th century, most of which
were given printed paper-covered mansard roofs. The double front
doors are again seen in these houses, which are often decorated on the
outside in soft pastel shades. Extra ornamentation was sometimes
provided by applied scrap-like flowers, lithographed panels or even
moulded relief decoration. Some of these houses lift apart into three
sections, presumably for ease of transportation, as a few are of a sub-

An attractive French house in fine
original condition from the collection
of Frau Verweyen. Note in particular
the painting to the rear of the
verandah and the elderly man with a
moulded beard.

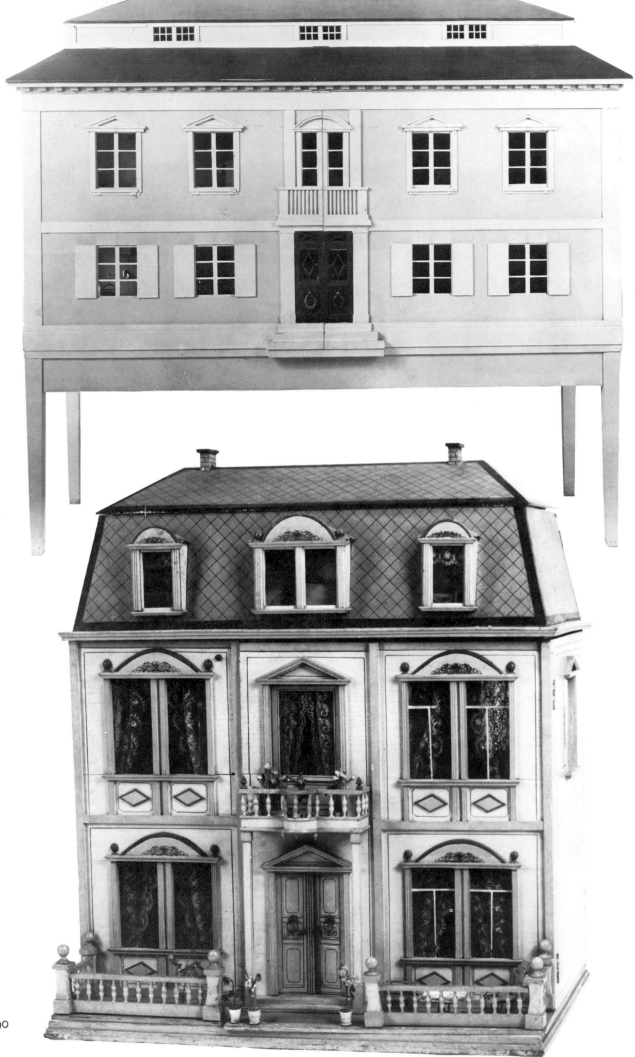

Left:
A joiner at Lidingo made this house around 1925. It was a copy of the Hersbyholm Manor at Lidingo near Stockholm. Nordiska Museet, Stockholm.

Below left:
Both the mansard roof and the double-opening front door are typical of late 19th-century French houses. The front of this house opens in two sections, and the roof also lifts off. Musée des Arts et Traditions Populaire, Paris.

Right:
The Grand Salon of the French 19th-century house, with its splendid matching mirror and clock. The miniature revolving photograph stand is very unusual. Musée des Arts et Traditions Populaire, Paris.

stantial size. The kitchen fittings, when still in place, are also particularly recognizable, as they consisted of a rather large-scale dresser and a large fireplace with an arched front, into which the range fitted. Both dresser and fireplace were painted either cream and yellow or cream and orange. Houses of this type are found in some number, and the manufacturer obviously used a limited number of basic units to create houses of varying size. Similar houses of the type were still appearing in the Schwarz Christmas catalogue for 1913, this American firm selling toys from several countries. Several of the houses share the same closely patterned flower wallpaper and the stairs are almost invariably a short flight leading to a mock door. Small pelmets were fitted over the windows and originally hung with silk curtains.

A range of silk-covered furniture is popularly attributed to France because of its light applied or printed flower decoration, the French appearance being further heightened by fringed fronts to chairs. Several types of metal furniture are also attributed to a French source, mainly because of their style, which is loosely based on Empire designs though no marked pieces have been found. The all-bisque dolls with short curly hair and beautifully made clothes are a particular feature of the late 19th-century French houses, though again no marked French examples are known. A range of all-bisque dolls of dolls' house size, and with moulded stringing loops at the base of the neck, are also popularly attributed to the French and certainly when found in original clothes do exhibit a peculiarly French flair for costume.

The French liking for model rooms extended into the 20th century and examples of the popular schoolrooms with their class of all-bisque dolls are seen in several museums and collections. As similar schools were made in Germany, their origin can only be ascertained when the original books and maps are present. Cardboard cut-out rooms and figures that were widely exported were published by Epinal, and at the *Musée d'Histoire de l'Éducation* is a most beautiful salon which was produced by this firm around 1900. A lavish Empire style room with printed silk gold-fringed curtains was depicted, a room that was peopled with effective cut-out groups representing men and women playing cards, while other groups engaged in animated conversation. The figures are all dressed in the costume of the 1860s and the whole arrangement is deliciously gaudy and animated.

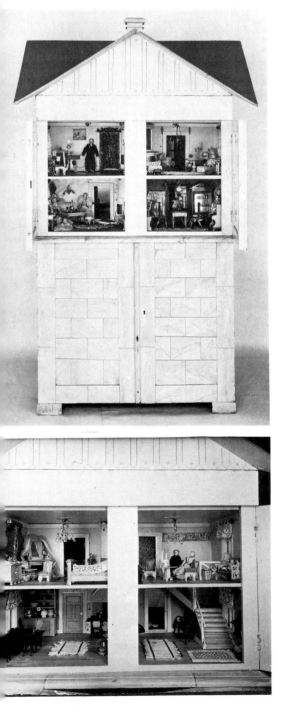

In 1976, the growing Continental interest in the subject of dolls and dolls' houses was reflected by several exhibitions, including one at the Hague and another at the open-air museum at Bokrijk in Belgium. At the Bokrijk exhibition, several houses were shown, including a charming two-roomed French house with a blue-painted roof. This house was obviously intended for children used to a warm climate, as the upstairs room led to a generous balcony furnished with bentwood chairs, while a similar area downstairs boasted a painted mural of a country scene on the rear wall. This complete house and its furnishings was still in a completely original state, even to the printed floor papers, and the silk, lace-appliquéd curtains. The general air of the house with its blue silk upholstered furniture was completely French, though the furnishings of the main living room downstairs were very much of German origin. The house contained several typically French all-bisque dolls and a few from Germany, including an old man with a moulded long white beard and twinkling blue glass eyes. An elderly lady with a lined face and similar eyes was obviously from the same series of dolls. The exterior of the cream-painted house, with its decorative moulding and neat dormer window was completely French in appearance and admirably set off the fussy interior.

At the same exhibition was shown a very unusual 19th-century German house with a bell on the roof, whose rope hung in the upstairs room. Inside the tower-like house there was only one room up and down, and the roof of the upper was domed, giving a completely unique effect. Behind this upstairs chamber, furnished as a living room, was a balcony that communicated with the ground floor by an entrancing spiral staircase. Among the furnishings was an unusual hanging key cupboard, still with its original filigree keys, of the gilt decorated imitation rosewood known to collectors as Walterhausen or 'Dolls Duncan Phyffe' and the only example of this particular model yet seen. Despite being well constructed, this house is surely a folly among dolls' houses, with its removable roof and decorative boarding, reminiscent of the balustrades in the Nürnberg houses, across the front of the upstairs room.

Much more conventionally Germanic was a dark brown house, almost every area of which was independently opening, making an amusing toy but, usually, an unsatisfactory collectors' piece, as it is almost impossible to accommodate a house that needs to be viewed from all sides in a modern room. The house, which dated from the late 19th century, was painted and varnished a dark brown and the façade, with cursive gables of a rather Dutch effect, was provided with both genuine and mock windows. The house was so rambling and complicated, with its small rooms and interconnecting corridors, that a

Above:
Detail of a room in Hersbyholm
Manor showing the Christmas tree
with parcels under its branches. The
parent dolls, with bisque heads, sit at
a table. Nordiska Museet, Stockholm.

Below:
The dining room of a house of the
1890s, which once belonged to the
daughter of State Councillor M.
Hallberg. The furniture was made at
M. Nordensvan's toy factory in
Kuopio. The small pieces are of
German origin. National Museum of
Finland, Helsinki.

Right:
The kitchen of the Hallberg house,
showing a particularly well-equipped
range. The kitchen is interesting, as
it is so typically Swedish. National
Museum of Finland, Helsinki.

Above:
Group of dolls' house furniture made
at M. Nordensvan's toy factory at
Kuopio in the 1890s. National
Museum of Finland, Helsinki.

Below:
A cardboard house with lavish surface
ornamentation made about 1840.
The house, which is 28 inches in
height, has a one-roomed interior
containing a sofa, chairs and tables,
a brass chandelier and a paper
carpet. Nordiska Museet, Stockholm.

complete shop contained on the ground floor of one wing was at first
unnoticed. A shop window was provided on each of the side walls of
the wing and the complete front of the area removed to reveal the
interior with the appropriate shelves and counters. Although the actual
furnishings of the house were not particularly interesting, the house
was arresting because of its typically heavy 19th-century Germanic
appearance.

The Nordiska Museet in Stockholm owns about thirty dolls' houses,
among which are several of the cabinet type, though not anything like
as fine as those in Nürnberg and Holland. The illustrated manor
house, with its strange tiered shape and in typical Northern style, with
the storerooms on the ground floor and the kitchen and living rooms
above, is again of interest as so obviously Scandinavian. It is also of
interest as, despite its late 17th century origin, it was completely in
the idiom of a play house rather than a collector's cabinet. The Dansk
Folkmuseum at Copenhagen also contains a number of houses, a few
of which date from the 18th century.

In Nürnberg, the Spielzeugmuseum displays several Continental
houses and rooms, all of which are furnished, though in several cases,
particularly in the rooms, the contents are later than the structures.
These model rooms are a particularly European toy and not encountered very often in England, where complete houses were
obviously preferred. One set, made between 1860 and 1865, represents
a large living room with a small bedroom; all the wallpapers are original,
though obviously intended for a normal house rather than a model, as
the scale is so large. The floor is covered with a printed leathercloth.
In the living room hang attractively coloured filigree pictures with
glass, while in a metal and wire doll's wheelchair sits a wan, blonde-

haired German boy doll looked after by his bisque-headed father. A set of commercial pieces made of gold-embossed card and panels of Berlin woolwork are also included in the setting. Although of fragile construction because of their card frames, these pieces must have proved costly to make, because of the small hand-stitching. A face screen, wall tidy and, in the bedroom, a much larger fire screen were all made in the same way. A set of hanging shelves made of threaded beads was seen on another wall, a set that is typical of many seen in European houses of this period. In the bedroom is a round, cream card stove that could have come from the same source as the face and fire screens.

Particularly 19th century are the rooms contained in children's books that could be opened to reveal different rooms, and the characters and furnishings pulled forward on tabs. The Spielzeugmuseum contains a very colourful example dating to 1908 that was entitled *The Doll's House. A Festival Gift for Good Girls* written by Lothar Meggendorfer and printed by J. F. Schreiber, Esslingen. This book was particularly effective as a toy, as the whole series of rooms could be opened out and viewed at once, and each was provided with a floor that folded forward. The scenes included a kitchen, a garden, a shop and a parlour and each room was provided with figures and pieces of furniture that could be pulled forward from the background.

Another, more realistic, set of rooms dates to just before the First World War, and a bathroom, bedroom, and dining-room are shown. The bathroom, by this time essential even in a set of rooms, was provided with Delft-tiled walls and a magnificent beaded lampshade while the washbasin that was fixed to the wall was supplied by a tank at the back. The wooden lavatory was supplied with neat squares of newspaper. A curtain could here be drawn across for privacy! The bedroom was furnished with the gold-lined white-painted furniture so often encountered in English doll's houses of the period. Printed tin pictures illustrate scenes of children at play. The dining-room is also of interest as it leads to another room at the back, an arrangement very rarely seen in model rooms as access would obviously present difficulties. In this small anteroom, a Christmas tree is displayed on a table, while dolls and doll's high chairs and prams stand about, obviously waiting for Christmas day.

The Spielzeugmuseum also owns a charming 19th-century dolls' house that is probably of French origin and is of the type that lifts apart in two sections. Again in the manner of so many French commercial houses, the upper and lower halves of the façade open separately and there is also the staircase that ends suddenly at a back wall. This house is effective because of the delicate light-red printed

Though very similar in concept to the Dutch cabinet houses, this example of about 1740 is of Swedish origin. The well-made furnishings include some fine silver and pewter pieces. On the third floor is a dancing room. Nordiska Museet, Stockholm.

decorative panels on the façade and the lightheartedly French metal balcony that is again so very typical. The conventional arrangement that places the bedroom upstairs is abandoned here, and the bedroom is next to the kitchen and separated only by the front stairs and hall. The house is furnished with several pieces of imitation rosewood furniture, among which is an effective tall and narrow display cabinet. This rosewood furniture, so popular among dolls' house collectors, was made over a considerable period, as it is seen in the original furnishings of houses dating from the early 1830s to 1905. The actual maker is as yet unidentified, but the quality is similar to that produced by the well-respected firm of Schneegass & Soehne of Walterhausen, who made the finest of Edwardian furniture. Although toymen's catalogues of the Edwardian period are available, in which illustrations of their contemporary work can be seen, earlier catalogues are as yet unavailable, though eventually it must be possible to trace the positive maker.

Dolls' rooms were still popular toys in Germany in the early 20th century, though the general standard was by then very much in decline. One more interesting example at the Spielzeugmuseum is skilfully made with marquetry panels not only on the floors but also on the actual furniture so that a good unified effect was achieved, despite the absurd oddities of scale. In the living room stands a Christmas tree, while on a table is a crystal wireless set with its earphones. A few older accessories have crept into the furnishings, which are of basic interest as they were especially made. The rooms are inhabited by bisque shoulder-headed dolls including a rather smooth, brown-haired man of a distinctly Noël Coward type of charm. An old lady has moulded grey hair and a very care-worn face. The scale of the furnishings of the bedroom is very amusing, as the bed is vast, as is the towering jug and basin with matching chamber pot, while the man who stands in the room is distinctly undersized.

Another late example of a much finer German craftsman's art is the house made between 1910 and 1911 by a cabinetmaker and furnished in a rather mild art nouveau style that is decorative and yet positively German. A stove that is situated in the heavily furnished upstairs study supplies water by means of a pipe to the bathroom next door; a

Right:
The façade of a house made in 1850 by Ludwig Adam Kelterborn, a Basel artist, for his daughters. Each section of this ingeniously constructed house opens separately. Historisches Museum, Basel.

Above:
Another view of the house made by Ludwig Adam Kelterborn, showing the more elegant rooms at the front of the house. The tradition of laundry rooms in the attics and storage in the cellar was still maintained at this time. Historisches Museum, Basel.

An early 19th-century Spanish or Portuguese dolls' house with a very unusual Chinoiserie lantern on the roof. The dolls are carved wood. Musée des Arts Decoratifs, Paris.

bathroom whose sparse furnishings are completely Spartan, including only a mirror and a bucket and chair in addition to the tin bath. In the kitchen the stove appears very small in comparison with the huge cooking areas of the 17th- and 18th-century houses, and space is allowed only for a dresser and a delft rack. A convenient stool matches the other furniture. In the roof is space for the drying of laundry, an engaging throwback to the attic laundry rooms of the Dutch cabinet houses.

Few European makers of dolls' houses, except when the house was locally or family made, are known, though in Germany Louis Lindner and Sons of Sonneberg are known as specialist makers. It was in the making of furniture that could be easily exported that the main German effort was concentrated and the catalogues of the various manufacturers enable many unmarked pieces of particularly idiosyncratic design to be attributed. Kindler & Briel of Boblingen, Würtemberg, made a range of furnishings including a lovely wooden washstand with bobbin-turned legs and china fittings. Schneegass & Soehne of Walterhausen in Thuringia was, in 1909, converted into a limited company, because of their swiftly increasing output and bought up another doll's factory in Walterhausen. Their agent in the UK was Bings of Ropemaker Street. After 1909, this old-established concern traded under the name of 'The United Toy Factories, Walterhausen' and advertised their wares in a trade catalogue of the period. 'We are specialists for

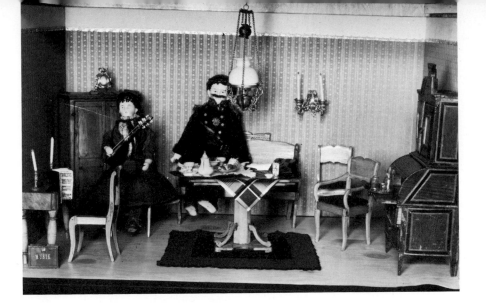

Above:
Two children, Barbi and Martin
Luther, played with this dolls' house
in the 1890s. In this room, a visiting
soldier sits at the table, and a girl
doll strums a mandolin. Some of the
furnishings are of an earlier date.
National Museum of Finland, Helsinki.

Left:
The nursery in the Luther children's
dolls' house, with its unusual closing
wash stand. Alongside this is a towel
rail and a sponge bag. National
Museum of Finland, Helsinki.

doll's house furniture of the highest standard. Bedroom sets, drawing
room sets, kitchen furniture.' Pieces were sold singly or packaged in
cut-paper decorated boxes. A very complete dining-room set advertised in 1910 offered fourteen pieces in a box, including a wall clock,
piano, an art nouveau table and a sofa. A writing desk of asymmetrical
design that was included was particularly evocative of its era, when
many of the conventions of furniture construction were questioned.

Many dolls' houses both of German and English origin contain
pieces made by the long-established firm of Märklin, which exported
its goods not only to Europe but also to America. This firm was founded
in 1859 by Theodor Friedrich Wilhelm Märklin, who held a master's
certificate as a sheet-metal worker. Their intention was to create
items for dolls' house kitchens, and his wife Caroline helped particularly in the organization of sales, travelling throughout south Germany
and Switzerland towards this end. Both Theodor and Caroline were
dead by 1893, and by this time the firm was in some decline, though
their sons, Eugen and Karl, who inherited the company, soon began
to expand its range of products and are generally known among toy
collectors for their fine trains and clockwork toys. It is one of the few
really old toymaking firms in existence, and has allowed some of its
early catalogues to be reprinted. We see in these pages that, though
different toys came and went, the production of a large number of
cheap dolls' house furnishings remained constant and that designs
hardly changed over the years, so that the flat pewter-like hot water
bottles that look so completely mid-19th century were still made some
sixty years later. In the earliest hand-coloured catalogues can be seen
the tin woodgrained buckets and baths so often seen in kitchens and

A dolls' house dating from the end of
the 19th century, containing individual
pieces from Germany, Italy, Spain
and Switzerland. Schweizerisches
Museum für Volkskunde, Basel.

bathrooms, together with an elegant piano and a parlour organ, both decorated with an applied bird motif. The thickness of their bases would suggest that these toys were made of wood. Also evident in these early catalogues are the shaped tin baths with one high side, slightly reminiscent of hip baths.

The 1895 catalogue includes an astonishing array of small kitchen ware, their range of moulds for instance including lobster, fish, pineapple and shell designs as well as the more conventional shapes. Cake tins, pastry cutters, iron and tin 'cake turners' and meat forks as well as cutlery trays and boxed sets of matching cutlery were all available for the model house. Tiny knives and forks were made with handles of bone, ebony or nickel, while bread boxes, Japanned bellows, brass and tin hot water bottles and a multitude of different ladles were offered to retailers. Five different types of iron were offered, including a very deep type for charcoal. Kitchens of a much larger scale as well as dolls' houses were popular toys, and many of the bigger items in the Märklin catalogues were intended for these models, whose contents were so quickly lost during play. It was for such kitchens that the miniature cookery books were provided, though these have often found their way into dolls' houses. Various pieces of furniture were sold, including kitchen cupboards and chairs in a wood described as Japanned maple. Their Japanned toilet sets are very recognizable, as the bases are made of bent wire with the basin fitting the top and the jug balanced in a lower ring. Many of the neat brush and mop sets on a wooden or card holder originated at the Märklin factory. Their 1902 catalogue illustrates a very pretty baby's bath with transfer-printed flowers on the sides and a similarly decorated bucket that stood on a wooden shelf beneath. The bath was fitted with a tap, so that it could be filled. The same catalogue shows a range of four fireplaces made of tin which are quite idiosyncratic because each has a small cauldron that hangs over the fire by thin chains. I have an example of the most ornate of this series in my collection, and this was provided with a brass rail at mantlepiece level and a similarly made fender. In the centre of the cream-tile-painted surround, a gilt metal angel's head was added and fire irons hang symmetrically from either side of the square fire opening. A series of rococo fire baskets was also made at this time as well as ornate metal stoves. An extremely progressive addition are the radiators of particularly interesting design. Their plant stands, shower baths with curtains, and 'cast iron' cradles, beds, and prams are very surprising in their wide variety and, judging from identified examples, very superior finish.

As in the late 18th and early 19th century, fine miniature toys made of wood were exported to equip baby houses, so in the early 20th century the German manufacturers were supplying mass-produced and much more ornate pieces in metal as well as the traditional wood.

An elaborate chimneypiece, 5¾ inches high, with enamelled and painted tiles and a copper fret fender and mantel rail. The cooking pot and the fire irons are also original. This item was made by Märklin, and was the most expensive of a range they were still producing in 1905. Author's collection.

American Dolls' Houses

American toy collectors are fortunate in having a native toy industry that is an amalgam of the tastes and skills of craftsmen who emigrated to the States from all parts of Europe. In the dolls' houses can be seen, perhaps most clearly, the influence of the Dutch and the English, though the furnishings were often imported from Germany or even France. The early colonists, arriving at Roanoke Island, off the coast of North Carolina, in 1585, carried among their gifts to the Indians a doll that was perpetuated in a contemporary drawing by John White of a little Indian girl clutching this treasure. It is probable that the children of early settlers were allowed to carry a few toys for their amusement, and certainly once fairly settled communities were established, elegant and frivolous items began to be shipped regularly from England to give a degree of sophistication to life.

A wide variety of toys, including dolls' house furnishings, were imported in the 18th century, a certain Mr William Price, Print and Map Seller, offering in July 1725, 'A great variety of fine looking glasses, tea tables and sconces, toys and small pictures for children.' The same shopkeeper was more specific in 1743 when he was able to offer 'English and Dutch toys for children.' An advertisement in a Philadelphia newspaper in 1785 for John Mason's shop mentioned 'Dressed Dolls, naked dolls and Lilliputian dolls, besides two new houses with gardens.' The dolls were almost certainly imported and it seems likely that the houses, despite their size, were also of English origin, as there is a great dearth of attributable American-made examples of this period. Though fine miniature furniture was made, in particular in western Pennsylvania and Philadelphia, there does not seem to have been much interest in the production of pieces small enough for dolls' houses, as early examples are as rare as the houses themselves.

The earliest known purely American house is that in the Van Cortlandt Museum, New York. This house stands uncompromisingly in the nursery of the old mansion, proudly exhibiting two dates 1744 and 1774. It has unfortunately lost its original furnishings though the carpets, which were painted on the floors, still remain. The house was made in 1744 for a member of the Homans family of Boston and it appears likely that the two dates indicate the births of the first two children to own the house, though without documentary evidence these dates will continue to tantalize collectors. The Dutch influence on this house is very strong, especially when viewed from the side,

The Rev. Dr Phillip Brett spent two years, from 1838 to 1840, creating this house. It was intended as a Christmas present for his daughters, and was complete even to the garden. The attic storey was added only for effect. Museum of the City of New York.

where a simplified effect of a canal house is given, even to a door in the attic where, in an actual Dutch house, goods would be hauled up from street or canal level by a pulley. Another example of the very strong Dutch influence is in the palings made of wood, which partly separate the upstairs rooms; similar paling is seen in the cabinet houses in the Rijksmuseum, Amsterdam, where this arrangement separates the utilitarian rooms at the top. The design of the Van Cortlandt house is simple but very practical, as two children could play with it at the same time. Extra furniture and dolls could be stored neatly in the two drawers that form the base and contribute to its stability. It seems strange that this is the only house of any note surviving from this period that is of certain American origin, as it seems improbable that all were imported.

The Philadelphia Public Ledger for December 1837 advertised Christmas and New Year presents that had just arrived: these included 'Fine toys, wax dolls . . . and furniture for fitting baby houses'. It might be thought that by this date the Americans would have made their own toys in quantity, but the German makers were able to employ peasant labour so cheaply and were so skilled at creating eye-catching playthings that there was, until the middle of the century, little point in competition. As dolls' houses took up considerable space when shipped, they appear to have been made in some number by native craftsmen before furniture was produced in commercial quantity. A fine dolls' house dating to 1810 can now be seen at the Independence National Park Collection and is believed to have been originally made for Sarah Emlen Cresson, who was born in 1806. It is reminiscent of English houses of this period with its twelve-paned windows and arched door. The carefully controlled proportions, so often seen in late 18th-century baby houses, are also much in evidence in this interior. As in the Van Cortlandt house, the floor coverings and even the hearth rugs are painted. The well-made cupboards fitted in the spaces on either side of the chimney breast in the downstairs rooms are an elegant addition, as are the neat shelves in corresponding positions upstairs. This is a curious arrangement, as the shelving would traditionally be expected in the downstairs rooms, for the display of china. The façade, that is provided with a lock, is of simulated grey stone with the interesting addition of miniature Green Tree Fire Marks, indicating, in a full-sized house, that it was covered by an insurance policy. These fire marks were very much a later addition by the

The drawing room of the Brett house contains some fine musical instruments and miniature books, some of which date from the 18th century. Museum of the City of New York.

Few dolls houses proclaim in uncertain terms both their date and the name of their original owner. Bessie Mitchell was given this 51-inch high house on Christmas Day 1879, when she was seven. It was built by a German carpenter employed by her grandfather. Lyme Historical Society, Connecticut.

doll's house owner, as one is very uncomfortably cramped against the original lock. This is the only dolls' house I have encountered with such an embellishment, though they were often found on actual houses. Fortunately a few pieces of the original furniture still survive, including a fine pair of four-poster beds of typical late 18th-century construction, and with bed rails pierced for the ropes that were stretched across, in lieu of springs, to support the mattress. The turned posts would probably have originally supported arched top-pieces to hold the curtains in position. The only discordant note in this elegant house is the 'Captains walk', a detail seen on several American dolls' houses, but which in this case detracts from the appearance.

Dolls' houses of this type did not necessarily depend on imported furnishings, especially for the kitchens, as pewter miniatures, for instance, have a long American history. The pewterer, Robert Boyle of New York, advertised 'Doll dishes, plates and platters' in 1781, while in the Philadelphia Museum is a miniature fireplace with accessories, dating to 1731. Among this group of early American pewter is a candlestick and, of much greater interest as only rarely seen in miniature, a candle mould. Tin equipment was also available by the end of the 18th century, from Stevens Plains and Maine, while the Patterson Brothers of Berlin, Connecticut, were producing toys that included miniature kitchens. Some of the better-known silversmiths also made small pieces though it is doubtful that they were intended for the furnishing of dolls' houses. Both Peter Oliver (1682–1712) and John Coney (1656–1722) are recorded as making miniature objects, while toy silver was also made by Elias Pelletreau and Ebenezer Moulton. Many of these pieces were too large in scale for dolls' houses though some eventually found their way into them, such as that made by the Rev. Dr Phillip Milledoler Brett, now in the Museum of the City of New York.

Another early 19th-century house, in the Shelburne Museum, has much of the detail painted directly on to the wood. The windows, fanlight, curtains and even the simple chimneypieces, are all painted in place, though the most charming feature of this house is the arched framing to each room. As the maker was trying to create his effect as simply as possible, these purely decorative arches seem a strange addition. Several of the early American houses exhibit this unevenness of quality which makes them particularly appealing.

The dining room of the house made at about 1836 by a Philadelphia cabinet maker named Vogler. Naturally, his main concentration was upon fine miniature pieces, such as the well-constructed table with its 7-inch chairs. Chester County Historical Society.

The Brett House is an endearing miniature building which was built by the doctor when a very young man in the sail room of the family shipping firm. It was played with by four generations of his family before it was taken, together with seventy boxes containing its furnishings, to the Museum of the City of New York. The house is enclosed by a sturdy wall of Indian red imitation bricks, with a lawn made of velvet, and a garden that includes a wide variety of potted plants. It measures some seven and a half feet long and, though not particularly elegant externally, is of a fairly complex arrangement—not for this maker the usual box type room setting! It is in its wealth of contents that the attractiveness of this house lies; a portrait of Brett hangs in the drawing room, while the Brett coat of arms graces the dining room, and there are many pieces of fine silver, early miniature books, Sèvres porcelain, and Bristol blue glass. Among the many 18th-century furnishings is a pine marriage chest with scenes painted on the sides while the musical instruments include a fine harp.

Possibly the most important mid-19th century American house was that constructed by a Philadelphia cabinet maker and upholsterer by the name of Vogler. The house was made as a setting in which to exhibit a cabinet maker's art in miniature and it now provides an excellent social commentary on the Philadelphia area, as almost all the accessories and types of furniture can be seen in standard form in the collection of the Chester County Historical Society. The importance of this house is underlined by the fact that it is the only American house to be included in Herbert F. and Peter B. Schiffer's *Miniature Antique*

A set of tin office furniture of about 1860, 10 inches high, made by Ellis, Britton and Eaton. The bisque-headed dolls are German. Wenham Historical Association.

Furniture, a book that illustrates the finest of pieces. The house, some eight feet high, has large rooms that form an effective setting for the furniture, which is in the large scale of two inches to the foot. An indication of the size is given by the fact that a ten-inch lady doll is perfectly appropriate. The atmosphere is quite unlike that of a play house, as the decoration is restrained and as logical as it would have been in a full-sized house. It is this very restraint that makes the basically equipped kitchen so disappointing, as the toy collector searches the bare walls in vain for the intriguing clutter found in doll's houses. The other rooms, however, leave little to be desired, as with the possible exception of some heavily framed pictures in the drawing room the illusion of an actual home in miniature is complete. Individual items, such as the four-poster bed and a detailed corner cupboard, are examples of the best American cabinet makers' art. Some of the larger pieces are made of mahogany-veneered pine, and among the greatest treasures is a long-case clock by Thomas Wagstaff, an English Quaker clockmaker who supplied full-sized clocks to American families of the same faith. Another fine treasure is a Tuckerware washstand set; this factory worked in Philadelphia between the years 1826–1838, and even full-sized examples are rare. The great interest of this house lies in the fact that it is so typically American in atmosphere and perfectly re-creates a house of the 1830s. The Schiffers' comment that good miniatures were made during periods when particular regions were prosperous and there was time for leisure and enjoyment; the charming details in this house, such as the steps at the foot of the bed, rare even in full size, certainly indicate that the maker had time to indulge in relatively fanciful exhibitions of his skill.

The American toy industry was well established by the middle of the 19th century, particularly in the making of tin playthings. Turners of Meriden, Connecticut, were utilizing scrap for toys in 1840, and the interest in their manufacture spread rapidly to New York and Philadelphia. An interesting model kitchen in the Metropolitan Museum is equipped with American-made pieces not only of tin but also of china, indicating a capability, even at this fairly early stage, of supplying their own needs even in the field of toys. Gaily decorated buckets, tea pots, and pails, all decorated in a manner reminiscent of English barge ware, were produced in Pennsylvania in the mid-19th century, and characterized by their brightly painted flowers.

The Patterson family of Berlin, Connecticut, had emigrated from Ireland to America in the late 1730s. Their interest was in the manufacture of tinware, a business they continued in for over a century. It was necessary, at first, to import the tinplate they needed, as no tin was discovered in America until the 19th century. Their toys were originally sold from pedlars' packs and later, as trade expanded, from wagons. Some of the men trained by the Pattersons carried their skills into other villages in the lower Connecticut valley and helped to develop the industry so that, by the early 19th century, there were several tinware factories in the area whose workmen sometimes travelled south in the winter and returned in the spring. The toys produced were of basically simple shapes with painted flower decoration that was often disproportionately large for the size of the object.

Francis Field and Francis, that sometimes styled itself The Philadelphia Toy Manufactory, is considered to have begun production in 1847. They advertised their products in the Philadelphia directory for 1848 and included tin chairs, tin clocks, bureaux and other furniture for doll's houses. In 1853 they were offering 'Clocks and other household pieces for the gentle girl to establish in her dolls' house.' Several firms produced tin doll's house toys as a sideline though their products, being generally unmarked, are virtually impossible to attribute. George W. Brown and Co. of Forestville stated in a catalogue of the 1860s that, 'To meet a want long felt, we have added to our list a number of tin toys expressly for girls.' Among the products listed were dust pans, coffee pots, cannisters, silverware, plates with the alphabet embossed around the rim, sprinkling cans, baking tins and sets of furniture for parlour or bedroom, 'The first imitation rosewood with velvet upholstery,' and the second 'oak grained'. Their complete tin kitchen was equipped with a water pump, stove and ice box! An example of the tin dolls' houses they mention in their catalogue would be an exciting find, as none are known to have survived.

Left and above:
The Warren dolls' house, which was planned by Mrs Annie Warren for her daughters in 1852. It was made by a Salem cabinetmaker, Israel Fellows. Note the Rococo chairs in the dressing room and the fine overmantel mirrors in the main reception rooms. Essex Institute, Salem.

Left:
The parlour of the Vogler house demonstrates that the scale is not always as perfect as might be expected of a craftsman. Most of the furniture is of pine with a mahogany veneer. Chester County Historical Society.

Below:
The scale of the kitchen equipment in the Vogler house is surprisingly accurate, and closely reflects the life style of the Philadelphia area in the 19th century. Chester Country Historical Society.

Architect's wooden model, 60 inches high, of a house built by Leonard Rosen of Philadelphia about 1876. The weathervane on top of the cupola is metal, as are the gas lamp standards. The sash windows all move and there is an exterior staircase. Smithsonian Institution, Washington D.C.

J. S. Stevens of Cromwell, Connecticut, included many dolls' house furnishings in their 1868 catalogue of iron toys 'All in the current adult styles and all in doll house size . . . bureaux, washstands, cook stoves, laundry stoves, Franklin stoves, coal hods with shovels, laundry tubs and washboards, sleds, . . . rocking chairs, cradles and dust pans,' give some idea of the vast range of metal toys available to American children at the time. Benjamin T. Roney, 'Tin and Sheet Iron Ware and Stove Manufactory' of Attlebrough, Pennsylvania, dispensed with such long lists of manufactures and stated grandly that they produced 'Everything in the tinware line that has ever been thought of.' After 1870, Hull and Stafford included dolls' house furniture among their toys. The pieces were simply made in two halves that were joined by metal tabs and made attractive by the decoration.

The tin dolls' house furniture of the type made by a whole range of firms such as I. F. Crocker of Rhode Island, and Stevens and Brown, was often of a very elaborate design, that would appear at first sight to be quite inappropriate for construction in metal; imitation silk or

The typically American bedroom of the Vogler house, with its unusual dolls'-house-size bed steps and a rare Tuckerware bowl and pitcher. The four-poster bed is well carved and a correct miniature. Chester County Historical Society.

The Brewster family dolls' house, dated 1873. It is made in the form of a simple cupboard with an unusual storage drawer in the centre. On either side are glass windows. Plymouth Antiquarian Society.

velvet finish was given to deep buttoned chairs, while a mock wood-grain effect was created in 'imitation rosewood' or 'oak'. Such pieces, if in good condition, are now very collectable as they are somehow more evocative of mid-19th century America with its great opulence in interior decoration than almost any other toy. In 1869, Ellis Britton and Eaton offered a tin office set that included an impressive desk, a table, a high stool for the clerk and, a typically American touch, a rocking chair. George H. Buck of New York who made 'Bucks Metallic Beds, the best selling line of metallic doll beds made', produced a piece of furniture much favoured by those disposed to 'Arts and Crafts', in the form of an 'Oriental Cozy Corner. A real new bunk for dolly. The only Toy Cozy Corner on the market.' Flora Gill Jacobs, in her *Dolls Houses in America*, shows this advertisement which illustrates a heavily draped and cushioned settle that relied on its metallic frame for its shape. The maker enthused about its black Venetian iron finish 'Complete with spears, battle axes, fairy lamps, oriental draperies and sofa cushions.'

Despite much patient researching among old catalogues and advertisements by American collectors, it is almost impossible to give a positive attribution to a particular piece unless it is marked. Edith Barenholz, in her book *The George Brown Toy Sketchbook*, remarks that it was a common practice for the larger tin manufacturers to provide parts for toys, and that entries in the ledger book of The Union Manufacturing Company, disclosed that eighteen shipments of 'Large and small horses in parts, men in parts, and ladies in parts,' were made to George Brown, of Stevens and Brown, between 1851 and 1861. Quite remarkable similarity is seen in catalogue illustrations of pieces made by, for instance, Stevens and Brown and Ellis Britton and Eaton, who both offered sets of parlour furniture in silk or velvet finish. Francis Field & Francis, and Hull and Stafford both advertised very elaborately embossed and Japanned furniture, which would now be extremely difficult to identify and collectors are now often of the opinion that there was some active co-operation between many of these apparent rivals.

Some help in the dating and attribution of tin pieces is possible by research in the Patent office, as the American makers seemed to register these with great enthusiasm, though obviously only the most idiosyncratic designs can be traced in this way. Some firms, such as Bergman and Co., who styled themselves 'Importers of toys', also made some toys themselves. Bergman promised 'To pay particular attention to avoid all sharp edges and corners ... We paint in bright brilliant colours.'

A writer in *Harpers Weekly* for 1900 stated that the pewter toy industry had been introduced to America around 1850 by an Italian craftsman, though it is now known to have started much earlier. The impressive parlour suites, 'Upholstered in plush and stamped with the most elaborate designs' were enthused about, as the metal pieces were still cast by hand, in brass and steel moulds. 'The pieces come out of these moulds in the flat and are then passed into stamping machines that produce at one stroke a perfectly made rocking chair or sofa.' In New York, Peter F. Pia had established a business in 1848 that ran for over a hundred years and produced pewter furniture. It is often difficult in these references to establish whether genuine pewter or some other type of alloy is actually meant. It is also difficult to distinguish between the genuine American pieces and those made at the same time in Germany, as the main difference is often only in the brightness of the metal, which is hardly a foolproof guide. F. G. Jacobs illustrates an advertisement dating from 1905 which actually shows a drawing of a dining-room set by Pia which does appear to differ considerably from the European white metal furniture, as the basic design is of a rather square and simple shape, though of course the work of this maker can hardly be judged by this single illustration.

The 19th-century American house most coveted by international collectors is surely that made, with a profusion of detail, by a silversmith, Benjamin H. Chamberlain, for his daughters Mamie and Millie, in 1884. The house was constructed secretly, in the best tradition of doll's house makers, in the silversmith's shop where his daughters could not discover his Christmas secret. Chamberlain really seems to have enjoyed the problem of constructing what must have been an unnecessarily complicated house, as he laid detail on detail. Eaves, balconies, and attic windows, though detailed in themselves, were made even more eye-catching by carvings and decorative metal railings. The final touch was a silver plaque, bearing the owners' names, that was fixed proudly to the door. The interior is packed with furniture that originated in several countries and was commercially available when the house was made. It is thought that the attractive

Above:
The Governor Ramsey dolls' house, which dated from 1887. The exterior is a simple pine construction. Minnesota Historical Society.

Left:
The interior of the Governor Ramsey dolls' house illustrates how a crudely made exterior often conceals effective work on the inside. The house was made for Miss Laura Furness in 1887 by the master carpenter. Minnesota Historical Society.

Right:
A house constructed in 1854 to raise funds for wounded Civil War soldiers at the Philadelphia Sanitary Fair. At the close of the Fair, it was given to Colonel H. S. M. McComb for his daughter Nellie, who was seven. The front opens in several sections. General Grant's name is on a silver nameplate on one of the entrance doors. Historical Society, Delaware.

Below:
Interior of the Philadelphia Fair house with paintings by well-known local artists. The circular ottoman or 'conversation' is a piece of furniture rarely seen in dolls' houses. Historical Society, Delaware.

chandeliers were made by Chamberlain himself while the soft furnishings were sewn by his wife. A house of this standard is surely the ultimate aim of every father who works in the winter evenings on a toy for his daughter, but how rarely is this aim achieved so splendidly.

One of the few dolls' houses that could be described as a commemorative piece is in the collection of the Delaware Historical Society, Washington. It was specially built for exhibition at The Great Central Fair for the US Sanitary Commission in Philadelphia in 1864, to raise funds for the sick and wounded soldiers of the Civil War. It is not a particularly attractive house nor is it very lavishly furnished but among its other idiosyncrasies is a picture gallery. The staircase in this nine-roomed house is particularly fine as are the marble fireplaces, one of which took a craftsman three days to make. After the fair the house became the possession of a child and was played with as a toy.

The number of American dolls' houses which survived increases steadily after 1840: life became more comfortable and the number of people with sufficient money to indulge their children with expensive presents multiplied. It is often extremely difficult to attribute a dolls' house to a particular country unless it is very fully documented. The task in relation to American houses is made even more problematical by the number of craftsmen from various European countries who settled and worked there. Houses that are home-made, or the work of a small local or family carpenter are perhaps the most difficult of this type. American houses have one great advantage over the British; they can often be traced by their architectural style to a particular region, a facet of attribution that is only very rarely possible in an English house. One that very closely reflects the architecture of the area where it was made is now in the Milwaukee Museum. It belonged to a child who later became Mrs Joseph E. Uihlein, and it is by this name that the house is known to collectors. Not only was this house painted in unusual colours, but the rooms were also given decorative arches ornamented with female heads in a classical style. Apparently this was a type of device often used as an architectural detail in the Milwaukee area in the late 19th century and certainly to European eyes the house exudes the atmosphere of this particular region.

Above:
One of the houses illustrated in R. Bliss Manufacturing Company's catalogue for autumn 1889. The lithographed upper windows and pillared door are both typical of Bliss. 14 inches high. Margaret Woodbury Strong Museum, New York.

Above:
The simple two-roomed interior of the Bliss house, showing the effective construction of the porch. Width 9½ inches. Margaret Woodbury Strong Museum, New York.

Possibly one of the most indisputably American houses is that
advertized in the 1904 issue of *Playthings*. Of lithographed paper on
wood and decorated with the heads of a deer and an Indian, it could
have originated in no other country. It was described as an 'Andiron-
dack Cottage–Novel Doll's House'.

Though many of 19th-century houses are different on the exterior
because of their regional style, the interiors are often very similar to
British and German houses of the period, as so many of the furnishings,
with the exception of most of the tin pieces, were often imported. We
see in their rooms the typical German wooden kitchenware, imitation
rosewood furniture, small French fringed chairs and the delicate pieces
of flower-decorated glass found in so many 19th-century houses. Tin
and iron furniture was, of course, made in Europe, but to nothing like
the extent of its American production and the chests of drawers with
flower painting on the front and parlour suites in pressed tin imitation
velvet are very characteristic of the American doll's house.

European collectors who perhaps know little of the carpenter or
cabinet maker houses of the 19th century have always heard of the
colourful lithographed fancies made by Bliss. This is a maker's name
that to many British collectors, epitomizes the American doll's house.
Yet Bliss was only one of several makers, some as yet unidentified, who
worked in a similar manner. So charming are the Bliss houses, and so
well known is the name, that almost every collector longs to possess an
example. American dealers even visit English antique shops in the
rather vain hope of satisfying one of their long list of collectors who
have asked for a house of this type.

The Bliss Manufacturing Company of Pawtucket, Rhode Island, was
established in 1832 and incorporated in 1893. Their range of houses,
all of lithographed paper mounted on wood, was popular from the time
of their introduction in 1895. The charm of these cheaply produced
houses lies in their wealth of colour and their convenient small size.

A most complex house dating from
the late 19th century and measuring
42 inches in height. The designer has
mixed almost every popular architectural device in the creation of this
engaging structure topped with a
small tower. Missouri Historical
Society.

A group of particularly elegant metal
pieces in high Victorian style with
cabriole legs and pressed-tin deep
buttoning. The 'Gothick' clock is
typical of a taste which prevailed
throughout the century both in
England and America. Museum of the
City of New York.

The maker also, obligingly for future collectors, printed his name on
the house so that the majority of examples are immediately attributable
even by the least knowledgeable. Bliss described their charming gingerbread houses as 'True to nature in all respects'. Their often improbable
architecture was described, a few years later, as 'Designed and modelled
by a practical architect'. Though several look fairly complex from the
outside, they are disappointing when opened as there is often only one
room up and down, though a 1901 catalogue describes a skyscraper
of 12 storeys that measured a sad 5 × 17 inches and cost a modest
10 cents.

It has not been established finally whether Bliss obtained the lithographed papers from American or European sources, but they do
appear to have been made to special order because of the characteristically complex decoration. The company seemed to have an inherent
dislike of any unpatterned surface, so that even the graining on the
front doors becomes stylized into a controlled design. It is only the
roofs that were economically treated. The Bliss name is usually applied
to a door or a pediment and unmarked houses have to be authenticated
by comparison with marked examples of identical design. Even here
there is sometimes difficulty, as the pirating of designs was not unknown, which is why a marked example is so much more valuable.
Some over-optimistic dealers describe almost any house that is of
lithographed paper on wood as Bliss but it should be remembered that
several other makers, such as Whitney Reed, also made similar houses.

The Bliss range included not only dolls' houses but also stables,
fire stations, warehouses, shops and mansions as well as the cottages.
All are characterized by their rich colour and decoration, utilized even
if a building such as a fire station might at first be thought an unlikely
candidate for such ornamentation. The houses are also characterized
by the bobbin-turned pillars that support the printed decorative ironwork veranda roofs. Most appear to stand on a lithographed stone or
brick base while cardboard dormers in the roofs are also typical. Small
printed windows on doors and gables are given a mock stained glass
effect, while the larger windows are made of mica. No house seemed
complete for Bliss without its veranda and railings, both usually
printed on, though in some the railings are of metal. On others the
pillars, instead of being bobbin-turned, are simply cut out and lithographed to resemble columns. As some of the houses measure as little
as 5 × 11 inches, it is not surprising that American collectors search
for fresh examples.

Left:
One of the most effective Bliss designs, with a small tower room and an ornate verandah, 28½ inches to the chimney top. The house is marked 'R. Bliss' in front on the second-floor door and just under the point of the gable. Margaret Woodbury Strong Museum, New York.

Below:
Three of the Bliss houses marked 'R. Bliss' on the doors. These highly colourful houses also appeared in the 1889 catalogue, which shows several versions differing in size by only a fraction of an inch. Margaret Woodbury Strong Museum, New York.

A small dolls' house—10 inches high and 11 inches wide—the decoration of which is lithographed directly on to the wood. It was made by Morton E. Converse, and on the back of the house is what appears to be the original shop price of 75 cents. Blanding House Museum, Wisconsin.

Although these toys were of a rather ephemeral appearance they were strongly made. In one of its advertisements the company claimed that the imported dolls' houses were 'unsatisfactory in every way'. Other manufacturers made houses that warped and cracked but Bliss houses were made of 'well seasoned lumber' that would not split. They claimed to make 'American designs to suit the taste of American children'. At first the interiors of the houses were lithographed but eventually mundane wallpaper was substituted for the more idiosyncratic design.

Folding rooms were included in the Bliss range of toys which also encompassed furniture. Most of their dolls' house furniture was not in itself of any particular merit but was made attractive by its effective lithographed decoration, not only on the pieces themselves but also on the boxes that contained them. Large letters of the alphabet and pictures of children at play, all of course in the characteristically lush Bliss colours, were the most typical decoration.

Toy folding rooms appear to have been a type of construction much more popular in the States than in Britain. Their obvious attractiveness, both to parents who could pack the toy away, and to children who could move it easily, would seem to have contributed to a toy that might have been as popular in England. Many patents were registered in the States for a variety of folding houses, but whether many of these were actually made is debatable. One of the earliest was patented in 1868 by Emily S. Russel of Plymouth, Massachusetts who laid claim to 'A toy house made of two thin sheets of material secured together, the outer sheet having swinging doors and blinds concealing and disclosing representations of apartments on the inner sheet. The space between the sheets being adapted to the movements of a paper doll.' This ingenious house was actually assembled by the designer, and a commercial house printed by G. W. Cottrell of Boston is believed to

have been made to this patent. On the back of the commercially produced house a number of verses telling the story of the cottage were printed.

A folding house that packed away into a box that formed the base, was made by Stirn and Lyon of New York in the 1880s. The detail on the surface of the house was pressure-printed on to wood and the pieces wcre joined by dowel, and tongued-and-grooved joints. Another firm that produced a house with a box container that formed a base for the construction, was Grimm and Leeds of New Jersey. Their house consisted of two rooms up and down and was given isinglass windows. Other ingenious houses included an example that was contained in an apparent book that when opened revealed a charming cottage with a small chimney and a neat hedge – all decorated in rich colours.

The complications involved in the designing of many of the complex patents seem to have attracted the American designers, though the products must have confounded many an unhappy child who was confronted with a structure full of tabs, dotted lines and minute instructions. Montgomery Ward, however, in 1894, described a paper house that was printed in bright colours on 'extra quality board' that could 'Be easily put together by a child'. In 1909 another manufacturer brought out a wide range of folding houses that included hotels, bungalows and 'Handsome residences'. In the 1930s Schoenhut produced 'Toy apartment house rooms' that were hinged so they could be folded away.

Of all the American folding rooms, those included among McLoughlin's range of products are the most popular. John McLoughlin was an engraver by trade and naturally became interested in the decoration of surfaces by various printing processes, so that his name is now linked by collectors with a wealth of gloriously coloured paper toys.

217

Left:
Exterior view of the house made by the silversmith Benjamin H. Chamberlain of Salem, Mass., between April and December of 1884 as a Christmas gift for his two daughters. 36 inches high. Wenham Historical Association.

Above:
The dining room of the Chamberlain house. The furnishings were mainly gifts from abroad given to the silversmith for the house by his customers. Wenham Historical Association.

Below:
Interior of the Chamberlain house with the dolls dressed by Mrs Chamberlain, who also made the curtains and soft furnishings. Wenham Historical Association.

A view of Coleen Moore's extravagant 'fairy castle', with Father Christmas and his sleigh flying to a tower. The highest tower stands 12 feet from the floor. The castle is made of aluminium, and was designed by Horace Jackson. Museum of Science and Industry, Chicago.

One of the most popular products was a set of four rooms, formed by slotting four pieces of card to a grooved centre. This design had originally been patented in 1894 by a Baltimore woman, and depicts a most elegant house with the whole of the wall and floor decoration printed on the cardboard. It is in the singing colours of interiors such as this that the rich atmosphere of the late 19th century can best be visualized. An elegant town house was here represented complete with its baronial fireplace surmounted with a stag's head. The use of patterned paper above the picture rail and the variety of decoration applied to the walls might be considered over-fanciful if they could not also be seen in interior designs of the period. In this folding room form, the line drawings, seen in contemporary women's magazines, come suddenly alive. Such rooms are of great interest to students of design as they show how curtains were draped, where carpets were laid and where *jardinières* were placed, all objects that tend to be moved about in a completely three-dimensional dolls' house. As furniture was also printed on the walls as well as ornamental items on sideboards and chimneypieces their interest as charming period sets can readily be appreciated.

The McLoughlin catalogue explained that the house was 'Designed to be played with on a table. A number of little girls may thus get around it to the very best advantage.' The set piece included parlour, dining-room, bedroom and kitchen. The firm's catalogue for 1896 described dolls' houses in two sizes, one costing 6 cents and the other 15. These were described as 'new folding houses'. A type that must have been made in some number, judging by the survivals, was the engaging 'Dolly's Play House', introduced in 1903. It was contained in an ornate box that showed the house in all its charming Empire style, economically constructed in strawboard and wood. Floors and walls were swung into position and slotted to the cornice. Fronts of rooms were elegantly arched so that the rather raw appearance a dolls' house made of thin board presents when open was avoided. The rich carpets, expensive mirrors, elegant sofa and opulent velvet curtains could be seen in all their extravagance through the ornamental arches. Such colourful interiors must have entranced their original child owners, though few in real life would enter houses of such perfection. Despite their obvious visual delight, the success as playthings is debatable. Presumably a few pieces of furniture in the same scale could have been added but as the rooms had such elegant printed accoutrements, odd pieces from the local toy shop must have looked decidedly shabby. For the display of beautifully-dressed small dolls, however, the houses must have been highly effective.

The chapel of Coleen Moore's dolls' house. The ceiling paintings are based on the illuminations in *The Book of Kells*, and the floor, designed by Bayard de Volo, is inlaid with biblical symbols. The stained-glass window by Helga Brabon shows scenes from the Old Testament. The baptismal font is gold, and the gold and ivory organ, with over 100 keys, was carved in Italy. Museum of Science and Industry, Chicago.

Some McLoughlin houses were much more restrained, as in an example the front of which when lowered formed a garden. This is a simple but ingenious device and one wonders why European makers of wooden houses failed to consider this solution when making a small house. McLoughlins provided great help to the collector by marking their work; the house with a garden for instance, states firmly 'McLoughlin, New York'.

It is thought that Clarke, Austin and Smith also produced a series of dolls' rooms and furniture in the mid-19th century while lithographed cut-out furnishings were made in several countries. Among those of American origin are the sets patented by F. Cairo and printed in 1892. Cairo's cut-out sheets did not only include furniture printed complete with tablecloths and ornaments, but also small details such as decorative wall tidies and even a thermometer. Cut-out sheets of German origin were sold in large numbers at around 10 cents a room, while a much smaller number of French settings were also imported. For the child who was skilful with a paint brush, the women's magazines provided cut-out pages. Unfortunately most of these were spoiled as collectors' pieces by the children who painted them, and it is usually only the uncut sheets that are desirable acquisitions.

A few folding rooms were virtually simple boxes that held pieces of metal or wooden furniture in place so that the product looked more attractive in the shops. Boxed sets of this type are rarely found, though of great interest as the packaging sometimes gives some clue as to the maker. Some paper furniture was given away in exchange for coupons or for a subscription to a magazine such as *The Ladies Home Journal*, which, at one stage, offered 'Letty Lane's' doll's house of 'Heavy printed cardboard' that was to be folded into shape. The 1912–1913 issue also contained a small bisque doll to 'inhabit' it. Many Americans must themselves remember playing with houses such as this and as a collector I hope that a few of these ladies will write on their experience of such houses as toys, so that toy historians of the future will not have to rely on surmise to discover whether a particular design made a successful toy.

Dolls' house furnishings such as 'Colonial pewter tea sets' and pieces of metal and wooden furniture were frequently given away as advertisement gifts, though unfortunately few were marked in any way. One manufacturer solved both his packaging and gift problems in the 1890s by placing his product in a container that became a dolls' house. Dunhams Coconut dolls' house was simply a container that was divided into four compartments each lithographed to represent a room. The outside of the box was also covered with lithographed paper, representing bricks. With an eye to future business, a packet of Dunhams coconut was printed on a shelf in the kitchen. This was quite a long-term advertisement, as individual pieces of furniture were to be obtained by sending off cake trade marks. Despite what must have been a widespread sale, few of these houses have survived, presumably because they were so cheaply made that the parents threw them away when no longer played with.

This house was given to the comedienne Zasu Pitts as a child, in about 1905. It is known as the 'Ramshackel Inn' (*sic*) after the title of a play. The furnishings date from several different periods, and include pictures of the comedienne as she appeared in various roles. Shelburne Museum, Vermont.

Fanny Hayes, daughter of President Rutherford B. Hayes, was given this house, one of her favourite toys, in February 1878. It was made by George C. Brown, a carpenter and contractor of Baltimore, Maryland. Rutherford B. Hayes Library, Ohio.

Dolls' houses were among the vast number of toys of all descriptions produced by Morton E. Converse. It is Converse who is said to have made Winchendon, Massachusetts into the 'Nürnberg of America'. The name of the firm changed several times, from Mason and Converse before 1883 to the Converse Toy and Woodware Company in that year. After several more changes it became, in 1905, Morton E. Converse & Son. Converse, who had originally made fruit boxes, is said to have almost strayed into toy production after making his daughter a table out of a collar box. His original idea was for a collar box that contained legs that converted it into a dolls' tea table; pieces of a wooden tea set were to be included. He is said to have used scrap materials left over from the making of large toys for dolls' house furniture, a range which he added to until it became the biggest in the country.

The early Converse houses are lithographed directly to the wood and are considerably less frivolous than those made by Bliss. Part of the charm of these houses lies in such detail as a cat that sits in perpetuity staring out from an attic window. Downstairs, two staid and printed ladies survey the world. The exterior decoration is rather more geometric than that on the Bliss houses and is reminiscent of the stencil type decoration seen on mid-19th century German Noah's Arks, this similarity being particularly noticeable in the stock farm they produced.

The basic dolls' house was simple and was composed of two columns, a veranda and windows, printed on a front that was hinged, while the interior was made attractive by printed decoration. In many examples the maker's name was printed on the border of a carpet. It is thought by American collectors that Converse and Cass of Athol, who worked quite near, engaged in some trading of parts, as it would appear that very similar lines were manufactured by both these companies. In 1913, 'Perfect models printed directly on wood by our new three-colour process' were sold. The advertisement related to bungalows that were available in five sizes. In 1931 the 'Realy Truly Doll House' (*sic*), made of fibre board and wood made its appearance. The house could be further equipped with the 'Realy Truly Doll Furniture'! This was claimed to be made of 'Beautiful mahogany woods, gum and walnut'. Converse even supplied miniature versions of packaged food for the fridges he made for the houses. The 'Realy Truly' range appears to have been among the last products of the firm as it went out of business in the 1930s. Though the Converse houses have less appeal than those by Bliss, the early types are eagerly sought because of their rarity value.

Though European collectors think of American dolls' house furnishings particularly in the context of the lithographed and tin range, individual pieces of very fine quality furniture were produced, in particular by The Tower Guild. The Guild, established in the late

The interior of Fanny Hayes' house was restored in 1960 and wired for electricity. None of the original furnishings have survived, and the house was refurnished with old pieces recently collected. Rutherford B. Hayes Library, Ohio.

1830s, endeavoured to pool the work of craftsmen in various fields in order to offer a more varied range of toys than could be offered by any individual. William S. Towers, said to be the founder of the toy industry in America, grouped craftsmen such as Cushing, Litchfield, Wilding and Jacob around him to form The Tower Toy Company, of South Hingham, Massachusetts. William Tower was a carpenter who also made wooden toys; Joseph Jacobs, who according to the McLintocks owned a hatchet factory, made toy tools and other novelties. Loring Cushing, who joined in 1861 made doll's beds, cradles and furniture. Some of his marked pieces are actually toy rather than dolls' house size but occasionally smaller pieces appear. F. G. Jacobs, in her book on dolls' houses, illustrates a small card table that bears the maker's label of Samuel Hersey – a founder member of the guild. Known examples of the guild's work are of exceptional quality and consequently much searched for by collectors, not only of toys but also of miniatures. Even during its period of activity, their work was highly thought of so that at the Exposition Universelle Internationale in Paris in 1878, the Tower Toy Company was one of only four American toymakers to exhibit. The French minister of commerce thought the toys beautifully made but too expensive in comparison with similar articles made in France.

Below right:
This house was made in 1877 by Maddison Magruder, a Washington carpenter-contractor, at a cost of $15. The exterior is well made and very typical of its period. Rutherford B. Hayes Library, Ohio.

Below:
The simple interior of the unfurnished house made by Maddison Magruder. Rutherford B. Hayes Library, Ohio.

Possibly the guild's most attractive products were the grandfather clocks that were made by Daniel Litchfield; these appeared to work as he set cheap watches in the faces. The guild continued to produce well-made furniture into the 20th century, though by this time it was run by Griswold of New York. *American Homes* and *House Beautiful* in 1912 and 1915, commented on the colonial style furniture made by Ralph T. Jones, one of the last well-known makers.

The fretwork craze of the 1870s and 80s caused a great increase both in England and in America of the output of home-made dolls' furnishings. A certain H. L. Wilde of New York revived the craft at this time and sold patterns, saws and accessories for models. Despite the large home production by this method a quantity of fretwork furniture seems to have been commercially made also.

American manufacturers in the late 19th century show far more imagination than the European in the variety of materials thought suitable for the construction of houses. In 1869 'Large houses of tin, painted to imitate brownstone' could be bought for $40, while in 1913 a silver wicker house was offered. Some of the luxury houses sold by Schwarz from their Fifth Avenue toy shop were fitted with electric lights just before the First World War, while other houses from about the same time boasted a bathroom. Some were quite good pieces of miniature plumbing, with a water tank in the roof that supplied not only the bathroom but the kitchen tap as well. Another advertisement of 1920 offered a house with a magic floor 'that moved the dolls around the house', while in 1928 a house was provided with a swimming pool, changing room and a shower that worked. A 1940s house even had an escalator. The rather economical houses of the present time sound drab in comparison.

The women's magazines carried advice on the making of houses from all sorts of materials that could be found in the home. The illustrations of such houses often look very splendid but must have provided much disappointment when the child attempted to copy it. The building blocks made by Crandall were suggested as a suitable material for a dolls' house builder, while another firm, French and Wheat of New York, sold a log cabin construction toy in the 1860s. One very ingenious construction converted from a doll's house to a nursery table!

Another famous American firm that produced houses was that founded by Albert Schoenhut in 1872. Schoenhut came originally from Württemburg where his family, for generations, had been carvers and toy-makers. It is not known whether the Schoenhut range of toys before the early 20th century ever included any dolls' houses, but in 1917 they were advertising 'Artistic high class dolls' houses and bungalows, new styles and Modern Architecture.' These houses were made of fibre board and wood and were embossed to resemble stone walls and roofs. These materials were chosen to that the houses should not warp or crack and were made to open at the side so that 'Children can easily get in at all the rooms. The front of the house remains stationary and therefore the appearance of the house is not lost by opening.' As the effect of so many doll's houses is lost when the front is hinged back, this is a particularly useful idea. On the inside the maker dispensed with the irritating problem of how to hang small doors from minute hinges and lithographed open doors 'Showing a perspective view of another room inside the doorway frame.' It was hoped that the illusion of a house that was full of fine rooms would be given; fireplaces were also printed on.

The Schoenhut houses were made in a wide variety of sizes and ranged from a mansion with eight rooms to a bungalow with only one. A strongly built house that would be 'More beautiful and Durable than the fine imported dolls' houses'was aimed at and the firm continued to market the same designs for some time with very little change. Once a design was popular the makers saw little point in change for its own sake. A similar continuance of old designs is seen in the catalogues of the producers of furniture, who often continued to sell identical pieces over a twenty-year period.

The 1927 Schoenhut catalogue is depressing, as the interesting perspective views were dispensed with and rather ordinary wallpapers substituted. New additions included window boxes and shutters, while the gardens could be provided with a shrubbery, trees, garage and a car. After 1928 they began to produce their own furniture and houses could be purchased completely furnished. This furniture is not as yet of any great interest to collectors as it is comparatively recent, though no doubt will be more appreciated in the future.

Another company whose work is of interest, though of minimal aesthetic appeal, is that made by Dowst Brothers of Chicago and sold as 'Tootsietoy Furniture'. In a 1923 advertisement they claimed 'All the strength of metal, all the beauty of wood–the newest and most complete line of all metal doll house furniture.' These pieces were faithful copies of the furnishings bought by middle-class parents– little here of the grandeur of the McLoughlin houses that must have inspired many a child to live in such a home herself one day. The 1920s house was such as the child lived in herself and this is possibly why houses of the period now hold relatively little magic.

After 1925 Tootsietoy houses were also marketed and included a washable mansion in heavy book board. A Spanish house with elegant mannered decoration has appeal though some of the furnishings, such as an all metal three-piece suite in imitation leopard skin, hardly lives up to the graciousness of such a building. Despite the fact that such houses are of a comparatively recent date, they are avidly collected, while in Europe toys of a similar date are still very lightly considered.

In the early 20th century, adults on both sides of the Atlantic began to consider dolls' houses in a new light and their artistic potential was re-examined to such a degree that even the advertisers of toy houses began to place more importance on the tastefulness of their products. One manufacturer claimed in 1919 that a leading country house architect designed his dolls' houses while another, in 1932, engaged unemployed draughtsmen and designers to build grand houses, no doubt in the hope that the more elegant products would appeal to parents. In 1900 a Chicago lady was featured in *House Beautiful* as a builder of houses that were replicas of the homes of famous people.

One of the adults who became fascinated with model houses was a Canadian, Percy Bland who, working from a print of an American country house, recreated it in miniature. The best known American adult to fall for the lure of model houses was Colleen Moore, a film star, whose house is to Americans what Titania's Palace is to the British. Colleen Moore's house was made of copper and aluminium and stood, complete with turrets some twelve feet high. Its actual construction was supervised by her father. Harold Grieve, the decorator of the house, claimed that he had set it in 'The early Faery Period'. No claim to any sort of accuracy is made as it is a purely fanciful work moving in time from 'The great dining room of King Arthur and his Knights' decorated with swords and heraldic devices, to a scene from *The Wizard of Oz*. On the dining table in King Arthur's room is gold cutlery, all appropriately monogrammed. There are eleven rooms including a chapel that contains a fine gold miniature organ that appears to play. The chapel also boasts stained glass windows that appear a little ill at ease with the architecture which is a strange amalgamation of very divergent tastes. The mass of details, such as a weeping willow that really does drip water, add to the fairy, or nightmarish, quality! This house is Hollywood kitsch at its most engaging.

226

British Dolls' Houses of the 19th and Early 20th Centuries

In considering the dolls' houses of this period which are available in some number for the collector, the problem of origin continually arises, especially with regard to the furnishings, as so many items found both in British and American houses originate from comparatively few sources. The number of furnishings that were commercially made in England is relatively few and though toys are sometimes found with tantalizing labels such as 'From Emma S. Windsor. Kindergarten and Toy and Crawling Rug Depot, 50 Harrington Road, South Kensington', the piano so marked, with an applied gilt motif, was of a similar type to those produced in such great numbers in Germany and the lady mentioned was in all probability only the retailer. In British trade catalogues and papers of the late 19th century much complaint is made regarding the number of foreign toys imported, but from the pages it is quite obvious that all too few were made here. As the actual houses were large and cumbersome, they were only occasionally imported and the majority were constructed as especial Christmas lines by toy factories whose main production was of rocking horses, mail carts and models of contemporary transport.

A few dolls' houses were imported both from France and Germany and, surprisingly, a considerable number came from the United States. In 1908 for example, out of $750,000 worth of American toys exported $231,000 worth went to the United Kingdom. Among the American companies whose goods were imported was R. Bliss of Pawtucket, whose toys were especially assembled in Britain. Judging by the low number of examples found, it would appear that the importation of their very desirable dolls' houses was small.

In the early 19th century there was a vast range of attractive furnishings available from the catalogues, distributed by the agents of the energetic German merchants whose wares were obtained from the traditional toy-making areas such as the Grödnertal, Berchtesgaden and Oberammergau. At the folk museum at Oberammergau is a set of unpainted day beds dating to the early 19th century, and of the same design as those seen displayed in groups in the Nürnberg catalogues. Such pieces were made to the specific designs of the merchants in the various toy-making areas, and exported in such vast quantities that competition from other European countries was uneconomic. Even in the 18th century Hieronymus Bestelmeier of Nürnberg was offering a fine display of glass chandeliers, while in his 1793 catalogue was offered a range in which a fire could be lit to heat the water available

Left:
Interior of the house known as Darley Hall after the house owned by the donor's grandfather in Lancashire. It was made in 1858, and some of the furniture is believed to have been purchased at the Paris Exhibition. The stonework is painted on the soft brownish-grey exterior. The inside doors are simply made of painted paper, but are given door knobs. Many of the furnishings are rather out of scale, but are interesting because of their variety. Blaise Castle House Museum, Bristol.

from a tap! This piece was intended for a fairly large-scale model kitchen, but is indicative of the standard available. Small tin and pewter plates, kitchen equipment, papier mâché washstand sets and simple, painted wooden plates were all available from German sources. It was interesting to see the name of one of the individual makers of the delicately flower-patterned wooden plates in a Nürnberg museum, that of Wilhelm Mederer.

Several of the commercially made early 19th-century houses are at first disappointing after the splendour of those of the 18th century, but it must be remembered that there was an ever-widening middle-class market to be catered for, a market that tended to keep even the rather mundane houses that were discarded almost completely in the 18th century. Some of the early 19th-century houses are extremely flimsy, and a few were even backed with cardboard for economy. The finely made Regency house, such as that exhibited at the tiny Southwold museum, is an exception rather than commonplace. This house is very obviously a transition between the structures common in the previous century, with its pedimented façade and the simplicity of the Regency. This house was once the property of the Runnacles family of Reydon Grove, and is at present on loan. The front opens in three sections, each of which is locked to close the house. The original paintwork is a soft brown and the windows all have mahogany frames. Inside are well-made stairs and, reminiscent of the 18th century, bone handles to doors and skirting boards that are correctly made. The house is again typical of the 19th century, as it contains items with a date span of some fifty years, reflecting several generations of children.

The simplicity of many Regency dolls' houses is reflected in contemporary prints; one in my possession shows a very basic toy with three windows on the first floor and two, together with a door, at ground level. The lady and child shown are obviously gentlefolk and the apparently cheaply made house, in comparison with the other extravagant toys pictured, is almost surprising. I recently purchased a very similar house at auction by one of those lucky chances that every collector sometimes experiences. I had viewed a large house and its furnishings but when collected it was found to be accompanied by another, much smaller, house filled with inches of dust that completely obscured the interior. When the dust was removed, the house was found to be of the most exquisite craftsmanship, though of very simple design. Each door has its own moulding and a neat bone knob,

Detail of the kitchen range in the house called Darley Hall, with a Dutch oven in front, a pair of miniature shoes, and cleaning equipment. Ranges in houses of this date are not often made in such precise detail. Note the decorative tap handle and the boiler lid. Blaise Castle House Museum, Bristol.

Above:
Interior of the early 19th-century
house at Audley End, with its family
of wooden Grödnertals. The furnishings date from early to mid-19th
century. Audley End, Saffron Walden.

Left:
The Runnacles family of Reydon
Grove once owned this house, which
dates from around 1805. The paintwork, of a soft brown colour, is
original. The house is constructed of
pine with mahogany window frames.
The two sides are secured from the
centre and the whole is locked by a
key in the middle panel. 34 inches
high. Southwold Museum, Suffolk.

Opposite top left:
The well-made staircase and metal
grates are typical of houses made in
the very early 19th century before
fine detail was abandoned in favour
of the commercial approach. The
pram in the hall is of a later date, but
a good example. Southwold Museum,
Suffolk.

Wykeham House, made about 1865, probably by a carpenter, and first owned by a Somerset family. The original paintwork is soft grey, and the front has a lock. It is an unpretentious house, but the details are well made. 36 inches high. Joy Stanford Collection.

while the original wallpapers and floor coverings were intact. The small fireplaces were of that pressed tin so often found in Regency houses and the tin kitchen range was still in its place. Unfortunately, all that remained of the furnishings was a bottle jack, a pewter type cover, a dutch oven and a few cooking tins. In an attempt to simulate a fire, the last child owner had snapped several small Grödnertal dolls to pieces and these still lay in place, representing in doll-buying terms of today some of the most expensive firewood yet seen! This sad fuel is now back in position in the cleaned grates as it provides such a completely authentic period atmosphere.

Changes in architectural taste spread only slowly to dolls' houses, and even the popular Gothick revival of the Regency is only occasionally seen in miniature and scarcely ever in furniture. A notable exception is the lively Gothick castle in the collection of Mrs Vivien Greene complete with battlements, windows with Gothick tracery, and the appropriate atmosphere of 'gloomth' pursued by Horace Walpole and others. In *English Dolls Houses*, written by Mrs Greene, another house is mentioned that was designed in the 1870s by John Hardman, the stained glass artist, for his family; this contained not only Gothick furniture but also a chapel in the same style, with an altar and censer. A heavy dark-stained house in my own collection again reflects the late Victorian taste for Gothick so exploited by Pugin and manifest in the detail of so many suburban houses of the time. With its castellated façade and a sinister black-painted room, the house swivels on a heavy screw that runs through the stand so that the child could have access to back or front without moving the heavy base. In the roof is a locking compartment, presumably for the doll's house silver, as the main doors do not have locks. No attempt was made to work to any kind of scale, so door frames are as high as fireplaces and the stairs and bannister rail, though very well made, are of gigantic size. All these contradictory effects combine to create a doll's house with an attractive air of mystery.

The simple four-roomed interior of Wykeham House contains items from various periods of the 19th century. The metal 'bent-wood' rocker is particularly effective. The large built-in dresser in the kitchen has opening drawers. Joy Stanford Collection.

231

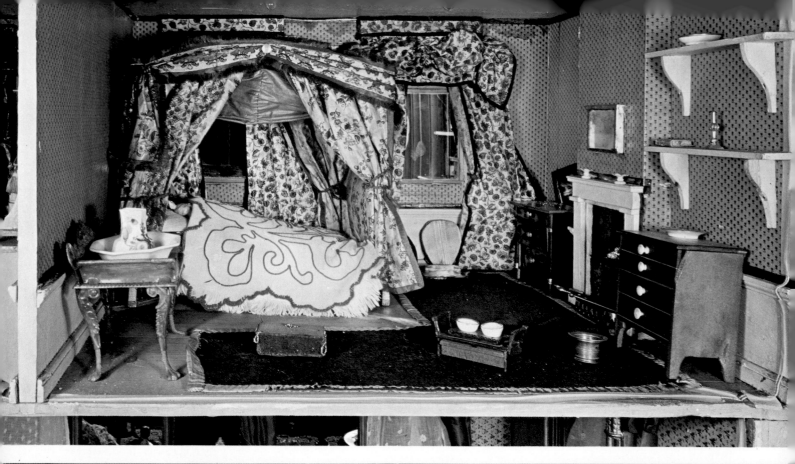

Top:
Bedroom of the Audley End house
showing the chintz-draped four-
poster bed and matching curtains.
Audley End, Saffron Walden.

Above:
The drawing room at Audley End,
showing the fine gilded overmantel
mirror and the unusual miniature
harp played by a wooden doll.
Audley End, Saffron Walden.

The dining room of the Audley End
house is furnished with pressed tin,
often described as Orley, and dating
from the middle years of the 19th
century. The impressive ornate clock
is probably of German make. Audley
End, Saffron Walden.

The Chinoiserie taste seems to have left dolls' house architects quite
untouched, except perhaps in an oriental fret to a bannister or applied
to the stand of another house. Some furniture was marketed in the
Edwardian period in this taste and included corner cupboards, dumb
waiters, writing desks and bookcases, all painted green and decorated
with gilt.

Again typical of Regency simplicity is the large dolls' house exhibited
at Audley End, Essex, and which contains echoes of the previous
century in its chintz-hung four-poster beds and impressive mirrors.
In the kitchen is a large hanging scale, again so typical of 17th- and
18th-century houses. Much of the remainder of the kitchen furniture
was added later but individual pieces such as the foot bellows are of
interest. One of the main attractions of the house is its generous compliment of Grödnertals, one of which plucks the strings of a harp in
the elegant drawing-room. Tin furniture, though common in American houses, is only occasionally seen in any quantity in British and the
Audley End house is of interest because of the number of pieces it
contains. Collectors often refer to furnishings of this type, with their
rather toffee-like finish and French Empire styling as 'Orley' though it
is again more likely to be of German origin.

'One of the few houses that is indisputedly a copy of a genuine building dates from the early years of the 19th century; this was made as a
copy of the Priory in the small town of Clare by a local cabinet maker
by the name of Mitson. This craftsman carved the family coat of arms
even on the miniature furniture that he constructed as copies of pieces
he had made for the actual house.

The most surprisingly simple of early 19th-century houses was that owned by Queen Victoria when a child and now on view at the London Museum. This house is a simple box arrangement with a dividing board forming the upper floor; it is without even the addition of a sloping roof. A careless decorator, even in early life, the Queen displayed the impatience that was later to try Albert. She papered over the windows on the inside and the house has an unkempt air. The kitchen boasts the usual fitted dresser and what appears to be some kind of much modified spit rack. Even in mid-Victorian houses the spit rack in a rudimentary form is seen, sometimes in the shape of a simple notched length of wood and probably always without the spits themselves. Most of the original furnishings of Victoria's house are lost and the structure is a reminder that not all royal toys are fine objects of great value.

A peculiarly English tradition is the estate or carpenter-made house which, despite its often modest construction, is passed down through the generations and added to by each so that the toy as viewed today resembles an actual home, lived in by the same family for a hundred years or more. Such a house was made in Hounslow in 1854 for a child by the name of Alice Chater. When she married and became a Robinson she took the house with her, again in classic dolls' house tradition, to her new home. Alice Robinson's eldest daughter was named Daisy and she inherited the house just after the First World War; it has since descended through the female line to its present owner, and all have added pieces to the contents. The majority of the furnishings were bought or made by Daisy and as she was a trained artist she found no difficulty in painting decorative panels on the drawing-room walls or in creating the tiny hatboxes for the top of the wardrobe. While the house was in her care she allowed the village children to visit and play with it and it is remembered in the family that it was at this juncture that the silver candle snuffers disappeared! Several pieces of glass, including the milk-glass candlesticks, were bought on visits to Paris, and the whole family was aware that she would be best pleased

Above:
The dining room of the Runnacles house with its marble and rosewood sideboard and miniature vases on the mantelpiece. These were not intended as dolls' house equipment, but are often included. The dolls with moulded bonnets are white bisque. Southwold Museum, Suffolk.

Right:
By the early 19th century, kitchens usually ceased to be as lavishly equipped, though there are a few exceptions. The rail for long-handled tools has here been utilized as a towel rail. The glass candlesticks on the mantelpiece are very fine friggers. The cook is papier mâché. Southwold Museum, Suffolk.

by a gift for the house. A small ivory man was brought back from China by her son, while the silver with which the house is almost ostentatiously supplied was all bought as individual gifts. She was a well read and amusing woman and the whole family was expected to share her enthusiasm, which even extended to her reproducing two family portraits in miniature. As I talked to her two daughters they vividly recalled the excitement engendered by the electrification of the house in 1939.

There was a great increase in the number of commercially made houses by the mid-19th century and though the rooms are frequently narrow and deep and staircases cramped, the general quality was improved as much thicker wood was again used, as the Victorians liked even their toys to be substantial. Lively surface ornamentation was also used, and though mainly machine-made, added to the interest of the façades, so that the dolls' house even when closed was still an attractive object. The very solidity of their construction was often their preserver, as once carried to an attic or store room they were left undisturbed as they were not easily chopped into firewood. Lavish furnishings were available, even from small country shops and the cluttered toys with their antimacassars, beaded lampshades, ornaments under glass shades and white bisque busts of Victoria and her relatives perfectly reflect the affluence of the middle classes of the period.

One of the most impressive mid-Victorian houses is that assembled in 1860 for Mrs Bryant and now in the Bethnal Green Museum, London. The house was made to her exact request by an unknown craftsman, and the contemporary furniture was also especially made. Though lacking the haphazard charm of the conventional dolls' house, her creation is of value for the way in which it perfectly mirrors an interior of the time. We see the heavily buttoned chairs, the bulbous legged sofas, the great wardrobe with its many cupboards and drawers and the magnificently broad half-tester beds, fit for the begetting of a large Victorian family!

The drawing-room, that runs across the width of the house, has that air of broad spaciousness usually associated with 18th-century interiors. On side tables stand impressive Chinese pots, while the rich effect is increased by the warm colours of the petit-point carpet and the foot stools, so essential in such an interior. In the dining-room on the ground floor is a child's high chair that is a well-made miniature copy of those in general use. The kitchen is small and its equipment modest when compared to the well-provisioned 18th-century examples. The façade of the Bryant house is also very simple with a balustrade at roof level and ten windows that are large enough for the contents of the house to be viewed when the front was shut: even the front door contained two windows with a further pair in the fanlight above. The front opens in two sections, the division going completely through the centre of the front door as in cupboard houses. In the integral base are two drawers for additional furnishings. As this house was an adult's preoccupation rather than a child's toy, the fronts could be locked to protect the contents.

Queen Victoria maintained the tradition of sending a dolls' house as a gift to the children of other Royal households, Princess Charlotte of Belgium being the recipient of such a present in 1848 and writing a charming thank-you letter. 'My dearest Cousin, I have received the beautiful doll's house you have been so kind as to send me and I thank you very much for it. I am delighted with it.' Unfortunately we are not told of the contents of the house as the Princess then goes on to describe her dolls and how she played at draughts with them.

The Rigg dolls' house in the Tunbridge Wells Museum is among the most impressive of mid-Victorian houses. It stands six feet high and is made in representation of the more substantial houses of the time. The problem of providing an aesthetically satisfactory base was solved by making this area an integral part of the construction and steps lead up to the portico, with its balustraded decoration, from either side, rather as in an 18th-century house the steps rose to the *piano nobile*. The Rigg house, with its arched lower windows and neat blinds, perfectly echoes mid-Victorian solidity and self-assurance. Inside the house this air of complete order is again apparent, both in its correctly organized

Above:
The simply decorated and sparsely furnished interior of Queen Victoria's house. There is a built-in dresser and a very generous cooking area. London Museum.

Right:
The house owned early in the 19th century by the young Queen Victoria. The front is painted bricks, with a painted fanlight over the door. The windows, at the sides as well as the front, would have originally made the house very light (the side windows are now papered over). London Museum.

kitchen and in the dining-room with its heavy and highly polished table. The large overmantel mirror in this room looks particularly effective. Upstairs, the draped half-tester bed is one of the most elegant seen in a Victorian house while the draped dressing table is reminiscent of those in 18th-century houses.

Many of the late Victorian houses were once avoided by the more serious collectors as the standard of workmanship, especially of commercially made examples, was considered poor. As toys in general have so increased in price a new generation of collectors is less concerned about fine craftsmanship and enjoys the eccentricity of many of these flimsy constructions with their cheap metal balconies, lithographed bricks and impractical decoration. Definite similarities are noticed between many of these houses and the number of actual producers was probably quite small. Firms such as Lines and Patterson Edwards

Right:
The house called Manor House was carpenter-made for Alice Chater in 1854. The interior shows the painted panelling in the drawing room. This was the work of Daisy Robinson, who also made the hat boxes on top of the wardrobe. The house, being mainly an adult's interest, is well equipped with silver, given to several generations of owners as gifts. Private collection (Georgia Palmer).

Below:
The very simple locking exterior of the house known as Manor House, gives little indication of the well-furnished interior. Private collection (Georgia Palmer).

Left:
Princess Mary of Teck, later Queen Mary, owned this house when she was a child. The mixed quality of the furnishings is typical of the late 19th century: those in the kitchen are of the cheapest kind, but the imitation rosewood secretaire is very well made. London Museum.

both produced dolls' houses and the larger stores such as Whiteleys and Gamages stocked both these and others especially made to their specific requirements. One manufacturer produced a complete range of very strongly made houses of different sizes but using the same component parts so that the same bay window might be seen on a small four-roomed house or an impressive tall town residence of the South Kensington type. This maker always supplied his work with a tin front door knocker in the form of a lion's head and the fire baskets were almost invariably made from the metal protectors used on wall thermometers. Some of the houses were papered on the ground floor with cream paper with green or blue lines representing large stone flags or tiles, while others were papered to look like brick. The manufacture of this particular line lasted for some years as some are found with their late Victorian furnishings while others contain items from the early 20th century. These houses are completely satisfactory from the collector's viewpoint as they are front opening and not too deep to be accommodated in a modern room.

A few late Victorian houses were beautifully made by indulgent parents, such as the very complicated model villa now in the Bethnal Green Museum that was made by Thomas Risley in 1889 for his daughter. A fanciful house of the period is represented with a 'cast iron' garden fence, an ornate conservatory and a neat coach house. The building is a charming mixture of architectural styles with deeply pitched roofs, an upper balcony and rather elegant downstairs windows. The house was painted in gold, black and blue, creating a very opulent effect.

The dining room of Darley Hall, showing a white bisque-headed doll with a moulded flower-trimmed bonnet taking tea. The original fireplace is tin. Blaise Castle House Museum, Bristol.

At the Holly Trees Museum, Colchester, is a very simply made house that is a complete treasure trove of miniatures. This model is complete even to its garden where bisque lady dolls are seen playing both tennis and croquet while a coach and pair set off on a journey. Few houses have so much incidental detail in their surroundings and the construction occupies a substantial area as not only a garden but even part of the home farm is shown. Inside, the house contains the usual wide assortment of items from different countries and periods typical of the majority of Victorian houses that were intended for children. The kitchen with its cluttered detail is typical of the best 19th-century toys and though the viewer is aware that the basic house is crudely made this is forgotten as the eyes feast on such an abundance of detail that new objects are discovered each time the house is seen.

The interest in arts and crafts engendered by William Morris and such groups as the Century Guild spread its influence even to the dolls' house and by the late years of the century cozy corners and medieval style furnishings were appearing in many toy boxes. With considerable misinterpretation of the intentions of Morris and his associates, many ordinary men took a renewed interest in the smaller home crafts and among several publications that supplied the new demand the most important was *Hobbies* magazine. In 'Frontispiece' by Marion Howard Spring, the writer, speaking of the 1890s – 'In winter my playroom was a deep recess on the landing. Here I had my dolls' house, made by brother Algy out of a large wooden stores box. He papered the rooms with pieces left over by house decorators and covered the floors with oilcoth. I cut out pictures of furniture from catalogues, pasted them onto cardboard and painted them. When Algy left school and got a job in an insurance office, he seemed to me terribly affluent. He bought a fretwork machine and made me some really beautiful furniture from patterns in *Hobbies*, which he took every month.'

Once a design, either for furniture or for a doll's house, was a success it continued to appear annually in the firm's catalogues. One house whose plans were offered in 1937 had a mock stone front and a fine portico; together with the gabled roof a completely 19th-century appearance was given. For this house the firm supplied a pack containing planed whitewood, mahogany, various mouldings and six

A late 19th-century house with an unusual double-fronted exterior. It was possibly made in this way so that it could be played with by two children. Holly Trees Museum, Colchester.

Left:
Exterior of the Rigg dolls' house, made about 1840 to represent a typical middle-class town house of the period. All the furnishings were made for it by craftsmen. The carpets are thought to have been specially made in Brussels. Tunbridge Wells Museum.

Below:
A group of five well-equipped rooms especially made for Mrs Bryant in 1860. The furnishings, correctly made and upholstered, were also specially made. The Chinese porcelain in the drawing room and the Doulton water filter in the kitchen are particularly noteworthy. Also interesting is the ivory birdcage in the dining room, which is lavishly supplied with armchairs for sitting at table. Bethnal Green Museum, London.

ornamental knobs – all for 8/6d. An even cheaper version could be made in plywood. Available on other pages were windowglass, wallpaper and hinges. Their red wallpaper, patterned with gold irregular blot-like shapes, is seen in dolls' house dining-rooms constructed over a period of some twenty years but was extremely effective. Kits for fretwork furniture were also supplied, those in oak with ready-cut ornamental motifs and a lighter wood looking particularly effective. Hall stands, tea trolleys and even standard lamps were all supplied to the busy fretworkers. In the 1920s and 30s, polished aluminium fittings were also supplied for bathrooms including sponge racks, clothes airers and a linen bin. Ground floors were provided with fireside companion sets, a letter box fitting and a metal mat. The influence of this magazine on dolls' houses of this period is considerable, and could in itself form the basis of a research project as the fretwork craze was pursued by such a variety of people.

Although fretwork furniture tends to be associated with amateurs a considerable quantity was also professionally manufactured. Audrey Johnson in *Furnishing Dolls Houses* illustrates a set made in the early 20s by Alfred Bowness, a craftsman who worked for Waring and Gillow. He constructed this particular set from tea chests and cigar

Above:
An elegant lacquer cabinet which was fitted as a dolls' house about 1835–38 by the wife and daughters of a Manchester doctor, John Egerton Killer. The interior has possibly too much order and control, but there are some good pieces, including a lovely overmantel mirror and a whole family of Grödnertals. Bethnal Green Museum, London.

Left:
The bedroom of Mrs Bryant's house, showing the high standard of the furniture and the attention given to detail, such as the beaded footstool in the foreground and the peculiarly Victorian wall-tidy. All the carpets were worked by hand. A glass-eyed bisque doll sits in bed. Bethnal Green Museum, London.

boxes. A number of German furniture makers also made use of fret-work-type furniture though the frets were more frequently used as surface decoration than for the complete construction.

As the size of many dolls' houses presented problems in storage, the folding room or house attracted manufacturers throughout the 19th century. An elderly Essex lady told me of one she had owned as a child that was made by her sea-captain grandfather in the 1890s. The house was some four feet high but folded into a large flat box. In assembly it was necessary to add the gables last as these finally linked the structure, which was front opening. As the unpainted mahogany structure was a work of fine craftsmanship, the children were only allowed to play with it and the rich furnishings which the grandfather had also provided when he was home from sea!

Among several firms producing cardboard folding houses in the early 20th century was Chad Valley, who offered rather insubstantial build-ings in their 1913 catalogue for 1/-. 'Each set comprises a large selection of printed card sections and clips to fix them together.' The house which they produced the following year sounded much more satis-

Above:
Even in the dolls' houses of the late 19th century, the lying-in room was sometimes included. Here a wooden mother doll wearing a warm dressing gown sits waiting for the maid to bath the baby. Holly Trees Museum, Colchester.

Below:
A late 19th-century house and garden. There is considerable activity in progress—croquet, tennis, farming, cycling and driving. Though the house itself is very poorly made, the general effect is lavish. Holly Trees Museum, Colchester.

Above:
The very elegant drawing room of
Miss Miles' house. The gilt furniture
includes an unusual 'conversation',
where visitors sat back to back so
that secrets could be whispered. The
walls are silk panelled, and the detail
is painted. The moulding is applied
and gilt painted. Bethnal Green
Museum, London.

Right:
The billiard room of Miss Miles'
house, made in 1890. In the room are
several bisque-headed dolls' house
men, one reading an 'Illustrated
London News', while on a chair in
the corner lies a copy of 'The
Graphic'. The chimneypiece is
roughly constructed from pieces of
plaster moulding. Bethnal Green
Museum, London.

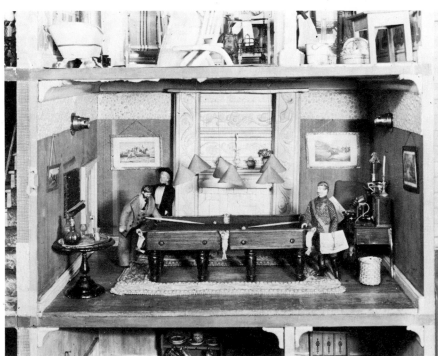

factory as it was described as 'A most realistic folding cardboard dolls' house with four rooms, printed in exact representation of a modern country house. Complete with walled in garden, rustic seats, etc.' The attractive container was labelled 'Dollies Home. (Her Country House)'. Gamages 1913 Christmas catalogue (now available in reprint), illustrates several constructional or folding houses including a lithographed collapsible village that was large enough to cover a dining-room table. More satisfactory as a play house, as it could open, was that made from 'Jean Jean' cardboard forms. These parts enabled a child 'To build houses complete with all details and inner walls' and towards this effect windows, outer and inner doors, gables, roofs and balconies were all provided. Three separate sets were available, the largest of which contained 320 single parts and 40 patterns that could be created.

Several of the conventional dolls' houses advertised in the Gamages' catalogue were made by Lines Brothers, such as one in a mildly Tudor style that opened in two parts at the front and whose roof was decorated by a printed clock. It was also Lines who produced 'The new screen doll's house, Improved' that was large enough for a child to play inside as it was constructed to fit across the corner of a room. It is of interest to note that such child-size houses were even at this time described as 'Wendy houses'. The screen dolls' house was provided with a locking front door and a neat letter box. The more conventional dolls' houses advertised included a good range that was described as 'Dolls mansions', one of which was completed by a distinctly American style widow's or captain's walk on the roof. This house, which cost 40/-, had a neat basement with two small windows almost at floor level. Another villa with four rooms and a staircase was provided with an electric door bell and all the windows were curtained. The design of this house is surprisingly progressive, and any collector buying such an example would surely date it at least ten years later. Gamages also sold much smaller lithographed houses costing as little as 5/11d and containing only two rooms. Such houses, because of their attractive colour lithography and conveniently small size, are now more sought after than the originally more expensive mansions and can now cost much more.

Left:
Late 19th-century dolls' house made of varnished pine, with the attic probably added for extra space. The stair carpet is of ribbon, with strips of gold paper as stair rods. Some of the floors are covered with printed cotton, and others with paper, while the wallpapers are hand painted. This is very much a home-made house, although the furnishings are commercial. Its great charm lies in the original creator's decorative work. Blaise Castle House Museum, Bristol.

245

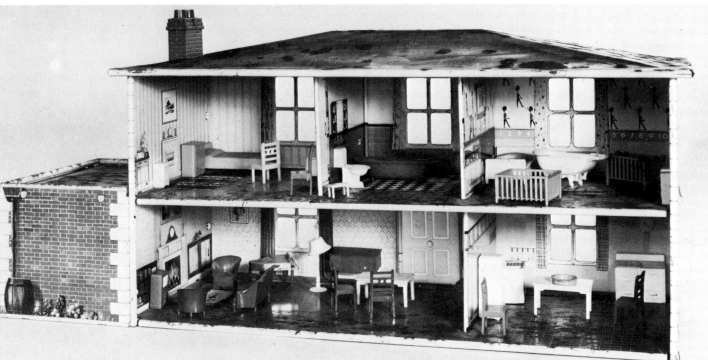

One of my own particular favourites among the late Victorian houses is that known as Miss Miles's House and on display at the Bethnal Green Museum, London. It once housed an artist's studio reached only by a ladder from the bathroom but this was demolished by enemy action in the 1940s! It is a detail that was only occasionally found in a dolls' house. The artist was an inappropriately dressed Edwardian lady with a lively skeleton that hung from the wall behind her. The paintings displayed on the walls, despite such useful equipment, were of the most amateurish kind.

This house is also a curiosity as it so obviously outgrew itself, and an extension was built on to the side, an extension almost half the size of the original commercially made house. Perhaps it is this obvious over-enthusiasm that gives the house such an attractive aura to the collector who knows only too well what disruption must have been caused when the kitchen was moved to the new part of the house and the bathroom moved next door. Besides the fascination of the basic construction the house contains an abundance of interesting pieces,

A stencil-decorated and simply made piece small enough for a dolls' house. It was originally sold at a price of sixpence with the cupboard and a drawer filled with Fry's chocolate. Author's collection.

Above right:
The schoolroom in Miss Miles' house, with a French doll and delicate metal chairs—probably also French. The schoolroom globe is metal, and over the door is an unusual metal-framed Rococo-style mirror. In the bay window stands a slope-top desk in imitation rosewood. Bethnal Green Museum, London.

Above:
The repainted façade of a house made between 1900 and 1905, known as 3 Devonshire Villas. The proportions now seem very ugly, though originally there was probably some painted decoration which helped to balance the arrangement of the windows. The fronts could be locked. Bethnal Green Museum, London.

such as a butler's tray in the dining-room and a tiny doll's house in the nursery. The dolls indicate the variety available when the house was furnished, and range from white bisque ladies with wigs to small French all-bisque children with their idiosyncratic costumes.

Plumbing was a newly important feature of houses by the early 20th century as most middle-class homes how possessed bathrooms and the child would not take easily to a model that was without. The *Royal Magazine* of 1907 described a house costing £25 that included not only a billiard room and a motor garage but also a lift to all the rooms. The bathroom of this impressive residence was supplied with hot water from a cistern heated by a spirit lamp. In more ordinary houses the baths were only occasionally supplied with water and then from a simple tank that fitted behind the bath. Complete tin bathroom sets could be purchased with a neat screen around the bath and washbasin which effectively concealed the tank. A few lavatories were also supplied with a tank of water and a working chain. These small water toys were of very obvious appeal to a young child and unfortunately many became disfigured with rust and were thrown away so that, in comparison with the number produced, few now remain.

Although metal furnishings were mainly imported from Germany, and to a lesser degree, France, there were several English firms making similar goods. The Reka Toy Company of Wimbourne Street, London, which specialized in light and hollow castings in metal included in their range of fancy goods kettles, teapots, toilet jugs and basins, and cooking equipment. The 'Holdfast' branded goods made by A. S. Cartwright Ltd of Birmingham also provided metal furnishings for doll's houses. This firm was established in 1880 but the earliest catalogue I was able to locate dated from the 1930s when they were selling bent metal furniture with enamelled seats. The sets usually included tables and chairs but clocks and pianos of less progressive design were also made. A set of eleven pieces cost 2/-. Cartwright also made sets that were marketed under the trade name of 'Gwenda' and included steel bedroom sets in rather cautious art deco style that were enamelled in pastel blue, pink or green. The arrangements were supplied boxed and accompanied by a neat patterned carpet. In the bedroom set was a tallboy, wardrobe, dressing table, two chairs, a stool and, a very up-to-the-minute touch, a cabinet radio set. This same cabinet radio, obviously by this stage an absolute essential in every household was also provided for the dining-room set. This firm is perhaps best known to dolls' house collectors for the working model mangles which are found in so many Edwardian doll's houses.

Even before the advent of Queen Mary's dolls' house there was an awakening of interest in the dolls' house as a work of good craftsmanship and in the opening years of the century a well-constructed house in the form of an Elizabethan manor was made by three boys from the LCC Pigott Street cripples' school at Limehouse. This large house, made as a prestige exhibit, contained an oak-panelled drawing-room that was furnished in Louis XIV style. In a bedroom was a large four-poster bed while the kitchen boasted a beaten iron fender. All this effective furniture was made by a fifteen-year-old boy who was presumably learning the trade. Sadly, after the great amount of work that went into such projects, the results were all too frequently given as generous gifts to hospitals where they survived for only a short period, as few children take great care of a toy they do not own.

There was still a considerable adult interest in dolls' houses in the 1930s and some effective commercial houses were made retrospectively with this market in mind. F. Tibbenham Ltd of Ipswich was among the firms making a few reproduction houses and they modelled a well-known local building, Sparrowe House, with its pargeted front. These models stood some eighteen inches high and one can be seen in the actual house, though the majority appear to have been sold to Americans. Other rather mannered furnishings were made by Eric Elgin who, in partnership with his sisters, worked from Enfield in Middlesex between 1919 and 1926.

From this brief survey of the development of the dolls' house it should be possible to see something of its continual fascination not only as a child's toy but also as an adult's preoccupation. The man or woman who buys one of the effectively made reproduction houses of today and spends hours searching for suitable furnishings should not feel shy at the peculiarity of the hobby, as it has an impeccable pedigree of several hundred years and some of the most intelligent and elegant of participants.

The interior of 3 Devonshire Villas, showing the large rooms that accommodate a huge miscellany of items. These are mainly contemporary, though the celluloid cook is later. The upholstered day-bed in the bedroom is well made. Bethnal Green Museum, London.

On Collecting

During the last five years the collecting of antique dolls has gained rapidly in popularity and it is no longer an enjoyable and inexpensive field for the amateur. Financial writers in national newspapers have even advised that, among antique objects, it is dolls that have most appreciated in value: the collector consequently finds himself in competition with the investor who often buys objects to store in a bank vault rather than for enjoyment. The individual has therefore of necessity, been forced into an awareness of current prices and even the fashions of the market. At present there is an upsurge of interest in fabric dolls, virtually unsaleable five years ago except at the lowest of prices, and in compositions made between the wars, though the latter are still very much the province of the American collector.

As with any antique object, it is very difficult to forecast the moment at which a particular type of doll will suddenly escalate in value. To the time of writing an actual drop in price such as is occasionally seen in other collecting fields has not been suffered, though the market does occasionally grow quieter for several months, which causes prices to level out for a while. Dealers are, however, beginning to feel concern that many of the traditionally cheap dolls have, in comparison with their availability, become over-priced, and this is preventing many would-be collectors from beginning.

When purchasing a doll it is advisable to buy from an established dealer rather than a general antique shop, whose owner cannot tell that what he is selling may be a marriage of pieces, perhaps composed of a baby doll's head attached to a jointed body, whose only real value would be for spare parts. Though the price of such a doll might initially appear attractive, the amount by which one has overpaid is made obvious when an attempt is made to sell. I frequently see dolls sold in country auctions and antique shops for double the price any specialist dealer would ask. Unless you are an expert on dolls, a very large amount of luck is needed to obtain an economic purchase in this way.

It is rare to find an old doll in absolutely perfect condition, as the object was, after all, originally a plaything. Most collectors are, for instance, prepared to accept some damage or restoration on fingers and toes, though any breaks to the head are considered much more seriously, especially on china dolls. If a bisque head is damaged, even by the most delicate hair-line crack, the purchase price should be as little as half that required for a perfect example. In dolls of extreme rarity, however, slight damage becomes comparatively less important. Many dealers now fix wigs down very lightly so that the purchaser can look inside the head for any damage or evidence of restoration. Some collectors like to ensure they are buying an unrestored doll by shining a light from the inside of the head. At sales of porcelain, auctioneers now frequently supply an ultra-violet lamp for examination of lots and it is rather surprising that this facility has not been extended to the buyers of the most expensive dolls at auction.

Restored items, though more attractive than a head with visible damage, should be purchased with great caution, as it is often difficult to establish the actual amount of damage after the bisque is resprayed. Porcelain dolls in particular are very difficult to restore perfectly, and an odd bloom is often given to the surface which is very unpleasant. After purchasing a very lovely but restored porcelain I found this surface so distasteful that I was forced to clean off the sprayed-on colour with petrol to reveal the cracked but beautiful face. Though the restoration on bisque can look very convincing when a doll is bought, it should also be remembered that after some years, colour changes might be evident, and it can also be difficult to remove dirty marks from parts of the head that have been treated. It is not always even possible to clean off this colour and reveal the original face, as in order to deal with cracks they are sometimes ground down so that a filler can be more evenly applied.

The buyer is given some protection against a bad purchase by the fact that most established dealers will offer a trade-back guarantee whereby a doll can be returned if wished, after a reasonable length of time, in part exchange for a more expensive item. If a seller is reluctant to offer this, some suspicion is justified since, with the fast escalation in doll prices he is almost bound to make a profit on the returned doll. If doubt is felt regarding authenticity then a receipt, stating the approximate date, price and any serious damage, should be requested. When spending a large amount on a good doll it is only logical to ask for some written authentication.

The new collector should also exercise great care when buying from the charming lady collector who, by a great favour, is prepared to part with some of her treasures. A sense of morality and fair dealing is sometimes sadly lacking in such circumstances and some of the most horrific mistakes I have seen have been sold to beginners by fellow-collectors whose experience made them perfectly aware of their deception. It is only prudent to learn as much as possible about the subject, by visiting museums and reading, before the actual collection is begun, as mistakes are now often too expensive to learn by.

Having negotiated the hazards of purchase, it is necessary to store or display the dolls with some care. Ideally, they should be kept in museum conditions with regulated humidity and temperature, though fortunately most dolls are not sufficiently valuable for this to be essential. The majority of collectors have to accommodate their acquisitions within the confines of ordinary houses and though it is sometimes possible to set aside one room solely for dolls with built-in cases around the walls, most collections are displayed in reception rooms or in a bedroom. Glass-fronted cases are advisable, as even the most gracious guests cannot be relied upon to handle dolls with sufficient care, and pick up porcelain dolls in such a way that their legs clatter dangerously together or will drag a fingernail down the surface of a composition doll to see if it is waxed! All dolls should be kept from direct sunlight as old fabrics fade quickly, papier mâché might warp and wax, of course, will melt. It is a sensible precaution, in case of theft, to photograph the more unusual dolls.

If a badly damaged doll is purchased it is often difficult to decide whether to use the services of a restorer. I feel that if damage is slight then it is generally better to leave well alone or simply undertake a cosmetic restoration with a little dental plaster or gesso that can be washed off at a later stage if not satisfactory. If a professional is consulted, then it is vital to see examples of his work in the material you need; those who work well on a piece of Derby porcelain frequently find bisque quite impossible. Having judged an example of restoration it is also necessary to ask for an estimate of cost. Restoration can take hours of patient work not only in filling but in matching colour, and what can appear a simple repair to the doll's owner can in some circumstances cost more than the doll would be worth. It is also advisable to tell the restorer very specifically what you require; if two fingers are broken off a wax doll a complete new arm is not necessary, even though this would often be easier as the wax would not need to be matched as perfectly. If the shoulder of a doll is cracked then the surface restoration should be confined to that shoulder and not extended, as so often happens, over the complete head. The wigs of old dolls are often in a dirty and untidy state; it is sometimes possible to wash them carefully and then separate the hair or mohair gently between the fingers. If a new wig or new costume is necessary then it is helpful to future collectors if the original items are retained.

Prices of dolls' houses have not undergone the dramatic rise experienced in the field of doll collecting and they have remained more in line with the general trend in antiques. As many are quite large, collectors are forced, through lack of space, to limit the number they possess, though many people collect the miniatures that came originally from such houses. As with dolls, the less restoration embarked upon the better, as it is very easy to over-restore and end up with a house that looks like a reproduction. A slightly shabby and chipped exterior is far preferable.

If a house is bought that has, over the years, been covered with layers of paint, then it is obvious that this must be cleaned away in order to discover something of the original which can occasionally be rescued or, more frequently, restored. Old paint will sometimes come away if scraped carefuly with a paint stripping knife, a flat piece of glass or even a not too delicate fingernail. If a modern paint has been used it is usually necessary to use a proprietary stripper that removes one layer of paint at a time, providing it is used with economy. Great care has to be taken not to damage the surface of the wood as it is very easy to suddenly penetrate several layers by over-enthusiastic scraping. If it is essential to repaint the dolls' house then water-bound colour is again useful as it can be cleaned off easily if another treatment is later discovered to be more suitable. If a rather more durable surface is required, a mixture of an oil-bound or white lead undercoat with powder colour gives a pleasant soft surface. Tins of very old paint are sometimes found with just enough colour, thinned with turpentine, to decorate a dolls' house. Brick papers can be bought from several craft shops, and that made in the traditional way in plain red and white, looks much better than a more natural type that is printed in shades of pink and red. Wallpapers for dolls' houses are sold in such a limited range that it is usually better to search for small prints on wrapping papers or in wallpaper shops which, with a little ingenuity can be adapted. If a suitable paper cannot be found then it might be possible to cut a stencil or a woodblock and print the lengths in soft colours; if a larger quantity is required a silk screen can be used. It is very difficult to paint a design directly on to the walls and it is usually advisable to paint a large panel, for instance, before it is pasted in position. If any scraps of the original papers remain they should be carefully preserved and kept in labelled envelopes, indicating their original position; it is better to keep these in the dolls' house itself as this type of item is so easily mislaid. Even if very stained and discoloured, original papers should never be removed, as particularly unpleasant areas can often be covered by a picture or a wall hanging.

Genuine old wallpapers are very difficult to find, and it is often easier to hang a room with period fabrics. Again, direct application to the walls is not recommended, especially in very early houses where paper should be cut to fit the various walls and the fabric glued to this with a PVA adhesive that should not mark the material. The complete piece can then be attached to the wall with a minute dab of glue that will not damage the wood.

It is often difficult to decide whether lighting should be installed. Sometimes, even in a very early house, with a little ingenuity, wiring can be carried up chimneys and under carpets to a candelabra or table lamp. It seems quite criminal to drive lighting holes through the ceilings of old houses even though the effect given can be pretty. One museum installed strip lighting in an early 18th-century house which, apart from giving too high a level of light and completely destroying the atmosphere, must have caused damage to the structure. If a house is purchased that already has lighting, then, the damage being already done, it might as well remain, though I would advise strongly against its installation in any pre-1900 houses.

Many collectors derive great enjoyment from making furnishings. While this is a pleasant hobby it should be indulged in with restraint otherwise an arty-crafty exercise rather than an antique restoration will be the result. I have seen houses filled with so many made-up items that practically the only authentic object is the house itself. As this type of reconstruction is enjoyed by so many people it is surely more logical to buy a well-made reproduction house in which all sorts of adventurous schemes can be carried out than to vandalize an antique.

Bibliography

Several of the books suggested in this list were written some time ago and sections of the information are now known to be incorrect, so it is advisable to read first the more recent publications. Newspaper and magazine articles, and toy-makers' catalogues are not included as they are not generally available; this also applies to a few very early books on the subject.

Angione, Genevieve *All Bisque and Half Bisque Dolls*. Thomas Nelson & Sons, Camden, New Jersey

Bachmann, Manfred & Hansmann, Claus *Dolls the Wide World Over*. George G. Harrap & Co. Ltd, London

Boehn, Max von *Dolls*. Dover Publications Inc., New York

Boehn, Max von *Puppets and Automata*. Dover Publications Inc., New York

Chapuis A. & Droz E. *Les Automates*. Neuchatel

Coleman, D. S., E. A., & E. J. *The Collector's Encyclopedia of Dolls*. Robert Hale & Co., London

Coleman, D. S., E. A., & E. J. *The Collector's Book of Dolls' Clothes*. Robert Hale & Co., London

Culff, Robert *The World of Toys*. Hamlyn, Feltham, Middlesex

Daiken, Lesley *Children's Toys Throughout the Ages*. Spring Books, Feltham, Middlesex

Desmonde, Kay *All Colour Book of Dolls*. Octopus Books, London

Baker, Roger *Dolls and Dolls' Houses*. Orbis (London) Ltd, London

Early, Alice K. *English Dolls, Effigies and Puppets*. B. T. Batsford, London

Eaton, Faith *Dolls in Colour*. Blandford Press Ltd, London

Fox, Carl *The Doll*. Abrams, New York

Fraser, Antonia *Dolls*. Octopus Books, London

Gerken, Jo Elizabeth *Wonderful Dolls of Papier Mâché*. Dolls Research Association, New York

Greene, Vivien *English Dolls' Houses*. B. T. Batsford, London

Greene, Vivien *Family Dolls' Houses*. G. Bell & Sons Ltd, London

Grober, Karl *Childrens Toys of Bygone Days*. Charles Scribner's Sons, New York

Hart, Louella *Directory of British Dolls*; *Directory of French Dolls*; *Directory of German Dolls* (all privately printed)

Hansmann, Claus & Roh, Juliane *Altes Spielzeug*. Verlag F. Bruckmann, Munich

Hillier, Mary *Dolls and Doll Makers*. Weidenfeld & Nicolson, London

Hughes, B. & T. *Collecting Miniature Antiques*. William Heinemann Ltd, London

Jackson, Mrs F. Nevill *Toys of Other Days*. White Lion Publishers, London

Jacobs, F. G. *A History of Dolls' Houses*. Charles Scribner's Sons, New York

Jacobs, F. G. *Dolls' Houses in America*. Charles Scribner's Sons, New York

Jacobs, F. G. & Faurholt, E. *Dolls and Dolls' Houses*. Charles E. Tuttle Co. Inc., Tokyo

King, C. E. *Dolls and Toys for Collectors*. Hamlyn, Feltham, Middlesex

King, C. E. *The Collector's History of Dolls*. Robert Hale & Co., London

Latham, Jean *Dolls' Houses: a Personal Choice*. A. & C. Black Ltd, London

Maillard, M. M. Rabecq *L'Histoire du Jouet*. Hachette, Paris

Mathes, Ruth & R. C. *Decline and Fall of the Wooden Doll*; *Doll Collector's Manual* 1964. Hobby House Press, Riverdale, Maryland

McClinton, Katherine *Antiques in Miniature*. Charles Scribner's Sons, New York

Mookerjee, Ajit *Folk Toys of India*. Probsthain & Co., London

Newall, Venetia (ed.) *The Witch Figure*. Routledge & Kegan Paul Ltd, London

Noble, John *Dolls*. Studio Vista, London

Noble, John *These Beautiful Dolls*. Hawthorne, London

Prasteau, M. *Les Automates*. Grund, Geneva

Roth, Eugen *Ein Kind ist uns geboren*. Prestel, Munich

Ruggles, Rowena Godding *The One Rose*. Oakland, USA

Schiffer & Schiffer *Miniature Antique Furniture*. Livingston, New York.

Schoonmaker, Patricia N. *Research on Kämmer & Reinhardt Dolls*. Charles Scribner's Sons, New York

Ringler, Josef *Alte Tiroler Weihnachtskrippen*. Universitats-verlag Wagner Innsbruck, Munich

Selfridge *Dolls' Images of Love*. Printed by J. & M. Selfridge, London

'Spinning Wheels' Complete Book of Dolls. Galahad Books, New York

Toller, Jane *Antique Miniature Furniture*. G. Bell & Sons Ltd, London

White, Gwen *European and American Dolls*. B. T. Batsford, London

Whitton, Barbara. *Paper Dolls and Paper Toys*. Jendrick, USA

Index